HEAVEN IS FOR ANIMALS TOO

HOPE AND COMFORT FOR BELIEVERS AND SKEPTICS

MELINDA CERISANO

Illustrations by Steve. A. Roberts

iUniverse

HEAVEN IS FOR ANIMALS TOO
HOPE AND COMFORT FOR BELIEVERS AND SKEPTICS

Copyright © 2015 Melinda Cerisano.

All rights reserved. No part of this book may be used or reproduced by any means, graphic, electronic, or mechanical, including photocopying, recording, taping or by any information storage retrieval system without the written permission of the publisher except in the case of brief quotations embodied in critical articles and reviews.

iUniverse books may be ordered through booksellers or by contacting:

iUniverse
1663 Liberty Drive
Bloomington, IN 47403
www.iuniverse.com
1-800-Authors (1-800-288-4677)

Because of the dynamic nature of the Internet, any web addresses or links contained in this book may have changed since publication and may no longer be valid. The views expressed in this work are solely those of the author and do not necessarily reflect the views of the publisher, and the publisher hereby disclaims any responsibility for them.

Any people depicted in stock imagery provided by Thinkstock are models, and such images are being used for illustrative purposes only.
Certain stock imagery © Thinkstock.

ISBN: 978-1-4917-2421-7 (sc)
ISBN: 978-1-4917-2422-4 (hc)
ISBN: 978-1-4917-2423-1 (e)

Library of Congress Control Number: 2014902166

Print information available on the last page.

iUniverse rev. date: 03/20/2015

*To my father, to the Ace of Spades (Blacky),
and to the little cat from Martins Ferry*

Contents

Preface ix
Acknowledgments xv
Introduction xix

Chapter 1: The Loss 3
Chapter 2: The True Meaning of Dominion 13
Chapter 3: A Place on the Ark and the Laws of Noah 29
Chapter 4: The Last Sacrificial Lamb 47
Chapter 5: Animals Have Souls and Spirits—What Original
    Translation Reveals 63
Chapter 6: A Free "Ticket to Ride" 89
Chapter 7: The Nature of Heaven 115
Chapter 8: Celestial Beings 139
Chapter 9: God's Animal Kingdom 149

Epilogue 177
Poem—Animals Not Forgotten 185

Appendix A: Other Opinions 187
Appendix B: Biblical Verses by Category 189
Appendix C: Recommended Reading 227

Bibliography 231
Index 243
Verse Index 253

Preface

It is in the glory of God to conceal a matter, but the honor of kings to search out a matter.
—**Proverbs 25:2 NIV**

I never expected to be writing a book that answers this often-asked question: Do animals go to heaven? When I was ten years old, a minister in our family's Methodist church told me that animals do not go to heaven because they do not have souls and are not made in the likeness of God. As an animal lover, I was disappointed in his answer. Even if I did not believe him, I figured I had to accept it because of his authority as a minister. After all, he knew the Bible inside and out, right? I remember thinking that I would ask another minister someday.

I never mustered up the nerve to do so. I have to admit that I really didn't know much about the Bible myself for many years. Being raised a Methodist, I thought I took my religion seriously; however, I fell short of having a secure grasp on biblical studies.

Then something changed. The year was 1998. Just a few months after appearing to be fully healthy, my father was diagnosed with Lou Gehrig's disease. There was a bit of ambiguity in the diagnosis, but it did not matter—it was too late. We learned that this disease progresses at a rapid rate, and we were advised to think about hospice.

This was devastating news. I dearly loved my father, who had been a constant presence in my life and who had always supported me in everything I tried to do. When I set out to become an airline pilot and others told me I would never make it because that was not a world for women, my father encouraged me. "You can do it!" he said. That meant the world to me because he had been a decorated air force fighter pilot for sixteen years. He was also a United Airlines pilot for thirty-three years. It was my dream to follow my dad's example.

Once I understood how fast his disease was progressing, I felt a call to action. For the first time in my life, I was going to read the Bible from front to back. Though I had tried many times before, I promised God that this time I would be successful. I was going to immerse myself in the Bible, and I was not going to quit. I truly believed that through the power of prayer, God could save my father. I would keep studying that Bible and have prayer chains going until he was healed.

I kept my promise. By studying the Bible, my eyes were opened to a greater understanding of the true nature and power of God. Something else happened, something unexpected. I began making discoveries in the Bible that shined a new light of awareness on the subject that I had considered settled. I stumbled upon several verses that made me question what I had learned from the Methodist minister who told me with such assurance that animals do not go to heaven.

Maybe our pets, and all the animals, really *do* go to heaven after all!

This discovery was a surprise and an inspiration. I copied those verses—I believe there were eight of them at the time—and put them in safekeeping. I did not even own a computer at the time. If I was going to write something, it was going to be on a typewriter.

Soon after, a friend suddenly lost her horse unexpectedly. She was crushed, and I yearned to find some way to comfort her. I understood something of her grief because when I lost my first dog as an adult, I felt almost suffocated by the enormous grief. There is no better way of saying it—when your best friend dies, it is heartbreaking. So I had an idea: I would take out those verses I had found, handwrite them out, and give them to my friend with my interpretation—that there definitely is an afterlife for our beloved pets; God will not forget his animals. I wasn't sure how she would respond. I was gratified to hear later that she put those verses in a personal scrapbook and even started to go to church.

Not long after that, another close friend lost his dog. This friend, a retired police chief, had seen a rough world through his lens, but he had a soft spot for his dogs. He had three dogs in his life, all of which lived to the age of fifteen. He'd come to the first party I attended after moving to our neighborhood with his dog, Max, his true friend.

By this time, word was circulating in our neighborhood that I had written something that might help him through this grieving process. My friend's wife called me and told me that after Max died, my friend stayed in bed for three days. She asked me for the "writing" she had heard about, saying that maybe it could help. I was scheduled to fly to Tokyo the next day. I had just bought my first computer, an Apple laptop, but I had no idea how to work it. Still, I promised to have my writing ready for my friend when I returned. I left for Tokyo, my four-pound Bible in tow. My intent was to type up those original eight verses, but by the time I returned home, I had written a twelve-page article.

Again, I was surprised and gratified by a friend's response to what I had uncovered about animals going to heaven. When my friend who had lost his dog came to my house for a visit, he told me, "If God is that merciful and graceful to the animals, and to Max, I will take him." Once again, the thought of animals going to heaven had shined a new light on God's grace. A friend had felt comforted by what I had shared, and a door had been opened to greater understanding of the nature of God.

There was more to this story. As time passed, this kind friend continued to ask me more questions about what the Bible said concerning the animal kingdom and going to heaven. Each time he asked, I plunged back into the Bible to find answers for him ... and for myself. Hence, the thirst for knowledge and comfort drew me into a research project that I just could not stop thinking about. It was incredibly exciting!

Soon, however, my enthusiasm was somewhat tempered. I began to realize that not everyone believed that our pets and all the animals go to heaven. For a time, I held back my sharing of what I had learned. Then I began to think about this Bible verse:

> *Each one should use whatever gift he has received to serve others, faithfully administering God's grace in its various forms.*
> —1 Peter 4:10 NIV

These words instilled in me a renewed sense of encouragement and a commitment to keep following the research trail I had set out on, to go on seeking answers to my friend's questions about what the Bible says regarding animals going to heaven. Before long, my process had evolved from simply writing up some of the evidence to give to individual friends to actually writing this book. I felt that I simply did not have a choice. Writing this book seemed to have become my *gift*, if I am to be so lucky. Perhaps writing about animals going to heaven and being remembered by a loving God really is my purpose at this time in my life. And better yet, it could be a way to serve others. This subject comes from the heart, and I simply have been unable to *not* write about the belief that animals really do go to heaven.

I certainly never expected to become an author. In fact, I was deathly afraid of writing when I was in college. I am a numbers person, not a writer! Yet every time I even briefly considered stopping this project, something or someone would come into my life to keep me going. I guess you could say that perhaps I have become a researcher of truth more so than a writer.

The journey for truth led me to extensive research. For seven years, everything in my life seemed to be on hold. I have conducted interviews with Hebrew scholars, ministers and pastors, priests and rabbis. I have attended animal theology seminars. I have been led to religious institutions such as the Dead Sea Scrolls displays and personal tours of the Vatican City.

It's not always an easy task, seeking the truth. Fortunately, I have been lucky enough to be surrounded by those who love animals and who are open-minded to a biblical perspective on this issue. I continue to be truly amazed by how many people have been willing to share with me their grieving experiences after losing a beloved animal. I've been gratified to see how deeply they are touched when they learn about the biblical evidence assuring them that their pets and all God's creatures will not be forgotten in the afterlife. Perhaps you too will be comforted by what you are about to read.

During my research, I had the most welcoming and loving experience when I visited the Vatican. When I called my father from Rome to tell him that the Vatican's position on this subject is that animals really do go to heaven, he struggled to hold back tears. He proceeded to tell me that the saddest day in his life was when Foxy, our family German shepherd, passed away. In his heart, Dad already believed that Foxy was in heaven. Now he felt deeply relieved to really *know* that she would be there waiting for him.

As for the power of prayer and the power of God himself, my father was with us for another thirteen years after the initial diagnosis. He was able to read some of the drafts of this book, and he found great comfort in the artwork. However, prior to the final editing of this work, in Jesus's arms, my father flew his final flight west. Foxy no longer waits.

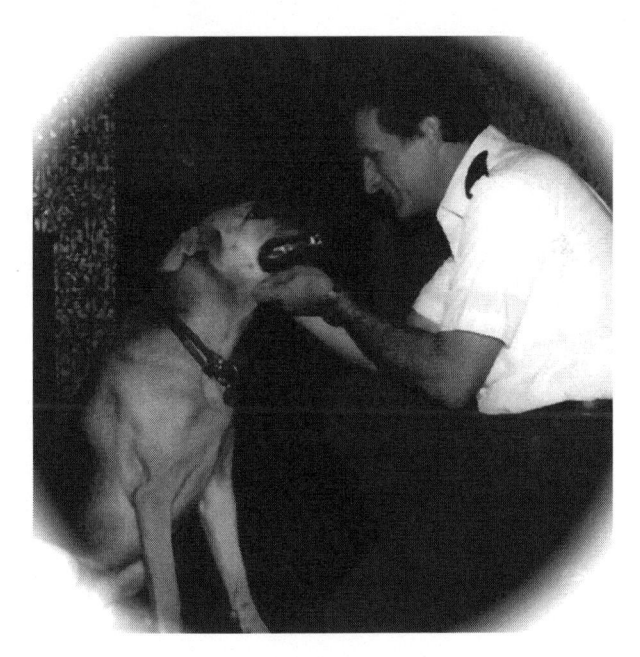

Acknowledgments

Thank you so much to all of those who stood by me as I attempted to execute the task of bringing this book to life. I am grateful to have such loyal friends to stand by and listen to the obsessive talks along the way and to continue to offer needed encouragement.

I thank my dear friend Sharon Conley for the conversations that birthed the idea of possibilities. Sharon, you are an inspiration. Pat and Marty Mitchell, Kim Carter, Scott and Lise Strumm, thank you for the motivation that brought this project from article to manuscript. I could not have done a project like this without the moral support of Kim Mason, Gloria Fuller, Laura and Ray Ogden, Vera and Roy Sciortino, Cheryl and Mike Stratos, Cathy Green, Christine Giraldin, Samantha Potter, and Leo Suglio. Thank you to Dr. Erick Cobb for contributing ideas. Thank you to Jill and John Baxter for the courage to make goals large! I thank my lovely bingo ladies for their interest and encouragement. To Bonnie and Russel Morris, thank you so much for taking the time to read through the "long version."

I would love to thank Karen and Ron Holliday for the many long-into-the-night kitchen-table chats about theology. I thank Jay Hollister for the privilege of "exchanging manuscripts" and hoping to receive honesty in return. I extend many thanks to Jack Kerr for the courage to continue when I wanted to quit.

I thank Renee Gerard for tending to the horses while I engaged in inspiration. I thank Jake Macken for allowing me to write when I should have been training K-9s at o'dark early in the morning. Jake, thank you for the inspiration to write poetry. Thank you to Yannay Moshe for helping me navigate through important concepts of the Hebrew heritage. I extend my thanks to Vicki McBride for helping me to see what a writer's life looks like. Thank you to Rhonda Sciortino for attempting to keep me on track. I thank my nephew JoJo for his kindness and for reserving judgment. And to Steven Haines, thank you for helping me navigate the clubhouse turn.

Thank you to Rabbi Hurwitz for your kind words, guidance, and understanding. To all the clergy I have met, thank you for your time. Whether we agreed or not, I have gained valuable insight by the contributing knowledge received. As for the Vatican, her graciousness and hospitality will always be cherished memories of my life.

I could not have done this without the help of the Laridian Pocket Bible. My life on the road requires that I have access to Bible verses at all times, and I surely felt 100 percent connected through this pocket Bible from Laridian. It is the best!

Thank you to Colin Dangaard for the recommendation to iUniverse. And on the iUniverse team, I extend a special thanks to Traci Anderson. I could always count on you for support. To Krista Hill, David Bernardi, Shellie Hurrle, and Amy McHargue, I thank you for the editorial insight.

And to the two people who would put the icing on the cake, Steve A. Roberts and Kevin Quirk, you have my gratitude! This definitely would not have been possible without you both. Steve, your artwork brought heaven home in our hearts and minds. I see color everywhere now, thanks to your perspective. My dad said that he hoped heaven is as beautiful as seen through your eyes. Kevin, as an editor, you were required to learn the material in order to construct a better outline to facilitate the reader. At a time when I was not able to concentrate due to my father's passing, you helped me navigate through the final process and get past the finish line with needed confidence.

Finally, for the grace, mercy, and blessings granted to me through God, and through Christ, I am eternally thankful.

INTRODUCTION

Introduction

And God said, Let the waters swarm with swarms of living souls, and let fowl fly above the earth in the expanse of the heavens. And God created the great sea monsters, and every living soul that moves with which the waters swarm, after their kind, and every winged fowl after its kind. And God saw that it was good.
—**Genesis 1:20–21 DAR**

Do our pets go to heaven? Will all animals have a place in the afterlife, where they will be welcomed and embraced by a loving and compassionate God?

Interest in the subject has never been greater than it is now. Both inside and outside the Christian community, we have seen a growing spotlight pointed at all matters related to heaven. At the same time, the specific issue of animals being included or excluded from heaven has been explored and debated in expanding circles, from Christian websites and magazine articles to dueling neighborhood church billboard postings.

I offer this book to the continued focus and exploration on this matter. I enter this public forum with a definitive point of view and a strong belief. I have arrived at my own resounding answer to this question, and I believe that clear, ample evidence in the Bible backs and supports it.

Yes, our pets and all the animals go to heaven! I do not mean doggy heaven; I mean God's heaven. I do not mean mankind's version of heaven but rather God's actual afterlife, a paradise of beauty and grace. To extend the phrase from the current popular book and movie, heaven is for real ... for animals too!

Allow me to share with you a little bit about who I am ... and who I am not. I'm not a theologian, although I have at times contemplated studying theology in school and may yet do so someday. I am not a noted biblical scholar, though I suspect that the amount of hours I've logged combing through the many versions of the Bible over seven long years could bring me close to becoming an expert on this subject matter. After all, this is not a subject taught in seminary. I am, however, deeply devoted to Jesus and to his teachings and with my devotion to this subject, I am a rare conduit of expertise in this matter.

Professionally, I'm an airline pilot. I fly 747s to such far-off destinations as Sydney, Hong Kong, Singapore, Shanghai, and Beijing. If you have ever worked under the union label, as I still do to this day, you can appreciate how I often tell those who know me that the Bible is my "union contract." As I have sought answers and evidence in response to the question of whether animals go to heaven, I have remained bound to the Bible as my guide and source.

I would also call myself a proud lifelong animal lover. Though I currently live in Southern California, I grew up in Virginia, in a region populated with equestrian racetracks. By age eight, I had progressed beyond pony rides to the point where I would walk right into a racehorse facility and insist to anyone I met that I could ride their horses. By the time I was twelve, I was riding those horses. I went on to become a competitor in jumping and eventually became a full-time dressage rider, competing at the international level and earning the Silver Medal Lifetime Achievement Award from the United States Dressage Federation. I have studied natural horsemanship under the guidance of renowned horse whisperer Pat Parelli. I have limited experience with marine mammals as well. I am a certified dog obedience trainer through the Animal Behavior College. Currently I own four horses and two dogs, including a German shepherd that I trained in police protection. I still own a dog training business, and I once was fortunate enough to receive many referrals through an organization recommended by Cesar Millan, TV's famed "Dog Whisperer."

Animals matter to me. When one of my pets or any animal I have loved dies, I grieve the loss. Most of us who love our animals mourn their passing as we would any departed loved one. The bond is that strong. Knowing that our animals will be in heaven with us can lift our spirits and inspire us to become ever more grateful for God's grace and God's mercy.

So if you have been guided to this book because you have lost a beloved pet or animal, I welcome you to the exploration. May you also be comforted by the many reasons to believe that God has not forgotten our animals. Perhaps you simply love animals and are concerned about their welfare, both on earth and in whatever you believe an afterlife may be. Maybe you are a minister or biblical scholar who is interested in discovering different views and possible new evidence that point to animals going to heaven. Perhaps you are in the camp that strongly contends that animals do *not* go to heaven and you are curious about the evidence and the beliefs you are about to encounter. If so, there's room for us all! You will find that I have provided my sources in a detailed manner so that they are available for you as well, should you desire continued study.

Let us prepare to journey down this path of understanding why we have reason to believe that animals really do go to heaven. As you travel with me, you may encounter evidence, ideas, and revelations that will surprise or startle you, perhaps even challenge preconceived notions you have held. That's okay. Even when I doubted what my Methodist minister told me about animals not going to heaven, I didn't initially know anything about why that was untrue.

As the chapters unfold, I will show you the following:

- Contrary to what you may have heard, animals do indeed have souls and spirits. The Bible clearly says so, if we take the time to navigate through the translations that have resulted in the original meanings getting lost or becoming significantly altered.

- God has always held animals in the highest regard, as evidenced by almost all the major stories in the Bible. From the start, he declared them "good," just as he did for Adam, when creating a paradise for Adam and the animals to share as neighbors. Examples abound throughout the Bible that build on God's love for animals, their important status, and how they honor God. You will learn why the evidence points clearly to the conclusion that it would simply be inconsistent for a loving, caring God to forget the animals or leave them out of the end times. To welcome and embrace his animals in heaven is simply in God's nature!
- The concept of "dominion" has been falsely used as a rationale to adopt an attitude in which we feel that animals are ours to do with as we like, believing that they are secondary characters on earth and simply have no place in God's heaven. This idea is critically misguided and cries out for reevaluation. The biblical evidence reveals that the word "dominion" really means that we are commanded to be good stewards to the animals, just as God is a good steward to us.
- Animals are not forbidden from heaven because they are not made in God's image or likeness. In fact, many inhabitants of heaven are not in God's likeness.
- Animals do not have to repent or claim Jesus to be admitted into heaven. They were victims of the fall of Adam and Eve in the Garden of Eden, so they do not have to be "saved" to gain entry to heaven.
- Before Jesus, sacrificing an animal and its sacred blood would atone for a man's sins. Jesus, through his death and resurrection, became the last sacrificial lamb. We will explore the intriguing and profound implications of this link, as well as how the story of Jesus provides multiple compelling illustrations of his love and reverence for animals. Remember, when Jesus was born in the manger, he was surrounded by animals. When he went to the wilderness after being baptized, he spent those forty days and forty nights living peacefully among the wild animals.

Heaven Is for Animals Too will also discuss familiar stories such as Noah and the ark, Moses receiving the Ten Commandments, the book of Job, the book of Daniel, and less familiar but equally important stories and Bible verses. We will consider the importance of angels and cherubim as well, and we will look at the relevant words and actions of such notable figures as Saint Francis of Assisi, John Calvin, John Wesley, and Pope John Paul II. Along the way, we will stop often to reflect upon the true nature of God and how that relates to his protection of his animal kingdom.

In building on the belief that animals do indeed go to "real" heaven, there is no silver bullet or one piece of evidence that tells the whole story and settles all arguments. As we build upon the body of evidence, the defense of our position will show strength. It may help to think of each piece of evidence in the Bible as a bead with which we are going to craft a necklace; only after all the beads are strung onto a single thread do we see a beautiful piece of jewelry. I hope this book strings an ornament of understanding and that some of the beads will represent for you a deeper love of God and the clarity that he loves all that he created.

The emphasis throughout this book is showing God's love, grace, and mercy for the redemption of our world and all that it contains within—and that includes our pets and all the animals. I have done my best to consider God's nature fully, especially as it shines over his animal kingdom. We also will consider the nature of heaven itself. It simply fits that if you're going to hold to a point of view on the question regarding an animal afterlife, whether on one side or the other, it would be an advantage to have a sense of heaven as part of the foundation of your belief.

As we dig into the biblical evidence that reveals that heaven is just as real for animals as it is for humans, we will chisel away the misconceptions and misunderstandings that have arisen through the many different translations of the Bible. Key words, phrases, and meanings have been lost, altered, or twisted far from the original intended meanings of the writers of the Bible. It would seem, unfortunately, that man and his pride can create a low-lying fog that can cloud what the Bible, especially the Old Testament, actually tells us. You may be quite surprised at what happened when the Hebrew words of the Old Testament and the Greek words of the New Testament were translated into English.

Then, of course, with the advent of many individual sects of the Christian faith, we have seen various churches attempt to shed their own light on what the controversial thoughts and teachings of the Bible really mean to that particular church. As a result, the question of animals redeeming the reward of becoming part of Christ's family in the afterlife has been cast in many different notions and often clung to with a general attitude that when it comes to animals in the stories of the Bible, animals are no more than "furniture in the room." They are present but not truly important. How sad it is that something God created, prior to the creation of man, is so easily overlooked and dismissed in the eyes of many theologians and clergymen.

My intent is not to be critical or judgmental of others and their personal beliefs but to seek the truth and shine more light on these nonhuman souls who feel joy and suffering, and who, as we will learn, honor God. I'm often struck by the response I receive in discussing my beliefs, and the compelling biblical evidence that supports them, from those who steadfastly insist that animals do not go to heaven. "Where is the biblical evidence to support your belief?" I ask. "Have you looked at the translation of the original words of the Bible, which confirms that animals have souls and spirits, and that they are fully included in God's plan for an afterlife?" Usually they simply say that their belief is true and well known, yet they are unprepared to present evidence. Some religious officials have even driven followers from their church with casual remarks about how they should not expect to see their pets in heaven. To me, that is such a shame.

From my perspective, those who dismiss the notion that animals could be allowed in "real" heaven may be making judgments from a human perspective, without taking into full account that God made this planet and only he really knows the answers to such complicated questions. What I have presented is my personal belief, based on my research. If you do happen to doubt that animals go to heaven, or insist that they do not, I humbly request that you take the time to look at the evidence that stems from this research.

In an attempt to simplify the journey, you will notice that when I address the Bible directly with quotations, I provide the version of translation. There are many different translations, and I have made decisions on which ones to use to: (1) facilitate understanding; (2) present a version that represents the original Hebrew, or the original Greek, more precisely; and (3) demonstrate how these versions differ, which can then develop into problematic issues of interpretation and understanding. For your clarification, these are the main versions I will reference: the New International Version (NIV), the King James Version (KJV), the New Living Translation (NLT), the New American Standard Bible (NASB), the Darby 1890 Version (DAR), the Darby New Translation (DNT), the Dead Sea Scrolls (DSS), and my favorite, the Interlinear Bible, Hebrew-Greek-English (LITV).

I have done my best to organize and structure this book so that it will be easy for you to navigate through it or simply skip around if you so desire. I also invite you to travel into the field of facts that I present in the appendices. Because *Heaven Is for Animals Too* is built around evidence in the Bible, we will start with the earliest Bible stories. After the initial chapter takes a personal look at the loss that we pet owners experience when our beloved animals depart, we will begin our biblical exploration by revisiting the Garden of Eden. We will consider the true meaning of the word "dominion." From there, we will go back to Noah and the ark to illustrate how animals, although suffering the same earthly consequence as humans, were granted an equal place on the ark to guarantee that they too would endure, and that even when Noah was granted permission to eat animals, they were protected by God's strict rules. Then we'll proceed to the glorious story of Jesus, stopping to pay careful attention to the prominent appearance of animals at almost every turn, and reflecting on the meaning of Jesus as the last sacrificial lamb. As our exploration continues, we will be moving more fluidly through both the Old Testament and the New Testament to cover the trail that we need to follow.

My desire is for you to find comfort in these words and discoveries when your beloved pet passes away. You can feel confident that what you will be reading is not simply comforting words but rather part of a real, substantive, biblically supported body of evidence that can bolster your belief that animals go to heaven, that heaven is as real for them as it is for us, and that we will share the same afterlife together.

So let's start down the trail to see what lies ahead, waiting for us to uncover.

THE LOSS

Chapter 1

THE LOSS

For the Lord thy God is a merciful God; he will not forsake thee, neither destroy thee, nor forget the covenant of thy fathers which he sware unto them.
—Deuteronomy 4:31 KJV

It is 2:00 a.m., and I awaken from a light, anxious sleep. Outside, fires are raging. Inside, Noel is coughing and gasping for air at my bedside. In a selfish way, I feel blessed that my dog is still with me tonight. I know it is close. Tears flow. I am agonizing over the decision process. Today? Tomorrow? When? Should the vet come to the house? He is only available on certain days. Noel needs to go out to the bathroom. I grab a flashlight. Her tumors are large and have grown aggressively within the last eight weeks. It started with a small bump on her leg. Now they are everywhere, from her lungs to her kidneys. Geez, she is only two years, eight months old. Are all German shepherds this susceptible to cancer? Her eyes are seriously bloodshot. She is exhausted by the simple act of breathing.

Outside, I see the orange glow of the fire in Camp Pendleton. I see the flames behind the mountain range that separates me from the marine base, a mere fourteen miles away. I am used to the routine activity of the base: the Hueys, the Cobras, the Black Hawks, the training exercises, the bombings. But this ... What is going on? There is no local news on the TV concerning this particular fire.

The horses? I only have a three-horse trailer, and I own four horses. I had better measure the side door of my horse trailer to see if one horse can fit into the tack room. I can't leave one horse behind. My husband is in Tokyo, and Southern California is riddled with fires. Evacuate?

Shoot. I can see with the beam of my flashlight that Noel is urinating solid-red blood. Her kidney tumor must have ruptured. Tears. Lord help her ... and me. Madness.

Have you lost your best friend? Have you experienced the anguish of losing a pet and the unconditional love that our animal companions bring to our lives? Bereavement can bring on intense, stifling emotions, and the feelings of loss can linger for a lifetime. When the storm clouds swoop over us in our time of loss, the thunder booms with frightening questions:

1) Does my pet have a soul?
2) Will my pet go to heaven?
3) Will I see my pet again in the afterlife?
4) What is my pet feeling as life on earth ceases? Is there pain?
5) If there is a God, where is he now?

Do animals have souls? In the beginning, God created the heavens and earth. This is the first line of the Bible. Nineteen verses later, God made the animals. Whether or not you believe in the creation theory or whether you see this as illustrative, there is a relevant fact regarding animal souls. And did you notice that in Genesis 1:20–21, quoted at the start of the introduction, animals' souls are mentioned twice? What is significant in this verse set at the beginning of the Bible is that it is a direct interpretation from the original Hebrew. In the common English translations of the Bible that we have come to know today, the word "soul" has been left out completely. This is something we will examine in detail down the road.

The second and third questions listed above are, for many people who love animals, the big ones: will my pet be in heaven and will I see my pet again? We will soon see that pets are given spirits as well as souls. Their spirits/souls will be lifted up and returned to God. But when you experience the death of a pet, you may naturally start to wonder about death and your own mortality. When we die, do we sleep until the coming of Christ? Do we go in spirit to heaven? Is there a third possibility? Many of these questions that beg for answers during the time of loss are mysteries, but they are mysteries that we can dive into together. We will soon look at many mysteries of the Bible, from Genesis to the book of Revelation, the last and most exciting book of the Bible. It includes details about the end times and the defeat over evil. Rest assured that there are animals mentioned in this apocalyptic story as well. This futuristic event, when redemption begets heaven and eternity is reality, has been described by several Old and New Testament prophets. They clearly include the animals in these predictions.

So what does a pet feel, and does it experience pain when death comes? As I held my dying dog in my arms, as my fingertips felt the weak heartbeat lapse into silence, I certainly pondered where her essence was as she took her last breath. We know that animals are sentient beings, and sentient beings have understanding. As John Wesley, founder of the Methodist Church, said in Sermon 60:

> What then is the barrier between men and brutes? ... It was not reason. Set aside that ambiguous term: exchange it for the plain word, understanding: and who can deny that the brutes have this? We may as well deny that they have sight or hearing.

I do not believe that anyone doubts whether animals feel joy, happiness, loneliness, hunger, shame, sadness, and pain. Because animals operate under instincts from God, their pain is not always obvious to us. The fact that animals are under instinct is actually an advantage in their case of inheriting eternity. When we look at man being the recipient of free will, accountability comes along with the responsibility of making a decision. Animals were not given free will, and therefore they are not under the same scrutiny that we humans are. Yes, they are under the earthly curses that we humans have lived with since the fall of Adam and the eating of the forbidden fruit. Yes, animals experience pain in their world. They hunt each other and eat flesh, also operating under the instinct or inclination that God gave them. This differs from us in that when they take their last breaths, their spirits and souls returns to God immediately. Our souls can do so also, but under different conditions. However, God is the Creator. He made the heavens and the earth. Therefore, in the end, he has all the sovereignty over all that he made. Keep these thoughts in mind when questions about your animal's fate begin to haunt you.

The last question on the list can be perhaps the most perplexing one, depending on your faith and your beliefs about God and his nature. As you watch your pet pass away, it's hard not to wonder where God is or ask the related questions: who is God anyway, and does he even know my pet? In my opinion, God does know your pet and will not forget your pet—the pet that he created. He sends his spirit to life; he gathers his spirit from life. In the Bible, God tells us joyously about how great his creatures are.

Every covenant and blessing God made included the animals. You will see through the stories of Noah and Jesus that God is intimately connected to the animal kingdom and always has been. "Is there anything too hard for God? Does the clay tell the potter what to do? God will show mercy to whom God will show mercy." These are God's words. Animals are important to God, and he uses them for his purpose. As Dr. Humphrey Primatt, an Anglican clergyman from the 1700s, noted in *A Dissertation on the Duty of Mercy and the Sin of Cruelty to Brute Animals*:

> All who share with us the divine spark of conscious life, given by God at the creation, are our neighbors. All fall under the protection of the commandment to love them as we love ourselves.

Questioning the Nature of God

I don't know what your religious beliefs may be. As for who God is, and what he means to you, the answer will always reside in your heart, for your heart only. I can only say that if you have been left questioning the nature of God while suffering the loss of a pet, you will meet a God you can fall in love with: a God who loves all that he created.

Allow me to share with you something that made me smile regarding the challenge of understanding God's nature. It's an excerpt from Lee Strobel's book *The Case for Faith*:

> Imagine a bear in a trap and a hunter who, out of sympathy, wants to liberate him. He tries to win the bear's confidence, but he can't do it, so he has to shoot the bear full of drugs. The bear, however, thinks this is an attack and that the hunter is trying to kill him. He doesn't realize that this is being done out of compassion. Then to get the bear out of the trap, the hunter has to push him further [sic] into the trap to release the tension on the spring. If the bear were semiconscious at that point, he would be more convinced that the hunter was his enemy who was out to cause him suffering and pain. But the bear would be wrong. He reaches this incorrect conclusion because he is not a human.

The analogy here is that the bear is a different species than the human and cannot see that the human is trying to be of some help. Is not God as different from us as we are from the bear? God is definitely not of the same species as we mere mortals. He is our maker. The vast difference in understanding between the bear and the human is smaller than the vastness between God and human. Therefore, God does not expect us to understand his ways completely as we read all the drama in the Bible.

I have come to believe that many of those who reject the notion of a loving God, a God who includes his animal kingdom in the afterlife, may be innocently placing God in a box. To suggest, as some theologians have, that animals are thought of by God as nothing more than furniture in the room seems to me to be a human-centered concept of God. As if we mere mortals can, with any accuracy, dictate what God is thinking … Yet that is what often seems to happen when the topic of animals going to heaven is addressed in our culture. We seem to be unable to think outside the box, and we attach *our* thoughts to what God would think and then pass a judgment. But we do not know God's thoughts, as the Bible reminds us:

> *For my thoughts are not your thoughts, neither are your ways my ways, saith the LORD. For as the heavens are higher than the earth, so are my ways higher than your ways, and my thoughts than your thoughts.*
> —Isaiah 55:8–9 KJV

I simply cannot believe that a God of this magnitude is capable of creating a world full of beauty and life and then permanently destroying its parts, namely the animal kingdom, in the life hereafter, with his total sights on the human likeness alone. I wonder if those who believe God will reject the animals may be assuming that God has limited power. I suspect that they may be unable to think outside the box about God, and I am sure that God doesn't ever think "inside" the box!

The first chapter of the Bible sets us up to understand God's original intention. From the beginning, God teaches us about his idea of dominion. He provides dominion over us, and his first request to the human race is to be fruitful and multiply and to have dominion over the animals. At that point in time, the animals were man's only companions. So in the next chapter, as we examine God's introduction to us through the book of Genesis, let us look at how past behavior predicts future behavior. How does the beginning of time relate to the end of time? How does dominion today compare to the dominion of yesterday—the dominion God imagined? Fortunately, God is very clear about his future behavior, and it includes the animals.

Fire burned in the hills. It burned to exhaust what was left of my emotions. I did not have to evacuate that night. An act of God did not take my house. However, God did take Noel, my dog, who would never forsake me. How horrible is the pain, the heartache ... the loss.

THE TRUE MEANING OF DOMINION

Chapter 2

THE TRUE MEANING OF DOMINION

> *And God said, Let us make man in our image, after our likeness; and let them have dominion over the fish of the sea, and over the fowl of the heavens, and over the cattle, and over the whole earth, and over every creeping thing that creepeth on the earth.*
> —**Genesis 1:26 DNT**

We're going to begin our exploration by examining an often misunderstood and distorted term. I'm talking about the concept of "dominion." In one form or another, the idea of dominion usually crops up in discussions with those who would believe that animals do not go to heaven. "We have dominion over the animals," many people say. "God gave us dominion over them. He gave the animals to us." No, he gave us the responsibility to be good stewards over the animals. We are to exercise command as benevolent *rulers* over the animals. This command was given in a paradise environment.

The distinction between mankind owning the animals and mankind acting as leaders and rulers over the animals is a critical line in the sand. To me, the first assumption reflects an attitude that easily leads to a belief that we can do whatever we want with the animals. That's an alarming idea by itself, as it potentially opens the door to the justification of a world of suffering and cruelty to animals. It invites mankind to develop an arrogant, self-centered regard for the animals, despite the reality that they are a vital part of God's creation.

Most important for us to consider in our quest is where this attitude leads in relation to animals having a place in the afterlife. If we own them and have dominion over them, then that means animals are simply not as important as we are, right? They're just background players on the big stage of life on this planet. And as that line of thinking goes, if the animals are secondary figures to humans, they certainly do not belong in the same heaven that is intended for us. When they die, that's the end of the line for them. But they are God's, not ours! He decides whom he will have mercy over. We are just caretakers.

The line of thinking that the animals were made for us, or are ours to own, both scares and disturbs me. Where this conclusion goes astray is that it stems from a major misconception of dominion. What does the word "dominion" really mean? How does it relate to God's original plan for us—and for his animal kingdom? These questions demand answers. As you follow the trail of where these answers take us, you will gain a better understanding as to the nature of God and how he really feels about the animal kingdom. Note that the emphasis here is on how *he* feels about the animal kingdom, not how humans feel about the animal kingdom.

The journey to understanding the true meaning of "dominion" takes us back to the beginning of time. Yes, that means Adam and Eve. Remember how the God of the Christian and Jewish faith created the Garden of Eden as a perfect paradise? There was no sadness, terror, fear, or death. It was an environment of pure harmony, and it served as a reflection of God's nature. And let's not forget that the animals were included in this original picture of harmony! God placed the animals there as companions for Adam. Animals got along with one another, as well as with Adam, the keeper of Eden. And consider this: as you may or may not recall, this garden was a vegetarian garden. There was no eating of flesh.

> **And God said, Behold, I have given you every herb producing seed that is on the whole earth, and every tree in which is the**

> *fruit of a tree producing seed: it shall be food for you; and to every animal of the earth, and to every fowl of the heavens, and to everything that creepeth on the earth, in which is a living soul, every green herb for food. And it was so.*
> —**Genesis 1:29–30 DNT**

So Adam's relationship to the animals was such that he was not to eat them. They were to be his companions—his neighbors, if you will. God, of course, regards man in a higher status than the animals; however, he expects Adam to act responsibly. As we are told, Adam was given the privilege of naming the animals—an intimate move on God's part, I would say. Adam had been appointed steward of the animals.

> *And out of the ground Jehovah Elohim had formed every animal of the field and all fowl of the heavens, and brought [them] to Man, to see what he would call them; and whatever Man called each living soul, that was its name.*
> —**Genesis 2:19 DNT**

This is an easy job so far. Here comes the catch ... God gave Adam one stipulation for this peaceful existence in the garden. One tree was forbidden.

> *... but of the tree of the knowledge of good and evil, thou shalt not eat of it; for in the day that thou eatest of it thou shalt certainly die.*
> —**Genesis 2:17 DNT**

Why did God put such a constraint on Adam and Eve, his two human occupants? Is this the first hint of the concept of "free will"? You bet it is! I suppose God could have created this garden and its perfect beings and just sat back and watched as nothing changed. That would be quite robotic—a garden of robots. God knew that he should give us choices. He also knew that evil could arise from our choices. Evil was birthed as the Bible describes, due to a group of fallen angels. The leader of this group is Lucifer, better known as Satan. God's design took into account this preexistence of evil, and he wanted us to do the right thing: to choose him.

Remembering the Nature of God

When God wanted Adam to do the right thing, to choose God, he was exhibiting his nature. Before we continue with the story of the Garden of Eden as it relates to the true meaning of dominion, allow me to offer a few further thoughts on God's nature while considering God's commitment to the animals.

The way the world exists today is not what God wanted, but it is by his design. He is omnipotent, which means he carries unlimited power, authority, or force. Let's think about this a moment. If God really created the planet, he is the intelligent designer.

> *But Jesus, looking on [them], said to them, With men this is impossible; but with God all things are possible.*
> —**Matthew 19:26 DNT**

> *He counteth the number of stars; he giveth names to them all. Great is the Lord, and of great power: his understanding is infinite.*
> —**Psalm 147:4–5 DNT**

> *Remember the former things of old; for I am God, and there is none else; I [am] ~ God, and there is none else; [I am] God, and there is none like me; declaring the end from the beginning, and from ancient times the things that are not yet done, saying, My counsel shall stand, and I will do all my pleasure; calling the bird of prey from the east, the man of my counsel from a far*

country. Yea, I have spoken, I will also bring it to pass; I have purposed it, I will also do it.
—Isaiah 46:9–11 DNT

God is also omniscient, aware of all that occurs among the seen and the unseen, visible and invisible. Think about what it would be like flying an airplane around a city at a lower level than an airliner at cruise altitude. You would get the bird's eye view, wouldn't you? Remember, God sees *all* from that perspective. He has knowledge of all.

Are not five sparrows sold for two pennies? Yet not one of them is forgotten before God. Indeed, the very hairs on your head are all numbered. Don't be afraid; you are worth more than many sparrows.
—Luke 12:6–7 NIV

This verse set illustrates that God is all-knowing. However, I believe there is another meaning to this set of verses. Could it be possible that this is a New Testament directive that animals are in God's plan too? Could this be a hint that God will not forget animals and sparrows in the afterlife? We find a similar thought presented by Matthew in his rendition of Jesus's quote:

Are not two sparrows sold for a penny? Yet not one of them will fall to the ground apart from the will of your Father.
—Matthew 10:29 NIV

Now Jesus is expressing the *will* of God. The first verse in Luke says they will fall before God, unforgotten. The verse in Matthew says that if one falls, it is the will of God. God's will is in command here! He decides their fate, and they will not be forgotten. It certainly leaves room to ponder whether that commitment extends to not being forgotten in the afterlife. Of course, we'll be looking at this issue from many different angles as we continue the journey.

To shed more light on the nature of God, consider this verse set:

> *In that day I will make a covenant for them with the beasts of the field and the birds of the air and the creatures that move along the ground. Bow and sword and battle I will abolish from the land, so that all may lie down in safety. I will betroth you to me forever; I will betroth you in righteousness and justice, in love and compassion.*
> —Hosea 2:18–19 NIV

God is making a covenant to the animals, as he also speaks "in love and compassion" about how he will "betroth you to me forever." Clearly, this is not a human-centered God.

Many verses illustrate the game plan that God intends to play out, showing his nature as omnipotent, omniscient, compassionate Creator. They remind us why it is unimaginable to match a God of this magnitude, regardless of all our human philosophies and intelligence. Yet many claim that they know exactly what God meant or intended, lending to the concept that the animals are for us to do as we please. The evidence, however, suggests that God's intention, true to his nature, was far more compassionate. God does not want to be forgotten, and he promises not to forget a single sparrow …

Returning now to Adam and Eve, we learn that due to the fall in the Garden of Eden, there was a severe departure from God's original game plan. It's important for our exploration to note that the animals had nothing to do with this fall. They were innocent! Yet from the very beginning, we see that the consequences of Adam and Eve were extended to the animals as well. Genesis chapter 3 tells us that after Adam and Eve ate from the tree of the knowledge of good and evil, they were then banished from the garden. Death became a reality. All that was made could now decay, including the animals that had been under Adam's care.

No longer companions in harmony, the animals become fearful of Adam. It is said in Genesis 3:21 that God made garments of skin for

Adam and Eve to cover their nakedness. The details of this particular act are unknown. However, some believe that perhaps God *made* them, as it is interpreted, and that he did not kill an animal for the skins, as many have interpreted. God had created the planet by that point in the story, so he could surely have made skins or garments as well.

However, may I share another possible explanation from a PhD in Hebrew whom I interviewed? He stated that the word for "skins" in Genesis 3:21 is a degraded form of skin. It is a lower form from which God originally made Adam and Eve. This perishable coating, if you will, is the physical/skin/body that will now decay and perish versus the imperishable physical body of spirit and light form, of which God had originally made Adam and Eve. The religion of Judaism does not consider this verse to be referring to animal skins at all. In this particular example, it refers to the physical degraded body from imperishable to the perishable physical state of Adam's and Eve's bodies. Literally, it means that Adam and Eve were beings clothed in light originally, and now they are beings clothed in skin. Isn't that an interesting point of view?

Let's peer closely into the picture that is beginning to emerge at this time. Adam and Eve were supposed to trust God and not be tempted by Satan. They thought that if they listened to Satan, disguised as the serpent, they would gain the knowledge that God himself had. Once they disobeyed God, the conditions of the garden completely changed. In a garden that began without death, death was now looming. A garden where the animals had been companions with humans was now a garden full of fear among the animals. Cherubim are introduced into the story to ban Adam and Eve from the garden. They will start life outside of the garden in conditions that will bring forth death and decay.

God had given Adam and Eve all that they needed and made just one restriction, and they violated it. Because of the way they chose to exercise their free will, there is now the need for curse and redemption. God was clearly disappointed in Adam and Eve. However, keep in mind that he was *not* disappointed in the animals. They had been betrayed just as God had.

Being Good Stewards

As we dig deeper into our considerations of the Garden of Eden and its importance in understanding why animals are included in all of God's plans, including heaven, we're going to look at the original translation of the word "dominion." In Hebrew, the word is not "dominion"; it is "rule." In our sinful world, to rule over someone often holds a negative connotation. How many rulers, whether now or in the ancient past, actually rule for the good of their people and not with a personal agenda? Very few. That is definitely not consistent with how God defined or described the word "rule" or "ruler." The Bible makes that very clear. Remember, Adam was given the role of ruler over the animals in a paradise environment. What does a ruler look like in paradise versus one in a fallen world? This can paint a very different picture of God's original intention versus how we view it today. If we track the word "dominion," or "rule," in Hebrew as it is in Genesis 1:28, we find descriptions of what a great ruler looks like. For example:

> *For he had dominion over all the region on this side the river, from Tiphsah even to Azzah, over all the kings on this side the river: and he had peace on all sides round about him. And Judah and Israel dwelt safely, every man under his vine and under his fig tree, from Dan even to Beersheba, all the days of Solomon.*
>
> —1 Kings 4:24–25 KJV

This next verse set goes on to say that King Solomon was rewarded with great wealth and wisdom as a result of his worthy ability to "rule" as a just king.

> *Give the king thy judgments, O God, and thy righteousness unto the king's son. He shall judge thy people with righteousness, and thy poor with judgment. The mountains shall bring peace*

> to the people, and the little hills, by righteousness. He shall judge the poor of the people, he shall save the children of the needy, and shall break in pieces the oppressor. They shall fear thee as long as the sun and moon endure, throughout all generations. He shall come down like rain upon the mown grass: as showers that water the earth. In his days shall the righteous flourish; and abundance of peace so long as the moon endureth. He shall have dominion also from sea to sea, and from the river unto the ends of the earth ... For he shall deliver the needy when he crieth; the poor also, and him that hath no helper. He shall spare the poor and needy, and shall save the souls of the needy. He shall redeem their soul from deceit and violence: and precious shall their blood be in his sight.
> —Psalm 72:1–8, 12–14 KJV

Both of these passages refer to King Solomon and point to the coming kingdom of Christ. It is King David's prayer for Solomon as he passes on the idea of how a great king should rule. This is how he hopes his son, King Solomon, will rule. As the story goes in the Bible, King Solomon becomes a great king and finds great favor from God.

Is this example of how to care for the king's people analogous to how we have dominion over our children, our planet ... and our animals? We don't own the animals; they are under our dominion. They are God's. Some would argue that God made the animals for us, but this is biblically incorrect. He did not make anything for us. He made the entire planet as well as the humans for himself. This means that animals are not ours for disposal. We have been commanded to be good stewards to them, as a good shepherd is to his flock.

> For every beast of the forest is mine, and the cattle upon a thousand hills. I know all the fowls of the mountains: and the wild beasts of the field are mine. If I were hungry, I would not tell thee: For the world is mine, and the fullness thereof.
> —Psalm 50:10–12 KJV

> *For by him all things were created: things in the heaven and on earth, visible and invisible, whether thrones or powers or rulers or authorities; all things were created by him and for him. He is before all things, and in him all things hold together. And he is the head of the body, the church; he is the beginning and the firstborn from among the dead, so that in everything he might have supremacy. For God was pleased to have all his fullness dwell in him, and through him to reconcile to himself all things, whether things on earth or things in heaven, by making peace through his blood, shed on the cross.*
>
> —Colossians 1:16–20 NIV

When we keep in mind that we don't own the animals, then the role of being good stewards to them becomes a greater awareness from within our souls. We will remember that we need to deliver them when they "crieth," as the psalm states. And we will move away from the mistaken use of the verse of Genesis 1:28 to give ourselves carte blanche over the treatment of the animals. Because look where that carte blanche attitude has often taken us. When we deprive animals of sunshine, food, humane shelter—when we cram them into concrete slaughterhouses, where they stand and feed in their own feces in environments so tight that their legs crumble beneath them—we are not operating within the concept of being good stewards. This is not an example of acting as a benevolent leader.

And what about hunting for sport, when chances are slim that the hunter will be able to kill the target instantly, without causing any suffering? Or paying a price to go on a safari in Africa to gun down a giraffe for a trophy to hang on your wall? Is that really the kind of dominion God had in mind?

Reverend Professor Andrew Linzey, PhD, DD, HonDD, a member of the Faculty of Theology at the University of Oxford, is one of my favorite authors in animal theology. In his book *Christianity and the Rights of Animals* he wrote:

The whole point about stewardship is that the stewards should value what God has given as highly as they value themselves. To be placed in a relationship of special care and special protection is hardly a license for tyranny or even ... "benevolent despotism." If we fail to grasp the necessarily sacrificial nature of lordship as revealed in Christ, we shall hardly begin to make good stewards, even of those beings we regard as "inferior."

The point that bears emphasis is that when we take the time to reference the Bible, we see that God views the word "dominion" with compassion and mercy. That, after all, is consistent with God's nature. Dominion does *not* mean that we can be thoughtless over that which we are instructed to act as stewards. Rather, it means that we are entrusted to exercise dominion over the animals as God would exercise dominion over us.

> *Your kingdom is an everlasting kingdom, and your dominion endures through all generations. The LORD is faithful to all his promises and loving toward all he has made.*
> **—Psalm 145:13 NIV**

God required us to act in servitude to him, as he has dominion over us. God wanted this relationship for Adam and the animals. If we choose to follow God, we are surely under his dominion, are we not?

Recall that when God offered up his blessings to Adam and the animals alike, he confirmed his validation that "it is good" for both. He asked Adam to give the animals names. He gave the animals herbs as food, just as he did for Adam. So at the time, prior to Adam's sin, the partaking of the fruit from the forbidden tree, God intended the world's inhabitants to be vegetarians and to live in harmony. Again, there was no eating of flesh, even among the animals. Adam, then, was to have been the first ruler—the first steward in the Garden of Eden.

We find that God spares no effort to show us repeatedly in the scriptures what a good ruler looks like. God also gives us strict instructions on how to care for the animals that are in service to us. There should be no question as to what a good steward is according to the Bible. Here are some specifics:

> *Thou shalt not plow with an ox and an ass together.*
> **—Deuteronomy 22:10 KJV**

An ass is much weaker than an ox. God does not want undo strain on the ass by not being able to keep pace with the ox.

> *For the scriptures saith, thou shalt not muzzle the ox that treadeth out the corn. And the laborer is worthy of his reward.*
> **—1 Timothy 5:18 KJV**

> *A righteous man regardeth the life of his beast: but the tender mercies of the wicked are cruel.*
> **—Proverbs 12:10 KJV**

And in Exodus, when the Ten Commandments are given to Moses, again the animals are mentioned:

> *But the seventh day is the sabbath of the Lord thy God: in it thou shalt not do any work, thou, nor thy son, nor thy daughter, thy manservant, not thy maidservant, nor thy cattle, nor thy stranger that is within thy gates ...*
> **—Exodus 20:10 KJV**

Through scripture, we have seen examples of what a good ruler looks like in God's eyes. We have noted in scripture that God established rules that dictated the fair treatment of the animals. All of this stands as further evidence that animals do not merit being referred to as mere furniture in the room. Why would one conclude that a sentient object that God calls "good" is of no value and therefore would be excluded from eternal oneness with God, the Creator, in heaven?

God's Game Plan

Those who have read the Bible from front to back understand that it can seem extremely complicated, with many strange customs or stories of the past. The challenge of referring to those stories while keeping the purpose of the Bible pure has spawned countless wars, denomination separation, feuds, and conflicts. That's sad because that is the last thing that Jesus wanted. He viewed things so differently. Jesus called himself a teacher and servant of God.

> *But Jesus knew what they were planning. So he left that area, and many people followed him. He healed all the sick among them, but he warned them not to reveal who he was. This fulfilled the prophecy of Isaiah concerning him: "Look at my servant, whom I have chosen. He is my beloved, who pleases me. I will put my Spirit upon him, and he will proclaim justice to the nations. He will not fight or shout; or raise his voice in public. He will not crush those who are weak, or quench the smallest hope, until he brings full justice with his final victory. And his name will be the hope of all the world."*
> —**Matthew 12:15–21 NLT**

And Jesus said:

> *Salt is good: but if the salt have lost his saltness, wherewith will ye season it? Have salt in yourselves, and have peace one with another.*
> —**Mark 9:50 KJV**

As we know, Jesus preached about peace and a new covenant. I have heard many argue that we as Christians should be in favor of war. With the current situation our great country finds itself, I am not taking position with the morality of being at war. That is another book entirely! For a moment, I invite you to ponder the reminder that Jesus came to bring peace on earth as it is in heaven. He preached repeatedly and consistently throughout the New Testament to love one another and to do unto others as we would have done unto ourselves.

Jesus, as prophesied in the Old Testament, brought a new covenant. He brought new rules. God's new rules! The New Testament lays them out with renewed intention. And he comes not fighting or shouting, as the previous verse states. He doesn't even defend himself when he is being questioned prior to his crucifixion. Why? Because that was God's plan. God would send a messiah to deliver us from evil. He did this to give us a chance at eternity. God realized that we as humans are imperfect and not capable of keeping the Ten Commandments. We became imperfect by the taking of the forbidden fruit and would forever live with the consequences on earth. But God had a larger plan. He would free us from that vanity and bondage by setting a messiah into the plan as a deity in human form. He is the ultimate display of a good ruler. To be included in the dominion of this shepherd we call Jesus, as faulty as we are, we can simply choose to follow him into eternity. We can use his name to gain a ticket to heaven. The animals, as we will learn, have a different means of gaining entry into heaven—the same heaven where we will be.

We will be looking at the story of Jesus extensively in a later chapter, as we will also revisit the Garden of Eden when we reveal more exciting and significant evidence that will strengthen our hope for reunion with our pets. As we conclude this initial stop in the Garden of Eden, we are left with this understanding: The choice to follow Satan's game plan or God's game plan rests now in our hands and our hearts. So too is the choice of whether or not to live by the true meaning of dominion, to be benevolent rulers over the animals, and to recognize God's actual intent for his animal kingdom—both on earth and in his heaven.

A PLACE ON THE ARK AND THE LAWS OF NOAH

Chapter 3

A PLACE ON THE ARK AND THE LAWS OF NOAH

You are to bring into the ark two of all living creatures, male and female, to keep them alive with you.
—**Genesis 6:19 NIV**

We move our attention forward now to one of the best-known stories of the Bible—Noah and the ark. This story occurs early in the Bible and is told in Genesis chapters 6 through 9. We will explore it here to further understand: (1) how important God's animals have always been to him and the high regard he holds for them; (2) how they play major roles in the most prominent stories of the Bible; and (3) how God displays his grace and mercy by maintaining an ongoing commitment to the animals' welfare and their future.

Shedding light on these matters will continue to reveal the picture of a God who will never forget his animals, a God who will welcome and embrace animals in heaven.

Let's begin by tracing the background of Noah and the ark. After the fall of the Garden of Eden, violence ensues among mankind. The human population has chosen to follow Satan's game plan rather than God's game plan. God is deeply disappointed in mankind and his choices. In fact, the earth has become so corrupt and filled with violence that God decides he would rather not have any humans around at all rather than watch them continue to act so contrary to his wishes.

> *The LORD saw how great man's wickedness on the earth had become, and that every inclination of the thoughts of his heart was only evil all the time. The LORD was grieved that he had made man on the earth, and his heart was filled with pain.*
> —Genesis 6:5–6 NIV

So God decides to destroy the inhabitants of the planet. The animals are also going to drown in the flood along with the humans. As we learned earlier, after the fall of Adam and Eve, the animals are subject to earthly consequences. However, not *everything* will be destroyed. As we know, God tells Noah about the flood that will wipe out the rest of the planet, and he makes it clear that Noah and his family will be saved from the coming destruction. Noah has a job: he must save two of every kind of animal. He will build the ark and take all those animals with him to safety.

How amazing and telling it is that God saves just one man and his family but commands this ark to be built to accommodate all the animal pairs. Think of it: *all* of God's animals will have a place on the ark! God is making a dramatic statement: the animals and their future well-being are *vitally* important to him. Again, this clearly is not a human-centered God. He is worried about the animals, and he will not allow them to be subjected to eternal nothingness. Animal life shall endure, just as human life shall. The animals will not be forgotten or left behind.

> *And they went to Noah, into the ark, two and two of all flesh, in which is the breath of life.*
> —Genesis 7:15 DNT

It appears that the animals were conscious of God's plan and appreciated God's grace and mercy. As we are told, the animals peacefully march onto the ark. Let's stop and think about the magnitude of this occurrence for a moment. It is really quite a miracle that all of these beasts, both vicious and docile, could harmoniously walk on board and then peacefully coexist together for this wild ride to come. Perhaps you've heard the verse "All things are possible through God"; this event is surely a good example, I would say.

As the story continues, the storm lasts 150 days, and Noah and all the animals continue to live in harmony on the ark. Noah sends a raven out, but it returns. He sends out a dove, and on the second flight, it returns with the olive branch. God finally instructs Noah to disembark the ark. The storm has subsided. Noah and his family are free, and they and all the animal pairs have been delivered safely. But God has something to say:

> *And God blessed Noah and his sons, and said to them, Be fruitful and multiply, and fill the earth. And let the fear of you and the dread of you be upon every animal of the earth, and upon all fowl of the heavens: upon all that moveth on the ground; and upon all the fishes of the sea: into your hand are they delivered. Every moving thing that liveth shall be food for you: as the green herb I give you everything. Only, the flesh with its life, its blood, ye shall not eat. And indeed your blood, the blood of your lives, will I require: at the hand of every animal will I require it, and at the hand of Man, at the hand of each the blood of his brother, will I require the life of Man. Who so sheddeth Man's blood, by Man shall his blood be shed; for in the image of God he hath made Man. And ye, be fruitful and multiply: swarm on the earth, and multiply on it.*
> —Genesis 9:1–7 DAR 1890

Here is the NIV interpretation for verses 3–5:

> *Every living thing that lives and moves will be food for you. Just as I gave you the green plants, I now give you everything. "But you must not eat meat that has the lifeblood still in it. And*

> *for your lifeblood I will surely demand an accounting. I will demand an accounting from every animal. And from each man, too, I will demand an accounting for the life of his fellow man."*

So here we are. Noah has docked safely ashore, and God is having a dialogue with him. Now that the earth has been flooded and Noah has consumed all the herbs that he loaded on board, God is now saying that he may use the animals for his food source. Yes, God has decided that he must let man eat animals now. He had created the Garden of Eden as a paradise where Adam and the animals were to live harmoniously in a vegetarian state. The fall of Adam and Eve changed all that, and the animals lived in fear of Adam. Now, because of man's hardened heart and his vile way of living, the earth no longer exists as it was before and God is allowing us to consume animals.

By the way, if there is evidence that other cultures were eating animals prior to the flood, it should be noted that was not in God's game plan until this time. And you can see what happened to those other cultures!

The animals, who peacefully boarded the ark initially, are now going to fear Noah and his family. But God is making strict rules on their behalf. Humans are going to be held accountable for every animal they kill. They must remember that when they kill an animal, the life they kill is not their own. It is to be done for sacrifice and food only. Also, man "must not eat meat that has the lifeblood still in it." God is very direct about this.

> *And every one of the house of Israel, or of the strangers who sojourn among them, that eateth any manner of blood—I will set my face against the soul that hath eaten blood, and will cut him off from among his people: for the soul of the flesh is in the blood; and I have given it to you upon the altar to make atonement for your souls, for it is the blood that maketh atonement for the soul.*
>
> —Leviticus 17:10–11 DAR 1890

You might already be thinking that this is surely not the focus of what we learn in school or church about the story of Noah and the ark. We get a pretty picture of Noah and the animals being saved, but we don't hear much about what's going to happen next. We don't usually spend much time talking about how God gave Noah a covenant that includes the animals as well:

> *And God spoke to Noah, and to his sons with him, saying, And I, behold, I establish my covenant with you, and with your seed after you; and with every living soul which is with you, fowl as well as cattle, and all the animals of the earth with you, of all that has gone out of the ark—every animal of the earth. And I establish my covenant with you, neither shall all flesh be cut off any more by the waters of a flood, and henceforth there shall be no flood to destroy the earth. And God said, This is the sign of the covenant that I set between me and you and every living soul that is with you, for everlasting generations: I set my bow in the clouds, and it shall be for a sign of the covenant between me and the earth. And it shall come to pass when I bring clouds over the earth, that the bow shall be seen in the cloud, and I will remember my covenant which is between me and you and every living soul of all flesh; and the waters shall not henceforth become a flood to destroy all flesh. And the bow shall be in the cloud; and I will look upon it, that I may remember the everlasting covenant between God and every living soul of all flesh that is upon the earth. And God said to Noah, This is the sign of the covenant which I have established between me and all flesh that is upon the earth.*
> —Genesis 9:8–17 DAR 1890

As we take a closer look at this covenant, we see that God repeats his central message five times. Each time, the animals are fully included: "every living soul of all flesh." As I have mentioned, in a later chapter we will dive deeper into the importance of the word "soul" in this particular case as well as in other biblical references. I will reveal how such critical terms were lost in translations of the Bible. For now, we'll stick with our focus on the repetition of God's central message in this covenant. That is certainly a sign that animals are of great significance to God, worthy to be addressed in the same way that he addresses humans. Even the animals are to be accountable for the taking of a life, as are men. God gave man specific animals to eat to survive, but the blood is not to be eaten, for the life (soul) of the animal is in the blood. God values life; he also owns life.

> *The Lord giveth and the Lord taketh away.*
> —Job 1:21 KJV

Perhaps this is a lesson that God wants us to understand. Man, because of his sin, can only live by the death of another. And as we have seen in the ending of the drama of Noah, man now survives by the death of an animal. The animals and their role in the Bible are pointing to future events and their significance.

The Noahide Laws

The covenant given to Noah is also significant because it is a critical component of what became known as the Noahide Laws. The first six laws were mentioned earlier in Genesis, but in chapter 9, the law of capital punishment and the law against tearing the limb of an animal and refraining from the eating of its blood were added.

The Noahide Laws were critically important at this time. They precede the Ten Commandments. The story of Noah, as narrated by Moses, is a preliminary story in the history of mankind. Therefore, at this point in the biblical story, all human beings are under the laws of Noah.

The *Encyclopedia Britannica* defines the Noahide Laws as "a Jewish Talmudic designation for seven biblical laws given to Adam and to

Noah before the revelation to Moses on Mount Sinai and consequently binding on all mankind." David Novak, in his book *Jewish-Christian Dialogue,* describes the Noahide Laws:

> The first explicit presentation of the Noahide Laws is in the Tosefta, a work commonly believed to have been edited in the late second century of the Common Era. There we read: "Seven commandments were the sons of Noah commanded: (1) concerning adjudication, (2) and concerning idolatry, (3) and concerning blasphemy, (4) and concerning sexual immorality, (5) and concerning bloodshed, (6) and concerning robbery, (7) and concerning a limb torn from a living animal."

The Tosefta is a compilation of the Oral Law of Judaism. Over time, the seven laws have appeared with minor variations in wording through many sources.

The Noahide Laws have maintained a prominent place through the passing centuries, especially in the Jewish tradition, where they are held in the highest regard. The seventh law, tearing a limb before killing it, or eating of an animal's blood, known as "strangulation," extends to the restriction of cruelty to animals. The foundation verse for the prohibition of cruelty and consuming an animal's blood is Genesis 9:4. Many Jewish documents, such as the *Encyclopedia Judaica,* go into great depth about cruelty to animals and the punishment that will ensue. Many Jews are vegetarian because of a mandate in the Torah to not cause any suffering to an animal: *tsa'ar ba'alei chayim*. The verse in Deuteronomy 25:4 that states that an ox may not be muzzled while he is plowing is an example and the foundation verse for this doctrine. To this day, due to these same laws, Jews are not permitted to hunt or consume an animal's blood. It is against their religion, said simply.

This theology has been respected long into the modern era. Many Christians followed the resulting dietary rules up until the seventeenth century. And here is an interesting twist! The Noahide Laws are still active today. President George Bush Sr., in 1991, officially recognized the Noahide Laws into a pubic law that reads, "Whereas these ethical values and principles have been the bedrock of society from the dawn of civilization, when they were known as the Seven Laws of Noah." Public Law 102–14, 102nd Congress, 1st session, H.J. Res. 104 also designates March 26 as Education Day. The law reads, "We turn to education and charity to return the world to the moral and ethical values contained in the Seven Noahide Laws."

Looking at number seven in more detail, you could certainly say that it is another way of emphasizing that we are meant to be caretakers of God's creatures—good stewards. By refraining from being cruel to animals through the act of removing flesh from a live animal prior to its expiration (death), we demonstrate our willingness to exist as partners with these creatures in God's world. We avoid suffering. An example of strangulation (law number 7) that has application in a modern world would be that of the cattle industry. For example, euthanasia of a cow occurs shortly before slaughter, and it is important that the cow is expired before the slaughter begins. There has been evidence that assembly lines accelerate so quickly that not all cattle have died before the process continues. This is a clear example of a violation of the Noahide Laws.

As many of you know, animal cruelty legislation applies to domestic animals but not necessarily to all farm animals. And as the intent of the Noahide Laws was to bring righteousness to both mankind and the animals, their practices are far from the letter of the law today. Factory farming of the current times is laced with atrocities and cruel practices that I am sure are against the nature of God. I believe Jesus would be against any suffering at all, human or animal, wouldn't he?

I could go on about animal rights, but I also need to acknowledge the reality of the covenant to Noah. God is indeed allowing us to consume animals, and for some animal lovers, this is a tough issue of the heart. But before we ask ourselves where God is when we are faced with examples of cruelty, let's ask ourselves, where is man? Be comforted in the reminder that this was not God's original intention.

And according to the Christian religion, one day, God's original Garden of Eden will return. When that happens, it will be a perfect environment. It was and will again be an environment free of eating flesh.

The story of Noah and the ark serves as another compelling reminder of how much God truly cares about his animals. He saved them from extinction in the flood. Every animal's future was preserved! He didn't simply single out the animals that would help humans survive. He included *all* of them. And even as he allowed Noah and his people to eat animals, God established rules to govern them.

Animals clearly have a prominent role in this important covenant. In fact, they are very much involved in every covenant, curse, and redemption in the Bible. That's how much they matter to God. But God does not stop there. What about the story of Moses? They are certainly included in the Ten Commandments.

Moses and the Ten Commandments

As the story of mankind continues in Exodus, Moses is given the daunting task of freeing the Israelites from the bondage of the Egyptians. God strikes the Egyptians with several plagues to convince the pharaoh to set the Israelites free. There is the plague of water becoming blood; the plague of frogs, gnats, and flies; the plague on the livestock of the Egyptians; the plague of boils, hail, locusts, and darkness; and finally the plague of the firstborn.

Amidst the plagues, there were opportunities to be passed over. For example, God gives the Egyptians the chance to move the livestock inside to be protected against the hail. And those who believed Moses did so. The pharaoh, however, is still not convinced after all these plagues upon his people and their animals. It takes the plague of the firstborn and the death of his own child to finally convince him to release the people of Moses. The details are covered in Exodus chapter 11, and we will revisit this plague in the next chapter.

So the people of Moses are now free, and it is time for Moses to receive the Ten Commandments. He is given instructions to climb the mountain, and no person or animal may touch this mountain at the time of this moment in history. There are also physical boundaries around the mountain because it is holy.

> *Put limits for the people around the mountain and tell them, 'Be careful that you do not go up the mountain or touch the foot of it. Whoever touches the mountain shall surely be put to death. He shall surely be stoned or shot with arrows; not a hand is to be laid on him. Whether man or animal, he shall not be permitted to live.' Only when the ram's horn sounds a long blast may they go up to the mountain.*
> —**Exodus 19:12–13 NIV**

We can see from this verse set another example of how the animals are included in every curse, as they are in every blessing. That's how important they were to God, and further evidence of the status they have always held.

So Moses receives the commandments. For our purposes, we turn our attention to the Fourth Commandment, where it states that the animals cannot be worked on the Sabbath: You must give rest to the animals on that day. Then, when we get to the Sixth Commandment, take a moment to notice that it does not say that you shall not kill your fellow man. It simply says thou shall not kill. Just a thought.

The Ten Commandments were given to the Israelites. These commandments, as well as the 613 laws that come along next, were not given to the other occupants of the planet, the Gentiles. They were bestowed upon God's chosen people: the Israelites. This is where we come to an important concept as to the "division" of the law, the differentiation between the Noahide Laws and Mosaic Laws. The Mosaic Laws, which are the Ten Commandments, are specifically and exclusively for the Israelites. It is thought that Moses wrote the first five books of the Bible. Therefore, Jewish law under Moses is the residing law of Judaism.

If you are not Jewish, then you are not, at this time, under Mosaic Law. You are still abiding by the Noahide Laws. The Gentiles, in fact, remain bound by Noah's laws throughout history, including the era both prior to and after the time that Jesus is resurrected, fulfilling the prophecies of the Old Testament and commencing the age of the new law under Christ.

Kosher Laws: Animals Protected Again

Allow me to stay with this discussion of ancient laws a bit longer so that we may see further evidence of how animals have been protected throughout biblical history. A part of the Mosaic Law that was given to the Israelites included many dietary rules. They are called "kosher" laws, and many of you may be familiar with them. Most of them are derived from the Torah books of Leviticus and Deuteronomy. Some of these rules include euthanizing the animals in the most humane and pain-free method, as well as draining the blood and prohibiting the eating of an animal's blood. They also decree that the animal to be consumed cannot have died from an accidental death or from a hunt, and that you cannot mix meat and milk due to the commandment not to cook a kid in its mother's milk.

It takes several years of formal schooling and apprenticeship to become a kosher butcher. Kosher law dictates that the animal be slaughtered with a deep, quick stroke across the throat with a sharp knife. It is thought that this method is painless and causes unconsciousness within two seconds, so it stands as the most humane method of slaughter. Jews do not eat the blood of an animal because they adhere to the Torah's prohibition of blood, for the blood contains the soul of the animal.

Judaism includes the belief that following these and all the laws of Moses makes one closer to God and perhaps worthy of inheriting an eternal life. The Israelites would regard a Gentile who is abiding by the

Noahide Laws as a "righteous" person. A Gentile following the Noahide Laws would also be seen as one closer to God, one perhaps eligible to inherit the kingdom hereafter. Interesting, isn't it? Those who abided by strict laws that included important safeguards for animals were closer to God. That's another illustration of the value that God placed on animals.

I'm going to conclude this chapter with my interpretation of one biblical story related to animals that is often misunderstood. This particular story is the basis for the justification that allows Christians to consume any and all animals without the restrictions of the Old Testament. Perhaps this justification is incorrect. You be the judge.

Cornelius and the Book of Acts

Let's take a quick quantum leap forward to the New Testament, stopping at the book of Acts. Jesus, of course, has already been crucified and resurrected. Christ has bestowed certain talents upon his disciples. They now are able to heal, and their mission is to spread the good news about Christ and his teachings. Peter has been given the keys to the kingdom, and all of the disciples have been given the Holy Spirit. Keep in mind that all of the disciples are Jewish, as was Christ, but the good news is being preached to all, Gentile and Jew alike. However, some issues are confusing to the disciples. They are still practicing some of their Jewish traditions.

This background sets the stage for the story of Cornelius the Roman centurion. What follows is my idea of what God or Jesus intended the story to mean. To walk you through this account, I am going to engage in a sample of some of the procedures that I will explain in more detail later regarding the tracking of original meanings from the Bible, and how the translations that followed sometimes confuse or obscure those meanings.

Peter gets a vision in which he sees animals both clean (kosher) and unclean (forbidden to be eaten by kosher law). All of these animals are being pulled down from heaven by a sheet. The actual Greek word for this sheet from heaven is *othone*, a fine linen. In the plural form, the word is *othonion*, which is described in *Strong's Expanded Exhaustive Concordance*, my primary source for translating Bible passages from the original language they were written in, as "strips of cloth with which the body of the Lord was bound." Here we have the same linen that was used to wrap Jesus's body being used to pull the animals down from heaven. This word is common to both animals ascending back and forth from heaven in the vision, as well as Christ's body when he is being prepared in death prior to his resurrection.

As the story continues, Peter hears a voice from God that says to "kill and eat." Peter refuses, stating that he has never eaten anything impure. The voice replies, "Do not call anything impure that God has made clean" (Acts 10:15). The sheet with all the animals is then "taken back up to heaven," as the Bible then clearly states.

A voice from God tells Peter that he will be summoned by three men to go to the home of Cornelius, the Roman centurion. Sure enough, the men appear and speak to Peter:

> *"We have come from Cornelius the centurion. He is a righteous and God-fearing man, who is respected by all the Jewish people. A holy angel told him to have you come to his house so that he could hear what you have to say."*
> **—Acts 10:22 NIV**

Peter now understands what the vision means. When he enters the house of Cornelius the centurion, he finds a large gathering.

> *He said to them: "You are well aware that it is against our law for a Jew to associate with a Gentile or visit him. But God has shown me that I should not call any man impure or unclean."*
> **—Acts 10:28 NIV**

By this verse, we see that Peter himself said that the vision is not about the killing and eating of animals at all. It is no longer prohibited by Jewish law to dine or associate with the Gentiles. It is about Hebrews and Gentiles being recognized by God alike under the new covenant of Christ. You see, the clean animals in the vision represent the Hebrew people and the unclean animals represent the Gentiles. This is of great significance because many Christians today use the vision of the animals, along with the phrase "kill and eat", as newfound permission to eat any animal and abandon the dietary laws of the Old Testament.

While we are here, let's also consider the severity of the English interpretation of the word "kill" in the phrase "kill and eat." We find that the Greek word for "kill" in this instance is defined with a softer meaning than the English word "to kill" or "to end a life". The Greek word *apokteino* means "to kill, to end a life, to slay" according to the *Strong's Exhaustive Concordance*. *Apokteino* is used often in the New Testament specifically for this meaning. But is not present in the verse we are addressing, "to kill and eat." The word present in this particular verse is *thuo,* which is used as the verb "to breathe hard" and "to sacrifice." It primarily means "to offer first fruits to a God," according to *Strong's Expanded Exhaustive Concordance.*

With this understanding in mind, I do not believe that this verse in the Bible frees us to consume any of the animals at free will without concession and, perhaps, without accountability. What if the original writer of the book of Acts meant for the statement to read as follows: "Sacrifice your traditions and go commune with Cornelius. Offer Cornelius's love unto Christ?" Is not one's love offered to Christ a fruit unto God? Wouldn't that change the entire meaning? After all, Cornelius was still practicing kosher dietary rules and preparing his meals in the style of representing life and in gratitude to God. And in actuality, regardless of interpretation, God does tell Peter that "nothing is impure that God created," and that it is now permissible to eat among fellow men in Christ.

But Peter is still on a mission. Why was Peter brought to Cornelius's house in the first place? You see, Cornelius is going to be the first Gentile to receive the Holy Spirit. Peter is to bestow this blessing upon Cornelius. At the time, only Jews had been brought to Christ and had

Heaven Is for Animals Too

received the Holy Spirit. And why did God choose Cornelius? Well, he was described as "righteous," and earlier we learned that a righteous Gentile was a non-Jew who was abiding by the Noahide Laws. And it is clear that Cornelius was honoring the seven Noahide Laws. We know this because later in the story of Acts, Peter is called to a Jewish council to explain why he entered a Gentile's home and, more so, why he bestowed the Holy Spirit upon a Gentile. Peter then responds to the council of Jerusalem:

> *"Brothers, you know that some time ago God made a choice among you that the Gentiles might hear from my lips the message of the gospel and believe. God, who knows the heart, showed that he accepted them by giving the Holy Spirit to them, just as he did to us. He made no distinction between us and them, for he purified their hearts by faith."*
> —Acts 15:7–9 NIV

Peter has just explained that God *showed* him, through the vision of clean and unclean animals, and by having him facilitate Cornelius receiving the Holy Spirit, that there is now "no distinction between us and them." He continues the explanation:

> *"It is my judgment, therefore, that we should not make it difficult for the Gentiles who are turning to God. Instead, we should write to them, telling them to abstain from food polluted by idols, from sexual immorality, from the meat of strangled animals and from blood."*
> —Acts 15:19–20 NIV

In this set of verses, Peter tells the council that any Gentile who is following these four points of the Noahide Laws is righteous and deserves to be a part of the following of Christ. (Did you notice that three out of the four points of the Noahide laws described in Acts 15:20 pertain to animals?) According to Peter, all have the opportunity to be purified by God. God, through this vision to Peter, is letting him know that all of mankind is welcomed into his kingdom. All should be given the opportunity to follow the new covenant of Jesus.

Now, because Cornelius was following the seventh Noahide Law, he would have been honoring some dietary restrictions related to animals, including avoiding cruelty. This is one of the reasons he was chosen as the first Gentile to receive the Holy Spirit. Why, all of a sudden, would Peter's vision change the law and allow newfound followers of Christ to kill and consume any or all animals, as many current Christians have concluded? It just does not make sense. And we should remember that the allowance to consume flesh was a concession by God, but not without consciousness as well as the restrictions that come with it.

The story of Cornelius is just one of the dozens of examples of how original meanings from the Bible were significantly altered through translations. I will spend more time with these translation issues in the upcoming chapter, in which I outline the clear and compelling evidence that animals have souls and spirits. You will see that many of our most common assumptions regarding God's perspective of the animal kingdom and whether or not they belong in the afterlife have stemmed from startling and dramatic changes in meaning due to translation.

Before we cover that ground, however, it's time to explore the most inspiring story of the Bible, a story that, like all of the most important stories of the Old Testament, includes the animals. Yes, we're going to look closely at the story of Jesus. We'll be stopping often to look for further clues that may shed light on our exploration of the status of the animals and how important they are to God, their Creator, and how God will remember them in the redemption of the world as well. May you find comfort in these words and the words to come.

THE LAST SACRIFICIAL LAMB

Chapter 4

THE LAST SACRIFICIAL LAMB

> *The high priest carries the blood of animals into the Most Holy Place as a sin offering, but the bodies are burned outside the camp. And so Jesus also suffered outside the city gate to make the people holy through his own blood.*
> —**Hebrews 13:11–12 NIV**

The dark stillness of the night looms. It is a stillness of terror, low lying like a fog stifled without wind. Ah, but there is a wind. It is wind from the breath of God. This black flowing fog surges through the pharaoh's kingdom like a powerful current. An angered God has become impatient. His numerous warnings have been rejected several times. And now the death of the firstborn of animal and child is slithering on into the night.

A single man's pride holds firm under his ignorance of God. This battle is the desire of that man, the pharaoh. The pharaoh, however, is not a matched gladiator for God, for he is but a mere mortal. It is God he is resisting, or perhaps he is resisting what he does not fully understand. Consequently, his kingdom will fall prey to this fog of God's breath in the night.

Yet there is a merciful undertow to this wave of death among the firstborn, for the enslaved townsmen have listened to God. In fear and anxiety, they have protected their homes with the blood of lambs. Sacrificial lambs' precious blood has been draped and painted and smeared on the entryways and doors of those who have chosen to listen. As the fog of death flows by and inhales the aroma of the blood-draped doors, both the firstborn children and animals that reside there will be spared. Those with the blood smeared on their doors have made a gesture of belief and will therefore be passed over by the fog of death that continues to hunt its prey.

The pharaoh has only one child, a child whose soul will now be kidnapped by the darkness of the night. As he mourns his lost child, he discovers that the pride that prevented him from heeding God's warning has been washed away, replaced by destitution and despair.

This is my own representation of that dramatic story from the Bible that we touched upon in the previous chapter, when we followed the trail that led to Moses receiving the Ten Commandments. It is the story of the Egyptian pharaoh who was warned but refused to listen when the fog of death came after his only son. All firstborns, both animals and children, were under the plague. The Israelites and their animals were protected, but the Egyptians who ignored these warnings, or who chose to follow the pharaoh, were not protected. Finally, after the pharaoh lost his child, he released the people of Moses.

Christians and Jews refer to this eventful night as the "Passover." To this day, it is a celebrated event. It is only one example of the many stories throughout the Bible in which the blood of the lamb has saved God's believers. In all of these stories, we find a common thread: the lamb's blood is an atonement. For hundreds and thousands of years, the Israelites used the blood of a perfect, unblemished animal to atone for their sins.

This is a significant ritual, but it was not what God originally desired. As the story goes, after Adam and Eve ate of the forbidden fruit, the world fell from grace. It became a fallen world, with humans for centuries living with these consequences. Thus the need for animal sacrifice as atonement became a religious necessity.

As God's story continues, however, we are given a sequel, a new means of atonement. And that brings us to the story of Jesus and the ongoing vitally important connection of the animals within that glorious story ...

The Animals and Jesus

Let us go back and recall how Jesus came into the scene. Jesus is born in a manger setting. Think about that for a moment. A manger setting, among the animals, in the animal's environment, is where Jesus is brought into the world. Of course, he is there with his earthly parents, Mary and Joseph, and others later come to see him. But those others are not present at his birth, only a large group of farm animals, so peaceful and gentle-looking as they have been depicted in thousands of manger scenes all over the world.

Years later, Jesus begins his teachings after John the Baptist baptizes him and the Holy Spirit descends on him like a dove (Mark 1:10). Did you know that doves were considered the first domesticated animal? In the book *The Bible According to Noah*, by Gary Kowalski, I learned that the wild rock dove of Eurasia was apparently one of the earliest animals to be domesticated and that terra cotta figurines of pigeons that are over six thousand years old have been unearthed in Iran. Doves, or pigeons, are monogamous and affectionate, and they mourn when their partners die—in a similar way that we humans mourn.

Doves also make great GPSs. They are a wonder, even to scientists. This bird displays the behavior of a loving, gentle, devoted being. Interesting that God would choose this bird as a representation to deliver the Holy Spirit to Christ himself. Even if the words "the spirit came down like a dove" are meant to be symbolic, it's fascinating to consider how God uses the analogy of one of his finer creations to symbolize the beginning of Christ's era. So for this vital passage point, as with so many important stories in the Bible, the animals are present.

There's more. After his baptism, Jesus commences his role as the Messiah by meditating in the wilderness and subjecting himself to Satan. This is one of Jesus's first recorded actions as told in the Gospel of Mark. Jesus chooses to take time away from the public, away from humans, in the solitude of the wilderness, to prepare for his teachings. And he is among the wild animals. For those forty days and forty nights, he lives safely among these wild animals.

> *And he was in the desert forty days, being tempted by Satan.*
> *He was with the wild animals, and angels attended him.*
> —**Mark 1:13 NIV**

The Bible is painting a picture of Jesus as a man of solitude and peacefulness. We see this consistent characteristic throughout his life. We move forward now to one of the many enduring messages from Jesus's teachings.

> *Blessed are the peacemakers, for they will be called sons of God.*
> —**Matthew 5:9 NIV**

Think about this verse containing these oft-repeated words of Jesus. Peacemakers—who are the peacemakers? Who will be called the sons of God? Let us peek into a few verses in the book of Romans:

> *For the creation was subjected to frustration, not by its own choice, but by the will of the one who subjected it, in hope that the creation itself will be liberated from its bondage to decay and brought into the glorious freedom of the children of God.*
> —**Romans 8:20–21 NIV**

This verse set is indicating that there will be a call to be brought unto the sons of God. That means to be brought to God into heaven and eternity. In Romans 8, Adam subjected the creation to bondage and decay, also bringing death into the world. Remember, there was no death and decay when Adam was directed to name and then rule over the animals. It was a perfect paradise. After the fall, the world and its contents were in peril. But the book of Romans says "they" live in the hope to be released from this bondage and "brought into the glorious freedom as children of God." The apostle Paul and Jesus are saying that peacemakers will also be in God's favor as his sons. With that comes an inheritance—a son's inheritance is what God has to offer. It is eternity.

Again, it is important to understand that Jesus came to bring peace. Throughout the New Testament, Jewish elders ask Jesus, "What are the two most important commandments?" Jesus explains that we need to love thy God with all our hearts and souls, and to love thy neighbor (Matthew 22:34–40). He then said, "On these two commandments the whole law and prophets hang." The apostle Matthew, in the Gospel of Matthew, reminds us of these characteristics of Jesus as prophesied by Isaiah.

> *He will not quarrel or cry out; no one will hear his voice in the streets. A bruised reed he will not break, and a smoldering wick he will not snuff out, till he leads justice to victory.*
> —**Matthew 12:19–20 NIV**

To simplify this, I would like to present the New Living Translation:

> *He will not fight or shout; he will not raise his voice in public. He will not crush those who are weak, or quench the smallest hope, until he brings full justice with his final victory.*

And this is how Jesus himself puts it:

> *"Come to me, all you who are weary and burdened, and I will give you rest. Take my yoke upon you and learn from me, for I am gentle and humble in heart, and you will find rest for your souls. For my yoke is easy and my burden is light."*
> —**Matthew 11:28–30 NIV**

You see, we often hear or quote the phrase "an eye for an eye." This phrase is actually from the Old Testament. Times have changed with the first coming of Christ. It is now out with the old and in with the new. It was Jesus who said to "turn the other cheek" in Matthew 5:39 and to "live by the sword, die by the sword" in Matthew 26:52. We are building upon the evidence that Jesus was here to bring a peaceable kingdom. Jesus did not come to condemn the world. He came to save it.

> *For God did not send his Son into the world to condemn the world but to save the world through him.*
> —**John 3:17 NIV**

> *Do not judge, and you will not be judged. Do not condemn, and you will not be condemned. Forgive, and you will be forgiven.*
> —**Luke 6:37 NIV**

How many of us can say, whether we follow any religion or not, that these words are even remotely similar to our thought processes in day-to-day life? It doesn't matter how you feel about religion—if you pick up a Bible and read only the red to distinguish the words of Jesus, you will find quite a peaceful picture of Jesus. You will find a man who preaches that we should love God, love one another, and forgive one another. He heals anyone who asks, and he feeds the poor. From a religious point of view, he is offering eternity to anyone who follows his teachings.

Now let's return to the trail of animals appearing so often at critical moments of Jesus's journey on earth. As you may know, in the Roman Empire of his day, it was common for leaders of regions to ride their horses into a city to display their might and power. After Jesus predicts his death, he rides into Jerusalem not on a horse but on a donkey colt. This is one of the few times that Jesus is recognized in his glory as Lord and King. Many of the people waved palms, bowed down, and praised Jesus. Of course, these same people did not stand up for him in the few days that followed this event, during which he was crucified. This is important because the prophet Zechariah prophesied this very act in the Old Testament. Christians today recognize this event as Palm Sunday.

> *See, your king comes to you, righteous and having salvation, gentle and riding on a donkey, on a colt, the foal of a donkey.*

> *... He will proclaim peace to the nations. His rule will extend from sea to sea and from the River to the ends of the earth.*
> —Zechariah 9:9–10 NIV

Again, keep in mind that Jesus rides in on a donkey, not a prestigious horse. You see, Jesus has been prophesied in the Old Testament, as many as three hundred times according to respected theologians. The Old Testament proclaims what will happen in the messianic era, which is the time when a messiah is on the earth and includes his legacy. In this case, we are considering Jesus the Messiah. The prophecies say he will be born among the animals; he will preach love and forgiveness; and then he will be rejected, beaten, and crucified. He will rise from the dead. He and those who follow his teachings will enter eternity, in a paradise where the "lion will eat straw like the ox."

As we follow the stories of Jesus, these prophecies are now beginning to unfold. During that period, the Romans were suppressing the Israelites and controlling Jerusalem. So the Israelites thought that Jesus was coming to lead them out of this repression by the Roman Empire. Jesus, however, makes it clear that he is not here to lead a war but to fulfill the prophecies of the Old Testament and to bring peace. Many people did not understand, however, that this was to be peace through God and not peace through a victory of war.

> *Do not think that I have come to abolish the Law or the Prophets; I have not come to abolish them but to fulfill them.*
> —Matthew 5:17 NIV

The Lost Sheep

The religious Jewish leaders, the Pharisees and the Sadducees, did not like what Jesus was doing in Jerusalem. Do you remember the story of the temple? Jesus goes to the temple and sees people using it as a market for the sale of sacrificed animals as well as the sale of innocent animals such as cattle, sheep, and doves. He believes that the merchants are taking advantage of foreigners with their high prices, and that they are crowding out the people coming to the temple to worship. In response to this disrespect in the house of God, he turns over the tables and runs the merchants off. Keep in mind that this is the only time in the Bible that Jesus displays anger. Note that in this case, he is unprovoked. In all other cases, when he is provoked, beaten, and later crucified, he remains quiet, with little words or defense. He simply states that one should love God with all his heart and soul, and one should love thy neighbor.

Now Jesus has brought even more attention to himself, and the Pharisees feel threatened. They are going to get rid of him. They accuse him of not following their traditions and accuse him of associating with people of ill repute. They want to crucify him for saying that he is the Son of God (blasphemy) and for not keeping the Sabbath holy by performing acts of healing the sick, which was considered work and therefore not to be done on the day of rest. In his response to this accusation, Jesus points to an example of a lost sheep. Thinking back to the earlier chapter on the true meaning of dominion, we can see this as Jesus proposing the idea of being a good shepherd.

> *He said to them, "If any of you has a sheep and it falls into a pit on the Sabbath, will you not take hold of it and lift it out? How much more valuable is a man than a sheep! Therefore it is lawful to do good on the Sabbath."*
> —**Matthew 12:11–12 NIV**

There are other examples of Jesus's words illustrating his kindness and compassion toward the animal world, as if they are models for how we also should regard God's creatures. He mentions in Luke 12:6 that not one sparrow falls to the ground forgotten by the Father (God). In Matthew 6:26 he advises us to "Look at the birds of the air, for they neither sow nor reap nor gather into barns; yet the heavenly father feeds them." In Matthew 17:27, he puts a coin in a fish's mouth to teach the disciples to pay their taxes. He sends his disciples out to teach and tells them to be as shrewd as a snake and as innocent as a dove. Remember, the dove is the representation of the Holy Spirit descending upon Jesus.

The Blood of Animals, the Blood of Jesus

What we've just been pointing out are individual, specific references to animals playing a part in the stories of Jesus. The next example that we will explore carries a deeper, more significant meaning concerning the connection between Jesus and the animal kingdom.

Jesus has come to fulfill the prophecies of the "renewal of all things" (Matthew 19:28). His second coming will bring a reconciliation between nature and mankind, as well as a reconciliation between mankind and God. How does this reconciliation play itself out? And why was Jesus so angry in the temple where the sacrificed animals were being sold? It may at first seem like an incredible twist, but I would like you to think about it as incredible clarity.

> *The high priest carries the blood of animals into the Most Holy Place as a sin offering, but the bodies are burned outside the camp. And so Jesus also suffered outside the city gate to make the people holy through his own blood. Let us, then, go to him outside the camp, bearing the disgrace he bore. For here we do not have an enduring city, but we are looking for the city that is to come. Through Jesus, therefore, let us continually offer to God a sacrifice of praise—the fruit of lips that confess his name. And do not forget to do good and to share with others, for with such sacrifices God is pleased.*
> **—Hebrews 13:11–16 NIV**

In this set of verses, the apostle Paul is speaking to the Hebrews, reminding them that Jesus died on the cross and shed his blood for them. Once he rose from the dead and was resurrected, the new law was in effect.

Notice what else Paul says. He symbolically compares the ritual of animal sacrifice to what happened to Jesus. He is telling the Hebrews that the old ways of the scriptures are over and we are to live as Jesus instructed. Animal sacrifice is not to be continued, for Jesus was the last sacrifice, as an atonement for us all and to clear all our past sins.

This is the genesis of the term the "last sacrificial lamb" in relation to Jesus. God is directly comparing the blood of animals to the blood of Jesus. The blood of animals and the blood of Christ are seen as one, in the likeness of Christ. Think for a moment about how significant this message is. God provides another sacrificial lamb. This new lamb will be sacrificed with his bloodshed, just as the lamb's blood was shed on the doors and entryways of the Israelites in the story of the Passover, which we explored at the start of this chapter. This blood is for us, so that we too can be passed over from the darkness of death and separation from God. This lamb was God's only son, a firstborn that God would give to us, just as the blood of the animals was given to God in the Old Testament. This blood of Christ will be the last bloodshed used for atonement.

Consider the implications of this profound connection. Before Jesus, God established the sacrifice of animals as the means to atone for our sins. With the death and resurrection of Jesus, *his* sacrificial blood has replaced the blood of the sacrificed animals. I don't know about you, but I am deeply stirred as I reflect on the kind of statement *that* makes about the importance of animals in God's plan! The sacrifice of the animals and Jesus's sacrifice come along the same continuum.

As we study this verse set from Paul and related biblical reference points, we learn even more about the strong, enduring link between Jesus and the animal world. And we find even more compelling reasons to believe that animals are included in the afterlife.

The Bible refers to the ancient practice of animal sacrifice in great length. It is a complicated act, with many parameters to it and several important ramifications for us. Originally, the blood of the animal to be sacrificed had to be sprinkled on the altar, and then the rest of the blood was to be drained at the base of the altar (Leviticus 8:15). The blood was not to be consumed, for the souls of the animals are in the blood. Yes, that is right—the *soul* of the animal is in the blood. The Bible is quite graphic about this.

> *And every one of the house of Israel, or of the strangers who sojourn among them, that eateth any manner of blood,—I will set my face against the soul that hath eaten blood, and will cut him off from among his people; for the soul of the flesh is in the blood; and I have given it to you upon the altar to make atonement for your souls, for it is the blood that maketh atonement for the soul.*
> **—Leviticus 17:10–11 DNT**

I need to point out that this Darby translation is a direct Hebrew translation. In the more modern versions of the Bible, the word "soul" is left out of these verses. As mentioned, I will cover in depth the problems of translation, especially as it relates to that key word "soul," in the next chapter. What's important to keep in mind here is that sacrificing an animal was a severe concession from God to mankind due to his hardened heart. There are many times in the Bible where God, through the prophet Isaiah or through Jesus himself, expresses his displeasure with sacrifice and his disappointment that it must be called into the game plan with man. He would much prefer a turn from sin by man.

One example of God's displeasure is when Isaiah addresses a rebellious nation and mocks the idea of animal sacrifice.

> *The ox knows his master, the donkey his owner's manger, but Israel does not know, my people do not understand.*
> **—Isaiah 1:3 NIV**

> *Hear the word of the LORD, you rulers of Sodom; listen to the law of our God, you people of Gomorrah! "The multitudes of your sacrifices—what are they to me?" says the LORD. "I*

> *have more than enough of burnt offerings, of rams and the fat of fattened animals; I have no pleasure in the blood of bulls and lambs and goats."*
> —Isaiah 1:10–11 NIV

> *But whoever sacrifices a bull is like one who kills a man, and whoever offers a lamb, like one who breaks a dog's neck; whoever makes a grain offering is like one who presents a pig's blood, and whoever burns memorial incense, like one who worships an idol. They have chosen their ways, and their souls delight in their abominations.*
> —Isaiah 66:3 NIV

So according to the Bible, breaking a dog's neck is like worshiping an idol. And we all know God does not like us worshiping idols. It's interesting to see that even the consumption of a sacrificial animal came with numerous rules. The animals had to be perfect and unblemished. God considered this a serious matter. His rules were designed to make those involved aware of his hatred for sin and death and of the price paid for the atonement of sin.

Animal sacrifice, then, can truly be regarded as an advanced look into what God had in store for the future. God had a larger plan. He would eventually send his only begotten son to be the *last* sacrifice for all people for their sins. This final sacrifice could allow us, in spite of our sinful ways, to continue to find God, to return to God.

I believe that when Jesus cleared out the merchants from the temple, he knew that sacrificial practices were going to be a thing of the past. Sacrifice had become a business. And soon all that would change forever.

At the Last Supper of the Passover tradition, Jesus tells his disciples to "take and drink, for this is my blood that will be shed for you" and "take and eat, for this is my body." Couldn't it be said that Jesus is going through the ritual of an animal's sacrifice? As eloquently stated by Norm Phelps in his book *The Dominion of Love*:

> By identifying his own execution with the killing of animals by human beings, Jesus was saying that, 'Just as my death is unjust, so is theirs.' This identification with all who suffer, which includes the poor, the oppressed, and the animals, forms the ethical text of Jesus's life and death.

Is this not a perfect example of the imitation of Jesus? Wasn't Jesus perfect and unblemished? Now we can partake in the blood of this past tradition, through Christ, once and for all, as the ritual of communion in remembrance of Christ's sacrifice for us.

Before we move on, let's take a moment to think now about the animals that had been sacrificed prior to Jesus. What if as soon as they were killed, their souls departed and went to be with the Lord? It seems cruel that God would eliminate many animals in the flood of Noah or, worse yet, advocate sacrifices that would permanently end the life of an innocent animal. But what if, in the picture of things unseen, the animal is released from the bondage of this world and goes on to heaven to be with God after he is sacrificed? From God's perspective, the animal would then be safe with him. It had fulfilled its mission and had lived under the inclination of God.

Sacrificial practices represented and pointed to the coming of the Messiah. The Messiah himself models suffering and death, just as the animals who were sacrificed did. They represented Jesus and what Jesus would do for us!

> *For God so loved the world, that he gave his only-begotten Son, that whomever believes on him may not perish, but have life eternal.*
> **—John 3:16 DNT**

So let's reflect on the ground covered in this chapter about Jesus and his major link to God's animal kingdom. When God came to the earth as a man, he was surrounded by peaceful animals. Jesus prepares to begin his journey by spending time in the wilderness among the wild animals, meditating with God and rebuking Satan. He lives his life preaching about peace and love. He does not fight or defend himself against his accusers. He blesses them, "for they know not what they do." He forgives us all and sheds his blood for us all, just as if he were an animal sacrificed. He was perfect and unblemished. He really was the last sacrificial lamb!

Seen through this lens, the story of Jesus shows us again just how significant animals are to God. After he made them, he said that they are "good." The animal's blood had the same purpose then as Christ's blood does now. This reincarnate deity become man, Christ, was the last blood to be shed. And now we are all welcome in heaven. As it states in Luke 12:6, not one sparrow is forgotten by God.

ANIMALS HAVE SOULS AND SPIRITS—WHAT ORIGINAL TRANSLATION REVEALS

Chapter 5

ANIMALS HAVE SOULS AND SPIRITS—WHAT ORIGINAL TRANSLATION REVEALS

> *We have not received the spirit of the world but the Spirit who is from God, that we may understand what God has freely given us. This is what we speak, not in words taught us by human wisdom but in words taught by Spirit, expressing spiritual truths in spiritual words.*
> —1 Corinthians 2:12–13 NIV

No matter what your religious affiliation or spiritual beliefs happen to be, there's a good chance that at some point you have heard the following common explanation for those who would argue that animals do not go to heaven: *Animals do not have souls. Therefore, they cannot inherit the kingdom of heaven.*

Maybe you have found yourself believing that explanation at some point, perhaps even until now. It sounds so simple, so clear, and so authoritative, doesn't it? Many ministers certainly proclaim that to be the case. They will tell you that this explanation should end any doubt or debate about the issue of animals going to heaven.

Ah, but if you ask them for the biblical evidence that supports their explanation, they do not sound as clear or authoritative. When persons occupying pulpits state that animals do not have souls and therefore cannot and will not go to heaven, they are not scripturally correct.

The reality is that animals do have souls, and spirits as well. It is plainly stated in the Bible. The existence of souls and spirits among the animal kingdom is just one more example of the body of biblical evidence that points us emphatically toward the conclusion that animals will be included in the afterlife.

In this chapter, we're going to take a close, detailed look at this evidence. We'll be on a "trip through translation" to fully understand the original meaning and intent of the writers of the Bible. We will discover the important changes and omissions that occurred as the Bible was converted from one language to another. Prepare yourself for some exciting discoveries that will be revealed as we hold up our magnifying glass to these ancient writings.

Evolution of the Bible

Before we begin this expedition, we need to address this question briefly: where does the Bible come from? Speaking for myself, I accept the Bible as an authentic document. More than that, I do solemnly believe that the scriptures are divinely inspired. However, some matters of the Bible may have been innocently ignored or omitted as the Bible matured into an English document. Through the many translations, there were poetic challenges to the process of interpretation. Ideas, thoughts, or words may have become lost or deemed irrelevant, leading to possible misconceptions, which took hold and lasted for centuries or even millenniums. Therefore, an understanding of the evolution of the Bible will be a precursor to unveiling these particular problems with translation that have clouded the concept of animals having souls and spirits.

When I began my own trip through the translation of the Bible, I often remembered the excellent advice that I received while developing my skills as an animal trainer: "Know the nature of the beast." A good trainer can capture the essence of the animal's nature and use it to train the animal in harmony and with mutual respect. Whether you're working with dogs, horses, dolphins, or killer whales, being able to communicate in their language with respect to their nature will surely elevate you from the average to the elite in the world of domesticating and training animals. That's why I think it's so important to take into account the nature of the Bible, its history, and its original languages while seeking clarity on the subject of animals going to heaven.

Where does the Bible come from? Here are some key points to keep in mind:

- The Old Testament comprises of thirty-nine books referred to as the Hebrew Bible. It is written in Hebrew and Aramaic. The word *testament* means "covenant," and the Old Testament is about the promises that God made to Abraham. The Old Testament is arranged in three parts. The "Law" is the first five books, believed to be written by Moses, also known as the Torah. The next two sections are the "Prophets" (Nebiim) and the "Writings" (Ketubim). Put those three names together and you have Tanakh.
- Another Hebrew version of the Torah is referred to as the Pentateuch.
- The Septuagint is a Greek translation of the Torah and the Pentateuch. The Septuagint later included the entire Old and New Testaments.
- Greek survived as the common language of the Roman Empire and through the birth of the New Testament. However, the order of the books of the Old Testament in the Septuagint has been changed. They are the Law, the Writings, and the Prophets. This is the order we have today; however, Jesus quotes them in their original order of the Tanakh.
- Before Christ, scholars were brought to Jerusalem to translate the Hebrew and Aramaic into Greek. There was a constant struggle to standardize the Hebrew Old Testament. Translation challenges were already underway before Jesus was even born.

- The New Testament is a new and last covenant God made with all people, through the life and death and resurrection of Jesus Christ. Jesus himself was a descendant of Abraham and referred to the Old Testament as "scripture" and the "word of God." Jesus rose from the dead in 30 AD. The New Testament books were written between 49–96 AD by Matthew, Mark, Luke, John, Paul, James, Peter, and Jude.
- The church then recognized the twenty-three New Testament books as canonical in 200 AD, but they are not yet collected into one book.
- The New Testament collection, as it is today, was canonized during the council of Laodicea and Carthage in the fourth century. Within these councils came the confirmation of the writings of Jerome and Augustine.
- Canon of the New Testament was confirmed by the Catholic Church (Council of Carthage) in approximately 397 AD.
- Translations of the Bible began in earnest when church scholar Jerome translated the scriptures into Latin in the fifth century.
- Parts of the Bible were translated into many different languages over the next several centuries, and in 1382 John Wycliffe translated the entire Bible into English from Latin. Think of it: more than a millennium had passed before the Bible ever had an English version!
- The popular King James Version was birthed in 1611, completing a mandate from King James of England, who appointed fifty-four scholars to complete the task.

New English versions followed the King James Version, but by then some fundamental changes had already happened and would not be altered. The King James Version and New Living Translation, for example, have much of the same meaning, but in many examples that I will present, the ancient Hebrew and Aramaic translations from the Old Testament, as well as the Greek translations from the New Testament, reveal something very different. Why? I believe that inaccuracies lie within the framework of the more modern translators and their cultural bias. The original Hebrew and Greek writings had far less room for the evolution of language to mask the original intent of the authors, who had been given the divine inspiration.

That's why it is necessary to explore the original languages of Hebrew and Greek to reveal the authenticity of meaning regarding animal souls and spirits. We will clear away all the dust that has covered over those original meanings so we can see them in the same light as the original authors.

Word-for-Word Translation

One may consider three primary approaches in understanding the Bible and its translation:

1) The thought-for-thought method. This approach is designed to help the reader understand the idea or equivalent meaning while maintaining the accuracy. Some examples are the New International Version and the New Century Version.
2) The phrase-for-phrase method. This approach, in which the meaning moves further away from the thought-for-thought style, is considered the most elementary version and thus the easiest to read. It allows for a wider sector of society, regardless of education level or language skills, to have the pleasure of reading and understanding the Bible. One example is the Living Bible, which is less complicated than the King James Version. It allows first-time readers to follow along with a better comprehension within the limits of everyday language.
3) The word-for-word method. I consider this approach the most accurate. How can we actually learn the intent of the original authors if we don't first interpret each delicate word unto its own meaning?

I will be consistently using the word-for-word method as I take you back to the original Hebrew words of the Old Testament and the original Greek words of the New Testament. A superior aid for this approach is the *New Strong's Exhaustive Expanded Concordance of the Bible: Red-Letter Edition*. You may recall that I have mentioned this document previously. Now it's time to take it a step further in our understanding.

Strong's Concordance assigns a numerical value to every word in the Bible, and then you are given the Hebrew and/or Greek words and their definitions. This allows you to then take an English word and look up the Hebrew or Greek equivalent. It is a milestone for navigating translations, a priceless way to sift through word choice conversion from English to original Hebrew or Greek. As I apply this method to our study, any number that I insert next to a referenced word will be referring to this particular *Strong's Concordance* numbering system. While referring to the concordance itself throughout, I will call it simply *Strong's Concordance*.

The actual name for the field of study of different versions or translations of the Bible to determine or validate the accuracy of a given meaning is called "textual criticism." According to Henry Hampton Halley's book *Halley's Bible Handbook*:

> Textual criticism involves the comparison of the various manuscripts or editions to determine as exactly as possible the original text.

I will be taking verses from the Bible and pointing out key words, then converting those words to Hebrew if a verse from the Old Testament and to Greek if it is from the New Testament. Then I will explain how the different versions of the Bible compare, to get back to that exact word choice of the original author before the meaning was obscured. Again, this is important because in English we may not be seeing the exact word choice of the original author. Variances may change the meaning or intent of the verse, or perhaps oversimplify its meaning. Perhaps there may even be a greater truth birthed from this process. We may realize that what we were taught in church or in a culturally biased society is not necessarily what the Bible actually says.

As we journey into translation, the message revealed is a strong indicator of a God of grace, mercy, and compassion, a God who would not delete the animal kingdom. As the Bible tells us, God is omnipotent and omniscient. He is all-knowing and has unlimited power and authority. The Bible also tells us about many miracles performed by God. Perhaps the biggest miracle God performed is the miracle of the creation. We will begin our biblical excavation in this chapter by looking at Genesis and the creation story because it has significant clues for us about the words "spirit" and "soul" and how these two words relate to animals.

The Soul and Spirit of the Creation Theory

Most people will admit that they believe in an intelligent design for the universe. Even scientists who find holes in the big bang theory fill their doubt with an intelligent design. The Bible goes into great detail to tell us about what God intended when he created the world. The Bible also says that there will be heaven on earth someday. There will be a new heaven and a new earth, and it will be a place of peace and harmony. The wolf shall lie down with the lamb. This new earth will be a return to the original paradise God created when he made Adam and Eve. Let's look at the Lord's Prayer, specifically the line "Thy kingdom come, thy will be done, on earth as it is in heaven." Like many of us, I recited this prayer for years without really analyzing what I was saying. If you consider it carefully, you will see that it means that someday earth will be as grand as it is in heaven. So if God created the planet and its occupants in the creation description in the first two chapters of Genesis, why would he only restore us and not the animals? Again, that is a human-centered perspective. Let's try to imagine a God-centered perspective.

As God began his most precious miracle, the creation, his spirit was engaged in the process of production.

> *And the earth was without form, and void; and darkness was upon the face of the deep. And the Spirit of God moved upon the face of the waters.*
> —**Genesis 1:2 KJV**

God (and God's spirit) goes on to create the light separate from the darkness, the firmament (the sky), the dry land, the vegetation, light from the firmament of the heaven, the animals of the sea, the animals of the sky and of the land, Adam and then Eve. By the way, it occurs in that order. The animals were created before Adam. Also note that the Bible does not say that God's spirit ever leaves the scene. God's spirit is always with his creation.

God's Spirit Never Leaves

Remember that in Genesis 1:2, God's spirit moved upon the face of the water, so his spirit is upon all that he created. And this spirit never leaves. In fact, it stays the same forever and ever. As the scripture says, God never changes. You see, the word for God's spirit in chapter 1, verse 2, is number 7307: *ruwach*. So the Hebrew word for "spirit" is *ruwach*, and the Greek equivalent is *pneuma*, number 4151.

> *And Moses spake unto the LORD, saying, Let the LORD, the God of the spirits of all flesh, set a man over the congregation ...*
> —**Numbers 27:15–16 KJV**

"God of the spirits of all flesh"—there it is! We see the word in Hebrew for spirits, number 7307: *ruwach*.

I would like to add here another term that will come up often, without controversy but significant to the animals. That term is "all flesh," which in Hebrew is number 1320: *basar*. It means "flesh of the body, both humans and of animals; of all living things."

> *And the Spirit of God hath made me, and the breath of the*
> *Almighty hath given me life.*
> —Job 33:4 KJV

If we understand Genesis in this light, we can see that the Holy Spirit is in all that God created. The Holy Spirit is in all flesh, so all flesh has the spirit of God. We know that the Bible tells us that the Holy Spirit gives eternal life, so that would mean that the animals are included in the picture of an eternal life—a place in the afterlife.

I invite you to reflect on those verses related to having a spirit and a soul for a moment. When I spent time considering the words as they appear in those verses, I found myself thinking of the Holy Trinity and how God the Father, the Son, and the Holy Spirit are all one being. According to the Bible, we as humans are also of three parts: the body, soul, and spirit. And as we're beginning to see, evidence in the Bible tells us that animals too have bodies (flesh), souls, and spirits.

Let us read what Flavius Josephus, a respected historian during the time directly after Jesus's crucifixion, wrote in his works titled *The Antiquities of the Jews, Book III*:

> However, he entirely forbade us the use of the blood for food, and esteemed it to contain the soul and spirit.

And we have this from the Bible:

> *And the very God of peace sanctify you wholly; and I pray God*
> *your whole spirit and soul and body be preserved blameless*
> *unto the coming of our Lord Jesus Christ.*
> —1 Thessalonians 5:23 KJV

The following verse specifically addresses animals and spirit:

> *I said in mine heart concerning the estate of the sons of men, that God might manifest them, and that they might see that they themselves are beasts. For that which befalleth the sons of men befalleth beasts; even one thing befalleth them: as the one dieth, so dieth the other: yea, they have all one breath; so that a man hath no preeminence above a beast: for all is vanity. All go unto one place; all are of the dust, and all turn to dust again. Who knoweth the spirit of man that goeth upward, and the spirit [ruwach, number 7307] of the beast that goeth downward to the earth?*
> —Ecclesiastes 3:18–21 KJV

So apparently beasts (animals) do have spirits. That is what the Bible says in this set of verses. Is the author of Ecclesiastes, Solomon, stating that we are being presumptuous to think our spirits go up and the spirits of the animals go down? Here is a great example of a common translation error. Many theologians use this particular verse set to actually say that animals or beasts are doomed to dust. Well, I would agree with "and the spirit of the beast that goeth downward to the earth" if it had finished with a simple period. But it does not. It ends instead with a question mark. This simple difference can change the whole meaning. This is why examining interpretation will give us a cumulative body of evidence that animals will be a part of God's grand finale.

Now, if God's spirit is in all he created, why would he not include a third of his creation (the animal kingdom) in the new heaven and earth?

> *Then shall the dust return to the earth as it was, and the spirit [ruwach, number 7307] shall return unto God who gave it.*
> —Ecclesiastes 12:7 LITV

To appreciate the meaning of this verse fully, it's time for some translation work. In the King James Version, specifically in Ecclesiastes

3, the word "beast" is the word used for animals. It is the only word used for animals throughout the KJV of the Bible. But there is more. Ecclesiastes 3:21 obviously makes note of a beast's spirit. In Ecclesiastes 12:7, the specifics of what happens to a spirit are explained. Notice that I have inserted the Hebrew word *ruwach* next to "spirit" with the *Strong's Concordance* number in both verses. So God creates his masterpiece as a Garden of Eden, and he breathes a soul and spirit into all the animals and Adam and Eve. That same spirit shall return to God who gave it. He loves his creation. He is steadfast and true … to all that he created.

References to the Animal's Soul

Let's get back to our close-up look at Genesis. I love Genesis because it gets right to the issue of the soul and the spirit. Genesis chapter 1 is the creation of the world. As I have mentioned, by day five, God made the first two sets of animals. What is so interesting in this context is that the same verbiage in Hebrew is used for the animals as it is for the creation of Adam.

I will be using a direct Hebrew-Greek-English translation to help define these verses for you. My favorite is by Jay P. Green and is a direct word-for-word translation of the Bible. It is formally named The Interlinear Bible, Hebrew-Greek-English (LITV). Another is the Darby 1890 version (DAR). The Dead Sea Scrolls (DSS) are often used to verify these choices. I have recently seen books interpreting the Dead Sea Scrolls; however, their authors make the same mistakes as the modern translators. As a result, I have interviewed scholars in Hebrew to validate these findings, and I have been blessed to have seen some of the scrolls.

Here's where the numbering system of *Strong's Concordance* gets interesting in terms of animals possessing souls. The Hebrew word *nephesh* is assigned number 5315, and it is directly translated as "soul." But watch what happens to the word *nephesh* in the English translations. In many cases, it is given another meaning. The word "soul" literally disappears!

Interestingly, this seems to be a common occurrence in the Bible when speaking of animals. In fact, the word "soul" is left out of modern translations such as the New King James Version, the New International Version, and the New American Standard Bible 195 times compared to pre-1611 versions of the Bible.

Let's watch the disappearing act in operation from two verses of the Darby New Translation (DNT) in comparison to the KJV:

> *And God said, Let the waters swarm with the swarms of living souls, and let the fowl fly above the earth in the expanse of the heavens. And God created the great sea monsters, and every living soul that moves with which the waters swarm, after their kind, and every winged fowl after its kind. And God saw that it was good.*
> **—Genesis 1:20–21**

The King James Version (KJV):

> *And God said, Let the waters bring forth abundantly the moving creature that hath life, and the fowl that may fly above the earth in the open firmament of heaven. And God created great whales, and every living creature that moveth, which the waters brought forth abundantly, after their kind, and every winged fowl after his kind: and God saw that it was good.*

Notice the substitution for the reference to "soul" and "living soul." That's how the question of animals having a soul gets obscured. But there is much more to this passage.

The New International Version (NIV):

> *And God said, "Let the waters teem with living creatures and let the birds fly above the earth across the expanse of the sky." So God created the great creatures of the sea and every living*

> *and moving thing with which the water teems, according to their kinds, and every winged bird according to its kind. And God saw that it was good.*

The word paired to number 5315 (*nephesh*/soul) is the word *chayyah* in Hebrew. It has been assigned number 2416. It is in the feminine form and means "living being" all by itself. In the original Hebrew, numbers 2416 and 5315 are together here in Genesis 1:20, 21, as well as in verse 24 of the Darby translation. All these refer to animals. Directly interpreted, these two combined words mean that they are "living beings with souls," as we see specifically in the Darby direct word-for-word translation. Here is another example of another verse, different translation; however, it reads similar to the Darby:

> *And he brought them to the man, to see what he would call it. And all which the man might call it, each living soul, that was its name.*
> —**Genesis 2:19 LITV**

The KJV and the NIV again leave the word "soul" out of this sentence and substitute it with "living creature." That's one more example of the animals being de-emphasized, which contributes to the mistaken notion that they will not have a place in heaven. If the modern translations maintained the "soul" reference to so many verses like these from Genesis, then clergy would have less rationale for rejecting the idea that animals will be included in the afterlife.

The Key Link: Adam and the Animals

Now take a close look at the wording of the first time God mentions Adam specifically, in Genesis 2:7. This is how it reads from a direct Hebrew word-for-word translation by Jay. P. Green, *The Interlineal Bible* (LITV).

> *And Jehovah God formed the man out of dust from the ground and blew into his nostril the breath of life; and man became a living soul.*
>
> —Genesis 2:7 LITV

The term "breath of life" in this verse is numbers 2416 and 5397. Number 5397 means "vital breath": *neshamah*. So we are reading it as "living vital breath." We can all agree that "breath of life" is a sufficient translation here. However, the last two words of this verse, "living soul," are the numbers 2416 and 5315, paired together. That just happens to be the same wording used to describe the animals in the earlier verses. So you see, the Hebrew verbiage is the same for Adam as it is for the animals! I can't tell you how significant this is. You may want to pause and reread this last paragraph.

We are seeing more clearly why translation variances are so important to our cause of finding evidence of animals having souls and spirits. This is why I am sticking to the original Hebrew. Remember, this part of the Bible was written approximately twenty-five hundred years before Christ. I truly believe in my heart that when the original authors wrote the word "soul" or "spirit," that is what they meant. It wasn't until the modern era that all the poetic variances came into play.

Next we'll point our close-up lens on verses 29 and 30 of Genesis chapter 1:

> *Then God said, "I give you every seed-bearing plant on the face of the whole earth and every tree that has fruit with seed in it. They will be yours for food. And to all the beasts of the earth and all the birds of the air and all the creatures that move along the ground—everything that has the breath of life in it—I give every green plant for food.*

This is the New International Version. In original Hebrew, however, those two words in the phrase "breath of life" (numbers

2416 and *neshamah*, number 5397) are not there. What is there in original Hebrew are the numbers 2416 and 5315. And as we know, 2416 and 5315 paired together equals *nephesh chayyah*: "living soul." So "breath of life" is clearly defined as number 2416 in combination with number 5397, as we saw in the first part of Genesis 2:7. In English, it has been improperly placed in this verse. Later, in Genesis, the NIV will use "breath of life" many times, when the actual word in Hebrew is "spirit." This is where I really have a problem with modern translations. In the NIV, this substitution of "breath of life" is not accurate at all, as I have stated, and it is continually used to replace the words "soul" and "spirit."

So it seems that when speaking of the animals, the word "soul" (number 5315) is substituted in English, even though in the original Hebrew or in the Dead Sea Scrolls (DSS) it is not "vital breath" (number 5397) but rather "soul." Now you can see how and why the word "soul" is left out so many times in modern translation.

Next we turn our attention to how verse 30 reads in original Hebrew (LITV):

> *And to every living thing on earth, and to every bird of the heavens, and to every creeper on the earth, in which there is a living soul, every green plant is for food. And it was so.*

Now look at this same verse in the King James Version:

> *And to every beast of the earth, and to every fowl of the air, and to every thing that creepeth upon the earth, wherein there is[c] life, I have given every green herb for meat; and it was so.*

The subscript *c* stands for the footnote in the King James Version that says that the literal translation is "soul." But how many people would take the time to look at that footnote? Not many, I imagine. As a result, most readers will miss the "soul" reference entirely.

The Mistake Clergy Make

So there it is. From the creation story of Genesis, according to the original translations of the Bible, animals do indeed have souls. When you take the time to examine it, the evidence is actually clear. You see, what I think actually happens to many clergy—innocently, I am sure—is that they read these modern translations and figure that the animals are of the "breath of life" and not of a soul, like Adam. This mistake often comes up during my discussions with ministers, pastors, and priests.

I remember one such discussion with a Protestant minister who strongly believed that animals do not go to heaven, solely because animals were given the "breath of life" and Adam was given a "soul." When I asked him what the Hebrew word was, he quoted me an incorrect word. When I gracefully corrected him, he got aggravated. He could not come up with one scriptural piece of evidence to support his position. In his Bible, the word "soul" was omitted, hence his conclusion.

Continuing our exploration into the word "soul," let's look closer at the *Strong's Concordance*. As we have seen, they assign this word as number 5315. The concordance goes into detail and devotes an entire column to this word as an object of eternity. However, in abbreviated versions of the concordance, I have seen it stated that "soul" is the inner person as apart from the outer person, and that it can be the act of breathing. That's curious because in the unabridged version of the concordance the word for number 5314, *naphash*, not to be confused with *nephesh*, is defined "to breathe; respire; to be refreshed."

In my 2001 edition of *Strong's Expanded Exhaustive Concordance,* we find this definition regarding the word for number 5315:

> In narrative or historical passages of the Old Testament, *nephesh* is translated as "soul". In Lev 17:11 "For the life of the flesh is in the blood: and I have given it to you upon the altar to make an atonement for your souls: for it is the blood

that maketh an atonement for the soul." The soul of the man that immaterial part, which moves into the afterlife (the body is buried and decomposes) needs atonement to enter into God's presence upon death.

Again, we see further backing of the conclusion that the Hebrew word *nephesh* means "soul," so when it's used in relation to animals in the Bible, it is a clear indicator that animals have souls.

Now, I need to mention that there is an argument that this dualistic theology of body being separate from soul was Greek and Latin in origin, not ancient Hebrew. As far as the question of animals having souls, this has led some naysayers to state that the word "soul" did not really mean anything to the Hebrew people back in that era. The concordance references this belief. I do not believe this to be true at all. The Hebrew people definitely believed in an afterlife and a release from the bondage of the human form.

Let's look at a translation issue that directly deals with the issue of dualism. In Genesis 35:18 of the King James Version, we read:

And it came to pass, as her soul was departing (for she died), that she called his name ...

The Hebrew word for "soul" is number 5315, and that is exactly how it is translated in Hebrew. But let's look at another translation, this one from the NIV:

As she breathed her last—for she was dying—she named her son Ben-Oni.

There are two important points to make in this example. One, the first verse verifies that the soul *does* leave the body upon death. Two, this is another illustration of modern translations leaving out the word "soul" again.

For direct evidence of the Hebrew belief in an afterlife, I learned about the next distinction from a PhD in Hebrew Studies, with whom I had the pleasure of spending a whole day in his company. Who better to teach me the ways of Judaism, and to verify much of my research, than a Hebrew scholar?

Let us turn to the book of Ezekiel, written in approximately 571 BC. The set of verses I am presenting appears in the *Life Application Study Bible, New International Version*. It explains how the prophet Ezekiel's purpose is to foretell the eventual salvation of God's people.

> *The hand of the LORD was upon me, and he brought me out by the Spirit of the LORD and set me in the middle of a valley; it was full of bones. He led me back and forth among them, and I saw a great many bones on the floor of the valley, bones that were very dry. He asked me, "Son of man, can these bones come alive?" I said, "O sovereign LORD, you alone know." Then he said to me, "Prophesy to these bones and say to them, 'Dry bones, hear the word of the LORD! This is what the Sovereign LORD says to these bones: I will make breath enter you, and you will come to life. I will attach tendons to you and make flesh come to life. Then you will know that I am the LORD.'" So I prophesied as I was commanded. And as I was prophesying, there was a noise, a rattling sound, and the bones came together, bone to bone. I looked, and tendons and flesh appeared on them and skin covered them, but there was no breath in them. Then he said to me, "Prophesy to the breath; prophesy, son of man, and say to it, 'This is what the Sovereign LORD says: Come from the four winds, O breath, and breathe into these slain, that they may live.'" So I prophesied as he commanded me, and breath entered them; they came to life and stood up on their feet—a vast army. Then he said to me: "Son of man, these bones are the whole house of Israel. They say, 'Our bones are dried up and our hope is gone; we are cut off.' Therefore prophesy and say to*

> *them: 'This is what the Sovereign LORD says: O my people, I am going to open your graves and bring you up from them; I will bring you back to the land of Israel. Then you, my people, will know that I am the LORD, when I open your graves and bring you up from them. I will put my spirit in you and you will live, and I will settle you in your own land. Then you will know that I the LORD have spoken, and I have done it, declares the LORD.'"*
>
> **—Ezekiel 37:1–14**

This demonstrates that the Hebrew people do believe in an afterlife. The word "soul" had an important meaning to them, as it does for all of us today. As we have been learning more and more, if you look at the original Hebrew and Greek, there seems to be a clear continuity while using the precious words "soul" and "spirit." Then came all the translations, and suddenly those two words were translated by various versions as "breath of life," "living creatures," "living being," "there is life," or "all that had life." In some cases, the words "soul" and "spirit" were completely omitted.

That's why, to me, in this situation, the Bible reads so much more logically and is much easier to understand in direct Hebrew/Greek versions. Again, if Moses called it a "soul" or a "spirit", then so be it. The Bible is telling us that animals have both a soul and a spirit. And because they do, they belong in heaven just as humans do.

Nephesh Means "Soul"

Before we conclude our discussion of the translation problems related to the words "soul" and "spirit," I'd like to bring in an interesting quote from the *New American Standard Bible (NASB) translation Key Word Study Bible: Key Insights to God's Word*. They are commenting about this verse:

> *The LORD formed the man from the dust of the ground and breathed into his nostrils the breath of life and the man became a living being.*
> —**Genesis 2:7**

Here is the quote from the Key Word Study Bible:

> The term "soul" has been used in a variety of senses by different writers in the Bible. The O.T. Hebrew word is Nephesh (5315) which means "that which breathes." It corresponds to the Greek word psuchē (5590) in the N.T., which is usually translated "soul" or "life." See the lexical aid sections for further definition. Here it is used synonymously with spirit. Both spirit and soul refer to the emotional life and also correspond to "heart" in a sense, which is the seat of all thinking, feeling, and purpose. "Soul" and "spirit" are frequently used interchangeably, and it is not easy to define the differences. Hebrew culture tended to view man as being composed of only two parts—soul (spirit) and body. The Greek concept of man was tripartite (see 1 Thess. 5:23). Broadly defined, the soul usually stood for life, the affections, the will, the consciousness, while the spirit stood for the higher elements by which we comprehend spiritual truths, and the body was, of course, the physical, material body. The author of Hebrews implied that there is a very fine line of distinction between soul and spirit (Heb. 4:12).

Out of curiosity, I looked at the lexical aid in the back of this same Bible and discovered a short paragraph that defines word number 5315: *nephesh*. It says the word only means "living creature" and does not once mention its relationship to the word "soul." In contrast, *Strong's Concordance* includes an extensive description of the soul translation, and it refers to Genesis 2:7 specifically. It mentions that the interpretation for *nephesh* is used 475 times in the Bible to mean "soul." And remember, the KJV agrees.

Again, you can see how the teachings of the modern era lead to extreme confusion as to what the Bible actually means. In this one specific example of the NASB version that we have just examined, Genesis 2:7, Adam himself was not even given a soul! The key point for us, though, is that the language that God used related to Adam, in its original form, through Moses, is the same language, combination of words, word for word, used for when he created the animals. Adam and the animals are linked. You see, everything God created is important, and loved, and shown his great mercy.

> *The LORD is good to all: and his tender mercies are over all his works.*
> —Psalm 145:9 KJV

The Souls of Noah and the Flood

Turning our attention to Noah, remember the covenant that God gave to Noah after he, his family, and the animals survived the flood?

> *And God spoke to Noah, and to his sons with him, saying, And I, behold, I establish my covenant with you, and with your seed after you; and with every living soul which is with you, fowl as well as cattle, and all the animals of the earth with you, of all that has gone out of the ark—every animal of the earth. And I establish my covenant with you, neither shall all flesh be cut off any more by the waters of a flood, and henceforth there shall be no flood to destroy the earth. And God said, This is the sign of the covenant that I set between me and you and every living soul that is with you, for everlasting generations: I set my bow in the clouds, and it shall be for a sign of the covenant between me and the earth.*

> *And it shall come to pass when I bring clouds over the earth, that the bow shall be seen in the cloud, and I will remember my covenant which is between me and you and every living* soul *of all flesh; and the waters shall not henceforth become a flood to destroy all flesh. And the bow shall be in the cloud; and I will look upon it, that I may remember the everlasting covenant between God and every living* soul *of all flesh that is upon the earth. And God said to Noah, This is the sign of the covenant which I have established between me and all flesh that is upon the earth.*
> —Genesis 9:8–17 DAR 1890

I referred to this covenant previously in the chapter on Noah, but here I would like to spotlight the word "soul" to emphasize a key point. In original scriptures, it appears in this set of verses four times. In almost all of the modern translations, including the King James, the New International Version, and the New American Standard, the word "soul" is left out of this particular piece of scripture the same four times. Once more, we see how the statuses of animals rise when the word "soul" is retained in connection with them. And when we clearly see that the animals do have souls, our belief in them being in heaven naturally rises. In this chapter, we've seen this repeatedly.

Remember also that this covenant is addressed to Noah five times and addressed to the animals five times as well. As we've seen throughout the Bible, every curse given to mankind also applied to the animals. All general covenants and blessings, including the Noahide Laws and the Ten Commandments, are also addressed to the animals throughout the Bible. To me, that's a powerful reminder that it is important to God to include, and be conscious of, all that he created.

Yet sadly, many people are so human centered that they fail to see the whole creation in God's teachings. They are filled with pride and believe that the world revolves around us. But with the recognition that animals possess souls and spirits, it's more and more difficult to hold to that anthropocentric belief and easier and easier to grasp the reality that animals are fully included in both our world and the world that is yet to come.

The Spirit Gives Life After Death

As we wrap up this examination of Bible translations related to animals having souls and spirits, I'd like to bring in an explanation in which I find great comfort. And it is truly a simple explanation. As we have seen earlier, in the beginning, God's spirit was upon all that he created. And consider Jesus's words as he took his last breath on the cross:

> *Then when Jesus took the vinegar, He said, It has been finished.*
> *And bowing His head, He delivered up the spirit.*
> —John 19:30 LITV

The word for "spirit" is *pneuma* in Greek, and it is number 4151. It is the equivalent word for *ruwach*, number 7307, in Hebrew, which means "spirit" also. Therefore, if Psalm 104:29, "You send out your spirit and they are created," is referring to the animals, then we have further biblical proof that animals do have spirits.

And here's more from Jesus:

> *The Spirit gives life; the flesh counts for nothing. The words I*
> *have spoken to you are spirit and they are life.*
> —John 6:63 NIV

It's an easy conclusion to draw here, isn't it? God sends his spirit and animals are created; Jesus takes his last breath and his spirit is released back to God. The spirit is what gives life after death. Having spirits and souls is what makes the animals and ourselves dualistic. This means that there is some aspect of the "being" that is more than dust upon death. The spirit/soul is the entity that moves to the afterlife. And as the Bible tells us, animals as well as humans have souls and spirits, and we will all be sharing heaven together.

Support from Pope John Paul II

In this chapter, you have been reading my firm and strong belief about animals possessing souls and spirits, backed by the abundant evidence in the original translations of the Bible. As we prepare to move on, I'd like to bring in another opinion on this question. Pope John Paul II spoke these words to a public audience in Italy on January 19, 1999:

> The animals possess a soul and men must love and feel solidarity with our smaller brethren.

The Pope's quote was featured in *Genre* magazine early that year, and even in the age before social media, his words were soon picked up in many places throughout the world. The Pope went on to say that all animals are "fruit of the creative action of the Holy Spirit and merit respect," and that they are "as near to God as men are."

If Pope John Paul II could make a statement like this, it speaks to a monumental position on behalf of the Vatican. The church itself does not teach animal theology in seminary, but the Vatican is very aware of animal issues and is not afraid to make a strong statement about their importance. The Pope's words were a great comfort to me. For those of you who love and cherish your beloved pets, perhaps you will find comfort in his words, and in everything we have been exploring, as we continue our journey.

A FREE "TICKET TO RIDE"

Chapter 6

A FREE "TICKET TO RIDE"

> *The LORD is good to all: and his tender mercies are over all his works.*
> —Psalm 145:9 KJV

There's another argument sometimes made by those who contend that animals will not go to heaven and be able to share an afterlife with us. This claim is not made nearly as often as the false declaration that "animals do not go to heaven because they do not have a soul," but it comes up often enough for us to consider … and respond to. Here's the basic contention: *Animals do not go to heaven because they cannot ask Jesus for repentance. They can't be saved.*

I'm going to invite you to accompany me on another trip through translation to learn why this specific argument about animals not going to heaven because they can't be saved just doesn't add up when we look at the biblical evidence.

The Unwilling

We know from Genesis 3:14–21 that we are cursed by the fall of Adam and Eve in the Garden of Eden. But what does the Bible say about that as it relates to the animal kingdom? I'll try to answer that question by looking at the following New Testament verse, which

I will interpret in the native Greek. The apostle Paul is speaking to the Romans:

> *For the earnest expectation of the creation is eagerly expecting the revelation of the sons of God. For the creation was not willingly subjected to vanity, but through him subjecting it, on hope; that also the creation will be freed from the slavery of corruption to the freedom of the glory of the children of God. For we know that all the creation groans together and travails together until now.*
> —**Romans 8:19–22 LITV**

Paul is speaking about the final coming of Christ. The Greek word for "revelation" is *apokalupsis*, number 602 in *Strong's Concordance*. It is defined as "disclosure, revelation, to be revealed." But there is a more interesting revelation about these verses in Romans, perhaps one that modern theology has overlooked. This oversight could be of importance to the truth about the animal kingdom's plight.

We're going to examine several versions of this writing, namely verses 20 and 21. Why? Not because of their differences but because of their similarities. This is so important because regardless of translations, the meaning is not lost. It is very clear.

King James Version:

> *For the creature was made subject to the vanity, not willingly, but by reason of him who hath subjected the same, in hope, because the creature itself also shall be delivered from the bondage of corruption into the glorious liberty of the children of God.*

New International Version:

> *For the creation was subjected to frustration, not by its own choice, but by the will of the one who subjected it, in hope that the creation itself will be liberated from its bondage to decay and brought into the glorious freedom of the children of God.*

New Living Translation:

Against its will, everything on earth was subjected to God's curse. All creation anticipates the day when it will join God's children in glorious freedom from death and decay.

Let's shine the translation spotlight on the word "creature" (KJV) or "creation." That word in Greek is number 2937: *ktisis*. It means "creature, creation or an act of creating by God." The word for "subject" is *hupotasso*, which means "to be subjected to." And "vanity" is referring to word number 3153, *mataiotes*, which means "emptiness as to the results" and is used regarding the creation. It is then specified in Romans 8:20 to mean "failing of the results of designed," owing to "sin" or simply "the fall." The line "of the one who subjected it" is referring to Adam.

What this verse set in the New Testament is saying is that all creation is waiting to be released from the hell that Adam subjected the world to, and to become a part of the children of God in heaven. The day of the second coming of Christ is the day that all creation awaits to be free again to enter into God's redemptive plan, to be at oneness with God versus separateness as it is now. This is what God desires and anxiously awaits.

I believe these verses are telling us that the animals were not willing partners in the offense that Adam and Eve created for themselves and all of humanity. And they anticipate a day when they too can join the glorious freedom from sin and evil as it is on the renewed "earth as it is in heaven."

I understand that some may argue that this verse set is just referring to a renewal of the earth and heaven when Christ returns. But why does Paul, who, like Moses, is divinely inspired, say that the creation is not guilty of the original sin but subjected to it? If we are talking about something as simple as a redemptive game plan, why is Paul being specific? And is he saying that the animals are not in the wrong by their own choice? If he is, then that is a clear indicator that animals do not have to repent as humans do.

After all, this "unwilling" can't apply to humankind, since man did take the fruit willingly. So man must repent. We Christians, because of our sinful nature due to the fall, must ask Jesus for forgiveness and attempt to live by his game plan to get to heaven. The animals, however, were just victims of the fall, not creators of it. They were supposed to be under our stewardship and care, in the true spirit of dominion. They have no need to repent or to be saved.

But there is more good news. You see, through Adam, we are now subjected to death, but through another "man," we are subjected to life everlasting.

> *For since death came through a man, the resurrection of the dead comes also through a man. For as in Adam all die, so in Christ all will be made alive.*
> **—1 Corinthians 15:21–22 NIV**

Let us look now at the translation of verse 21 of Romans from a direct Greek interpretation:

> *That also the creation will be freed from the slavery of corruption to the freedom of the glory of the children of God.*
> **—Romans 8:21 LITV**

Check out the word "also." It is *kai* in Greek, number 2532. It means "copulative and cumulative force, also, and." I would say that this means the animals are included, in addition to the believers about whom the apostle Paul is speaking. Remember, Paul is addressing the believers in Christ in Rome. The animals are in addition to this group. Perhaps animal fate is that of humans due to the human indiscretion, so therefore they await the release from bondage. They will be freed, as will the children of God. As humans, we have to become children of God. The creation or animals will be freed with us. To me, this means that the animals are not under the same rules that we are. We have to choose God and Christ, but they do not.

They have been subjected to the pitfalls of our doing but are released from it along with the children of God. Therefore, they need *not* be saved, as in a conscious act of receiving or accepting Christ, as it is defined in the Christian religion.

Now that we have a better understanding as to the meaning of Romans 8, let us examine what other theologians have said in past centuries concerning this set of verses in Romans. I choose John Calvin (1509–1564), a famous Protestant reformer, Bible theologian, and commentator, and Reverend John Wesley (1703–1791), also a reformer and the founder of the Methodist Church. Both of these men have had significant roles in the evolution of religion throughout the centuries to the present time. Here's their take on animals in the afterlife.

As noted from the Christian Classics Ethereal Library (www.ccel.org), John Calvin comments on Romans 8:20:

> He shows the object of expectation from what is of an opposite character; for as creatures, being now subject to corruption, cannot be restored until the sons of God shall be wholly restored: hence they, longing for their renewal, look forward to the manifestation of the celestial kingdom.

And this is what he has to say about verse 21:

> He shows how the creation has in hope been made subject to vanity; that is, inasmuch as it shall some time be made free, according to what Isaiah testifies, and what Peter confirms still more clearly. It is then indeed meet for us to consider what a dreadful curse we have deserved, since all created things in themselves blameless, both on earth and in the visible heaven, undergo punishment for our sins; for it has not happened through their own fault, that they are liable to corruption. Thus the condemnation of mankind is imprinted on the heavens, and on the earth, and on all creatures. It hence also appears to what excelling glory

the sons of God shall be exalted; for all creatures shall be renewed in order to amplify it, and to render it illustrious.

Let us turn our attention to Reverend John Wesley's Sermon 60, written in the mid- to late 1700s, in which he emphatically states:

> To descend to a few particulars: The whole brute creation will then, undoubtedly, be restored, not only to the vigour, strength, and swiftness which they had at their creation, but to a far higher degree of each than they ever enjoyed. They will be restored, not only to that measure of understanding which they had in paradise, but to a degree of it as much higher than that, as the understanding of an elephant is beyond that of a worm. And whatever affections they had in the garden of God, will be restored with vast increase; being exalted and refined in a manner, which we ourselves are not now able to comprehend. The liberty they then had will be completely restored, and they will be free in all their motions. They will be delivered from all irregular appetites, from all unruly passions, from every disposition that is either evil in itself, or has any tendency to evil. No rage will be found in any creature, no fierceness, no cruelty, or thirst for blood. So far from it that "the wolf shall dwell with the lamb, the leopard shall lie down with the kid; the calf and the young lion together; and a little child shall lead them. The cow and the bear shall feed together; and the lion shall eat straw like the ox. They shall not hurt nor destroy in all my holy mountain." (Isaiah 11:6 & c.)

After some analysis of a New Testament set of verses in Romans, we can see that our hope to see our pets in heaven has support from famous theologians. For there have been great theologians in times past that have portrayed the same notion. Funny that being reminded how my story begins with a minister from a Methodist church created this need for inquiry. And now we learn that John Wesley himself, the founder of the Methodist Church, was supporting, back in the 1700s, the idea that animals would be in heaven.

All Flesh shall be Included

During our close-up look at biblical evidence of animals possessing a soul and a spirit in the previous chapter, we spoke briefly about the concept of all flesh having the spirit of God. Let's now revisit the term "all flesh" in a different context as we continue to use the method of word-for-word translation to uncover evidence about animals going to heaven and not needing to be saved to gain entry.

> *And the glory of the LORD shall be revealed, and all flesh shall see it together: for the mouth of the LORD hath spoken it.*
> —Isaiah 40:5 KJV

> *Let the LORD, God of the spirits of all flesh, set a man over the congregation, which may go out before them, and which may go in before them, and which may lead them in; that the congregation of the LORD be not as sheep which have no shepherd.*
> —Numbers 27:16–17 KJV

As we mentioned earlier, the word for "all flesh" in Hebrew is *basar*, number 1320. It is defined as "the flesh of the body, both that of humans and animals." It is also used to describe flesh that is both alive and dead. In the case of dead flesh, that is usually referring to animals. We see "all flesh" used many times throughout the Old Testament. When it is used in the equivalent manner in the New Testament, the Greek word is *sarx*, number 4561.

In the verse from Isaiah 40:5, it states clearly that all flesh shall see the coming of the Lord and his glory. How much clearer can this powerful statement be? We know that "all flesh" means both animal and man. Why did the author not say "mankind" instead of "all flesh" if the reference was intended to exclude animals?

We can back up this assertion by bringing in more scripture. In the New Testament, Paul talks specifically about flesh. He states that there are different types of flesh, but that they are of "all flesh."

> *But someone may ask, "How are the dead raised? With what kind of body will they come?" How foolish! What you sow does not come to life unless it dies. When you sow, you do not plant the body that will be but just a seed, perhaps of wheat or of something else. But God gives it a body as he has determined, and to each kind of seed he gives its own body. All flesh is not the same: Men have one kind of flesh, animals have another, birds another and fish another. There are also heavenly bodies and there are earthly bodies; but the splendor of the heavenly bodies is one kind, and the splendor of the earthly bodies is another. The sun has one kind of splendor, the moon another and the stars another; and star differs from star in splendor. So will it be with the resurrection of the dead. The body that is sown is perishable, it is raised imperishable; it is sown in dishonor, it is raised in glory; it is sown in weakness, it is raised in power; it is sown a natural body, it is raised a spiritual body.*
> —1 Corinthians 15:35–44 NIV

It's interesting to note that Paul is specific in referring to the same three animal groups mentioned in the creation story in Genesis chapter 1 when he referred to "every living thing on earth," "every bird of the heavens," and "every creeper on the earth." We are biblically confirming the consciousness of animal flesh in scripture. Not as a "splendor" like the sun and the moon, but as flesh, as are the human "bodies." And note that as this verse concludes, the "all flesh" is sown a natural body and raised a spiritual body. I find that incredibly powerful!

We move on now to consider new pieces to the puzzle in which animals will see the salvation of God, noting use of the phrase "all flesh":

> *All flesh shall see the salvation of God.*
> —Luke 3:6 KJV

> *And the glory of the Lord shall be revealed, and all flesh shall see it together: for the mouth of the LORD hath spoken.*
> —Isaiah 40:5 NIV

> *O thou that hearest prayer, unto thee shall all flesh come.*
> —Psalm 65:2 KJV

Some theologians may deem the word "see" in this context, referring to the coming of Christ, as witnessing the salvation of God but not being *redeemed* by it. I would simply remind them of the verse in Romans 8:21 NIV:

> *Because the creature itself also shall be delivered from the bondage of corruption into the glorious liberty of the children of God.*

In my research beyond the Bible, I came upon another compelling and relevant reference to Romans 8 in the excellent book *There Is Eternal Life for Animals*, by Niki Behrikis Shanahan:

> What creature or part of creation will be delivered from the bondage of corruption?
> Using the process of elimination we know who it could **not** be:
> 1. **The Angels**, because they are not subject to corruption and they are not longing for another state.
> 2. **Demons/Fallen Angels**, because they will never share in the glorious liberation. They have been sentenced to eternal bondage.
> 3. **Believers**, because Paul distinguishes the believers from the "**creature or creation**" by saying in verse

23 **"and not only they but ourselves also."** It is obvious that "ourselves" means the believers.
4. **Non-believers**, because they have no hope (John 3:18).

Who is left? Paul is referring to the animals.

Therefore, the evidence is building that the animals will not only *see* the coming of Christ but will also be released from this world unto the redemptive afterlife the Bible speaks of.

> *O thou that hearest prayer, unto thee shall all flesh come.*
> **—Psalm 65:2 KJV**

In this psalm, the word for "come" is the Greek word *bow*, number 935. It is defined as "to enter or to come in." I believe that this verse by King David, of the Old Testament, is referring to "all flesh" coming unto the Lord. Again, this is referring to the second coming of the Messiah, Christ Jesus.

Speaking of Jesus, here's another intriguing "all flesh" reference from the apostle John, of the New Testament:

> *As thou hast given power over all flesh, that he should give eternal life to as many as thou hast given him.*
> **—John 17:2 KJV**

As God has given Christ eternal life, to all flesh, he has the power to bring them unto himself for eternal life. Breaking down the Greek here, we find that the word "all" is *pas*, number 3956, meaning "the whole"; and "flesh" is *sarx*, number 4561. The apostle John is referring to "all flesh" here. Why did he not say "all mankind" if that is what he meant? Perhaps because he meant that Jesus has the power to bring the animals unto himself as well, in the final coming. And again, they would not need to repent for that to happen.

> *Behold, I am the LORD, the God of all flesh: is there anything too hard for me?*
> —Jeremiah 32:27 KJV

Let's examine another set of verses by the apostle Luke, the author of the book of Acts:

> *And he shall send Jesus Christ, which before was preached unto you: Whom the heaven must receive until the times of restitution of all things, which God hath spoken by the mouth of all of his holy prophets since the world began.*
> —Acts 3:20–21 KJV

The apostle Luke of the New Testament is describing the fact that Christ will remain in heaven until it is time to restore all things, as promised by the Old Testament prophets. We are talking about restoration of all here. The Greek word for "restitution" is number 605, *apokatastasis*, also meaning "to set in order"—not the making of new animals but the restoration of that which was.

Here is a comparable set of verses coming from the prophet Isaiah, of the Old Testament:

> *The wolf also shall dwell with the lamb, and the leopard shall lie down with the kid, and the calf and the young lion and the fatling together; and the little child shall lead them. And the cow and the bear shall feed; their young ones shall lie together: and the lion shall eat straw like the ox. And the sucking child shall play on the hole of the asp, and the weaned child shall put his hand on the cockatrices den. They shall not hurt nor destroy in all my holy mountain: for the earth shall be full of the knowledge of the Lord, as the waters cover the sea.*
> —Isaiah 11:6–9 KJV

Remember, the apostle Luke is a writer in the New Testament and the prophet Isaiah is from the Old Testament, yet I believe that their words can be seen as consistent with the idea that animals are included in God's game plan. We will explore the implications of this important verse set from Isaiah in the following chapter, when we discuss the different theories about the end times and the second coming of Christ. For our reflection in this chapter, we will next consider these verses from Hosea:

> *In that day I will make a covenant for them with the beasts of the field and the birds of the air and the creatures that move along the ground, bow and sword and battle I will abolish from the land, so that all may lie down in safety. I will betroth you to me forever; I will betroth you in righteousness and justice, in love and compassion.*
> —Hosea 2:18–19 NIV

God is again specifically speaking about the three animal groups, as in Genesis, as he promised to honor another covenant to them. In that time (after the return of Christ), "all may lie down in safely. I will betroth you to me forever in righteousness and justice, in love and compassion." That is the English version. The Hebrew version says the same thing. Once again, there is no mention of these animal groups needing to be saved to merit this commitment.

So when Christ returns, there does not seem to be any doubt, according to Hosea and to Isaiah, as to who will be included. The animals indeed will have their place!

God Preserveth All

Let's look at one of my favorite verses, one of the earliest indicators to me that the words of my Methodist minister from childhood about animals not going to heaven were very much misguided. For years, this verse set gave me particular comfort. The key word here is "preserveth."

> *Thy righteousness is like the great mountains; thy judgements are a great deep: O Lord, thou preserveth both man and beast. How excellent is thy loving kindness, O God!*
> *—Psalm 36:6–7 KJV*

The *Strong's Concordance* designation for "preserveth" is number 3467: *yasha*. It means "to save, be saved from moral troubles, to be delivered, to be liberated, to be victorious, to give victory to." It does not mean "to feed or provide for." Therefore, this verse does not mean that God is providing sustenance for the animals, as some might claim. The word *yasha* is actually referred to as "salvation" five times elsewhere in the Bible. King David is writing about the future of Christ's second coming. You see, this verse in Psalms can only point to the eschatological theology, meaning "the study of end times." We know it is not about current times, for we are not enjoying liberation from moral issues. But we, as well as the animals, will be delivered, liberated unto the Messiah, as the Messiah again restores the whole creation unto himself.

Since we are in Psalms, let's look at Psalm 104. I will use the *Interlinear Bible, Hebrew-Greek-English*, by Jay P. Green Sr. (LITV), my favorite and dear to my heart! This version does such a wonderful job at navigating the journey through the Hebrew and Greek languages so as not to lose the original meaning in the way that other translations do.

> *O Jehovah, how many are your works! You have made all of them in wisdom; the earth is full of your riches. This is the sea, great and wide on both hands; there are creeping things even without numbers; living things small and great. There the ships go: You made the great sea animals to play in it. All of them wait for you to give them their food in due season. You give to them, they gather; you open your hand and they are filled with good. You hide your face and they are troubled: You gather your breath*

> *and they expire and they return to their dust. You send out your Spirit, and they are created; and you renew the face of the earth.*
> —**Psalm 104:24–30 LITV**

As you read this set of verses, think for a moment. Perhaps the animals already know God. Can we make this assumption from these verses? "You hide your face and they are troubled …" This line from the previous psalm suggests that animals can see God's face and would be troubled if they no longer could. If this is the case, they have a real advantage over humans because, as you may not know, God's face is strictly prohibited from us humans. Do you know why the devil cannot return to being an angel? Because he saw the face of God and he still rejected him. Did you know that when Moses took the Ten Commandments, he could have been put to death if he saw the face of God? In fact, any animal or human that touched the mountain at that time would have been put to death. The deliverance of the Ten Commandments was a holy event, and God was exercising restrictions. Throughout the Bible, God is adamant about restricting anyone from seeing his face.

Interestingly, when you read the accounts of people who have had near-death experiences, they consistently say that they have seen Jesus, but when they saw God, they could not make out his face. Remember, these people came back to life here on earth, so perhaps God was still restricting his face from them.

According to Psalm 104, we can entertain the idea that the animals are not under this restriction. In fact, this is the only reference in the Bible of anyone other than the devil, the angels, and Christ seeing God's face. So this again supports the belief that animals have a type of connection with God that we do not have. The animals may know of their maker in a sense or in a way that we are not capable of as humans. Whatever they may be aware of, regarding God, the animals will surely serve him well, as we will see.

> *The wild animals honor me, the jackals and the owls, because I provide water in the desert and streams in the wasteland, to give*

> *drink to my people, my chosen, the people I formed for myself that they may proclaim my praise. Yet you have not called upon me, O Jacob, you have not wearied yourselves for me, O Israel.*
> —Isaiah 43:20 NIV

> *The ox knows his master, the donkey his owner's manager, but Israel does not know, my people do not understand.*
> —Isaiah 1:3 NIV

Let's consider what is happening in these verses. God is upset that his people of Jacob's heritage, the Israelites, are not honoring him or living by his game plan. Notice that he is expressing the fact that even the animals honor him but the prideful people do not. To me, that's further evidence that perhaps the animals know God in a way that we do not.

God Gathers up a Spirit

Returning to Psalm 104, note the use of the word "gather." It is used twice, once in verse 28 and again in verse 29. The word in verse 28, in the Hebrew interpretation, is number 3950, *lagat*, and is referred to in this passage as "the animals gather up food that is provided by God." In verse 29, the number for "gather" is 622, *acaph*. It is referring to "gathering of souls" by definition, in this particular passage or verse. "You gather your breath and they expire." Number 622 is defined as "to bring objects to a common point" or "to gather one's soul." According to *Strong's Concordance*, "God can also be the agent who gathers or takes away a soul." So God is "gathering" a spirit and then giving a spirit to the animals in these verses.

In the second half of verse 29, however, we need to note some differences. Most versions, such as the KJV, quote verse 29 like this:

> The KJV: *Thou taketh away their breath they die, and return to dust.*
>
> The NIV: *When you take away their breath, they die ...*

But the word used for "breath" here is *spirit*, number 7307 in original Hebrew, as I have mentioned, the same number used for verse 30, when God "sends forth his spirit." So here we can go from "you take away their breath and they die," as we see in the NIV and the KJV, to "you gather your spirit and they expire and they return to dust," as seen in the Bible's original language. I would say this is a big difference, isn't it? As the verse continues, "you send forth thy spirit and they are created." Most versions do agree that God can send forth a spirit. So is he taking away a breath or gathering up a spirit? According to the original Hebrew, God is gathering up a spirit. Can we conclude that God's spirit is within the animal's dualistic body? Apparently we can, according to the original language of the Bible. We see how minor interpretation variances can contribute to a loss of true meaning. Unfortunately, this is at the expense of the animals.

Continuing along this trail, let's bring in the New Testament. I will point out verses that address such inclusive language as "to gather," "all things," and "the whole world."

> *That in the dispensation of the fullness of times he might gather together in one all things in Christ, both which are in heaven and which are on earth; even in Him ...*
> —Ephesians 1:10 KJV

Here we see the English word "gather," which in Greek is the word *anakephalaiomao*, number 346. It means "to gather together as one," "to sum up to gather up to present as a whole." Again we find the words "all things," or *pas*, number 3956. That Greek word *pas* means "all, any, every, the whole." This time "gather" in Greek is equivalent to number 622 in Hebrew. I believe the meaning in Psalm 104:29, when the Ephesians comparison is considered, sounds more like "the gathering unto himself." For clarity, the animal spirits will be gathered unto God. I believe this verse in the New Testament Ephesians is a confirmation of our understanding of Psalm 104. It is all-inclusive.

Here's another verse that appears to be all-inclusive, from the apostle John:

> *For God sent not his son into the world to condemn the world;*
> *but that the world through him might be saved.*
> —John 3:17 KJV

The "world" that might be saved is the Greek word *kosmos*, which means "inhabitants of the earth." Again, according to the Bible, we humans may have to receive the grace to be saved, but not all flesh is under the same rules. Jesus came to give us all the opportunity to be restored unto himself. His atonement, or sacrifice on the cross, provides that opportunity. The author of this verse states that all inhabitants can be saved. The Bible does go on to be specific about what this means to humans, but perhaps this verse and others like it are not specific to humans only and actually refer to the whole *kosmos*.

> *That God was reconciling the world to himself in Christ, not counting men's sins against them. And he has committed to us the message of reconciliation.*
> —2 Corinthians 5:19 NIV

> *For it pleased the father that in him should all fullness dwell;*
> *And, having made peace through the blood of his cross, by him*
> *to reconcile all things unto himself; by him, I say, whether they*
> *be things in earth or things in heaven.*
> —Colossians 1:19–20 KJV

As mentioned earlier, the word for "reconciliation" in Greek is *apokatallasso*, which means "to bring back a former state of harmony."

Remember that verse from the prophet Isaiah about the "wolf will lie down with the lamb"? In this case, these verses are about Christ. They were written in the first century AD, after Christ had been present on earth and after his resurrection. Christ is the messiah that the Old Testament prophets such as Isaiah prophesied about. Through Christ the reconciliation will occur.

Now in the New Testament, the men who walked with him are sharing and spreading this good news throughout the Roman empire.

> *In the past God spoke to our forefathers through the prophet at many times and various ways, but in these last days he has spoken to us by his son, whom he appointed heir of all things, and through whom also he made the universe. The Son is the radiance of God's glory and the exact representation of his being, sustaining all things by his powerful word.*
> —Hebrews 1:1–3 NIV

> *He must remain in heaven until the time comes for God to restore everything, as he promised long ago through his holy prophets.*
> —Acts 3:21 NIV

> *And he is the propitiation for our sins, and not for ours only but for the whole world.*
> —1 John 2:2 KJV

> *And that he died for all, that they which live should not hence forth live unto themselves, but unto him which died for them, and rose again.*
> —2 Corinthians 5:15 KJV

The word for "all" is *pas* in Greek, and the word for "they" is *zao* in Greek, meaning "to live." Taken together, the meaning is "all living things."

We are confident, I say, and willing rather to be absent from the body, and to be present with the LORD.
—2 Corinthians 5:8 KJV

So if all things that inhabit the earth are a part of the mercy and grace of Christ and his sacrifice for the whole world, then perhaps the animals, when absent from the body, are in the present with Jesus as well. They do not need to repent to be included. They already *are* included.

The Three-Tier Theory

I'm going to escort you down a different avenue to view this question of whether animals need to be saved to gain entrance to heaven. I've been pointing to evidence in the Bible that, in my opinion, suggests that animals do *not* need to be saved, or repent, because they were victims of the fall in the Garden of Eden. We as humans can go to heaven if we follow God's game plan. Yet under the radar and rarely addressed in this capacity, there is one entity that will never gain entrance to heaven under any circumstances. I am referring to Satan.

One way to organize these three different scenarios of the prospects of going to heaven is through what I have coined the "Three Tier Theory." Here's how it looks:

Tier 1: If Satan wants to go to heaven, can he? *No*
Tier 2: If we want to go to heaven, can we? *Maybe, if we ask*
Tier 3: Can the animals go to heaven? *Yes*

Let's look at this theory and consider how it may shed further light on our broader exploration. We know that as humans we have the opportunity to gain access to the afterlife. That opportunity is God's grace and mercy at its best, and it is for you and I and anyone who asks, as we have seen in the Bible. As for the animals, we have pointed out in many different contexts that they are not the ones who sinned and therefore do not have to ask Christ for repentance or mercy. They are not under the same game plan that we are as far as having to know the secret knock to gain access into the best party in town. Remember, they are unwilling victims of the fall. They are subject to the fallen world that we created, but it is not their fault. That is biblical. We also know now from our studies that they too await to be released from the bondage of this life. There is no need or biblical requirement for repentance on their behalf, or that they are or will be held accountable for the indiscretions of the human condition that resulted from the exile from the Garden of Eden.

As for the devil, that is a different story. You see, the devil is a fallen angel. The angels do not have the opportunity to repent. If they act in rebellion to God once, it is over—no chance to return to heaven.

> *He [Jesus] replied, "I saw Satan fall like lightning from heaven."*
> **—Luke 10:18 NIV**

Christ also spoke in this conversation:

> *But he who rejects me rejects him who sent me.*
> **—Luke 10:16 NIV**

Christ is talking with his disciples as he is sending them out to teach others. So he is telling them that they will have the ability to perform miracles in his name and ward off demons, for Christ himself saw Satan fall from the heavens. But he is also saying that one who rejects Christ rejects God, as Satan rejected God, the Father. This line in Luke is in regard to humans, but in the case of the devil, who was originally an angel, the consequences are under a different game plan. You see, as we know for sure, the angels can see the face of God!

> *See that you do not look down on one of these little ones. For I tell you that their angels in heaven always see the face of my Father in heaven.*
> —**Matthew 18:10 NIV**

So once you have seen the face of God and then choose to reject him, you become a fallen angel with no parole, no possibility to gain access back to the heavenly kingdom. As for the "little ones" in this verse, Jesus is describing the parable of a lost sheep and how the shepherd rejoiced in finding one lost sheep. Jesus does not want one lost soul among us humans either, as he is our shepherd. Be comforted, for his angels are looking after us—angels who see the face of God.

Earlier in this chapter, we mentioned how we as mere mortals are forbidden to see God's face. However, we will see God's face after Christ returns and we awake as a part of the heavenly kingdom. This is illustrated in the following psalm by King David:

> *And I—in righteousness I will see your face; when I awake, I will be satisfied with seeing your likeness.*
> —**Psalm 17:15 NIV**

In the devil's case, the privilege to be amongst God, be able to see him face-to-face, and then decide to reject him is quite the atrocity. The devil was prideful and rejected God, and therefore he is no longer able to repair the damaged relationship with God. Hence we get the fallen angels and the birth of Satan. Therefore, the battle between good and evil and the struggle of a prideful angel, Satan, to be like God, begins.

Moving on to Tier 2, we are reminded that we, unlike the devil, can ask God to forgive us, and he will. In all cases in the Bible, he forgave everyone who asked. We have the ability to rebuke the devil's grip. We can choose God's game plan. God grants us that privilege. He does not grant this to a fallen angel.

Here's how the renowned Billy Graham describes this distinction in his book *Angels*:

> God made provision for salvation for fallen men, but he made no provisions for the salvation of fallen angels. Why? Perhaps because unlike Adam and Eve, who were enticed toward sin by sinners, the angels fell when there were no sinners, so no one could entice them to sin. Thus, their sinful state cannot be altered; their sin cannot be forgiven; their salvation cannot be achieved.

A Link Between Angels and the Animals?

Now it's time to focus on Tier 3 and our friends in the animal kingdom. I'd like to share a conversation I had while interviewing an orthodox rabbi to verify some of my Hebrew research. When Rabbi Hurwitz happened to mention the Jewish view concerning heaven, you can bet I was intrigued and wanted to hear more. The rabbi asked me whether I think humans have a "sense" of God, and he spoke of his belief that very few have this sense. Perhaps those who try to become close to God, perhaps those who are crazy, and perhaps the prophets are this privileged, he suggested.

Then he went on to say that the angels have this "sense" of God, and he added that the animals have this sense of God as well. Wow! He explained that what he meant was that angels and animals have an instinct and are here for God's purpose. Under this "instinct," or "sense," you do as God intends. We as humans were given free choice and do not sense God, for the most part. We are allowed to follow our own inclinations, or free will.

As we continued our discussion, he revealed that our views on the evidence of animals having souls were very much in sync. He emphasized a combination of two words in the creation story: *nephesh chayyah*. As we discussed in the chapter on animals having souls and spirits, those two words mean a "living soul." But the rabbi added a new twist to that meaning. He told me that he had named his daughter Chayyah because that is a word synonymous with an angel. He stressed that this combination of words carries a deeper meaning. A "living soul" is one "that God lives within." It is not a "breath of life" or just a "living being," as some translations have reduced it to. It is a "soul that God lives within." I was awed by his poetic and loving explanation.

I'd like to pick up on his mention of the word "instinct" in connection with the animals. There are two verses in the Bible often used to discredit the belief that animals go to heaven. Let's see what they are really telling us.

> *But these men blaspheme in matters they do not understand. They are like brute beasts, creatures of instinct, born only to be caught and destroyed, and like beasts they too will perish.*
> —2 Peter 2:12 NIV

> *Yet these men speak abusively against whatever they do not understand; and what things they do understand by instinct, like unreasoning animals—these are the very things that destroy them.*
> —Jude 1:10 NIV

I got a little nervous when I first read those verses, until I went back to my tried-and-true method of translating key words. First, the word "instinct" is *physica* in Greek and means "inborn or by nature," according to *Strong's Concordance*. So what we have here is a situation in which these vile men are saying things that are not thought out, nor are they correct. They are being compared to animals that are in the wild and who operate under instinct. As Norm Phelps wrote in his book *The Dominion of Love*:

> This instinct is a part of the world that allows bigger and stronger animals to have victory over their prey and hence

some animals die and perish under the harsh laws of the animal world.

Thanks to Adam, it is an animal world that is now subjected to the eating of flesh to survive. The verse does not mean that they will perish eternally. Rather, these men referred to are acting inappropriately and therefore are subjecting themselves to the ravages of others who could also cause them to perish. Sin begets sin.

Now that we have the idea of "instinct" under control, can this understanding be turned into something positive related to the animals in our Tier 3 examination? Ah, to me the answer is again clear and obvious. Since the animals did not make any choice in their fate, and since they are victims of the bondage of this planet, and since they are like the angels in that they are under God's command and intent, they have a free "ticket to ride" to heaven! Yes, if you were born a simple animal, you would go to heaven.

I believe, from what I have researched from the Bible, that the free pass means that once an animal expires, its last breath is taken/gathered by God and its spirit is one with Christ immediately. Being of the nature of instinct, they have a different purpose under God than that of human beings. They are not under the same set of rules as mankind. Hence, that is their distinction in Tier 3 of my Three Tier Theory.

As we conclude this chapter, we hold a firmer grasp on how God loves all his creation. I believe the evidence confirms for us that God will call all things unto himself in the end, in *his* end.

Behold, all souls are mine ...
—Ezekiel 18:4 KJV

THE NATURE OF HEAVEN

Chapter 7

THE NATURE OF HEAVEN

> *"Therefore every teacher of the law who has been instructed about the kingdom of heaven is like the owner of a house who brings out of his storeroom new treasures as well as old."*
> —Matthew 13:52 NIV

So what is heaven, anyway? Do you remember what you were taught about heaven in church? What cultural assumptions have you heard about heaven, and to what degree have you accepted or rejected those concepts?

I remember what I believed about heaven when I was a child. I imagined it as a place full of angels and clouds, with white-robed beings floating around. I'm not sure that anything about heaven was ever taught in any of my church classrooms. I just knew somehow that if I followed Jesus, I would be in the right place when I died.

It wasn't until the first dog that I owned as an adult passed away that I really began to sink my teeth into the question about heaven. Roxanne, a Rottweiler mix, had been my faithful companion though many difficult times. We had weathered a tough marriage and divorce together, as well as a move across the country. We had palled around as buddies for a solid eight years—jogging together, going to the barn together, going for oil changes together. The list goes on. When Roxanne's end came, I experienced a gut-wrenching loss for my canine companion. That's when heaven started to look extremely important to me. And for years, it's been at the heart of my research for this book.

Yet I'll be the first to admit that heaven can be a tough subject to wrap your head around. There have been so many images and ideas about it tossed around by various religions. It can seem that everybody has a different answer about what heaven is or, more commonly, no real answer of any substance or comfort at all.

So we ponder the questions: How will we get to heaven? Is it somewhere out there in the extraterrestrial realm or is it here on earth someday? What do those words "on earth as it is in heaven" truly mean? Will we go to heaven immediately when we die or later, when Christ returns? When we arrive in heaven, who or what else will be there?

In the previous chapter, we zeroed in on the question of whether animals need to be saved to gain entry to heaven or, as I conclude, they have a free "ticket to ride." But this is a good time to further our knowledge and gaze up at the big picture about the nature of heaven itself.

This is an important step to take for all of us who firmly believe or yearn to have a reason to have faith that our pets and all the animals go to heaven. I would suggest that it's just as important for those who still may argue that animals do *not* belong in heaven. After all, if one does not know what the Bible says about heaven, how can one contend that animals don't have a place in it? I find that many Christians are unclear about what they believe about the second coming of Christ. They're often not familiar with such terms as the rapture, the tribulation, a millennial reign, or the book of Daniel or the book of Revelation. They may not even know what their denomination's dogma is ... or what their specific church believes about these concepts and theories related to heaven. So we're going to dive into this terrain now.

Heaven in the Bible

You may be surprised to learn that the Bible actually has a lot to say about heaven. While there may be ideas about heaven that are not easily or fully understood, there is enough said to provide true comfort. I believe that by examining what the Bible says about heaven, you will see how biblical prophecies line up with the fact that animals are included in the apocalyptical detail. Isaiah says the wolf will lie down with the lamb and all will live in harmony. The lion shall eat grass as the oxen. Let's decipher how all of this fits into the puzzle about the reality of heaven.

I'd like to start this exploration into the confusion and disagreement about concepts of heaven by bringing in one of my favorite verses in the book of Revelation: verse 19:11. This is where Christ is returning from the heavens, in the end times story, on a white horse. Ah, so there must be horses in heaven if Christ is *returning* on one, right? Actually, many theologians say no, arguing that this is just symbolic and then they go into long explanations as to what this metaphor means. In fact, this kind of response is common in most interpretations of the apocalyptical book of Revelation.

In this situation, however, why is it so hard to believe that Christ could descend from heaven at the second coming on a horse? Did he not ride a colt into the city of Jerusalem in John 12:12–16? Yes, that act was symbolic in meaning, but still, he did actually come in on a colt. Here in Revelation, Christ returning on a white horse is an event to come in the future. So the question is, will he really come down from the heavens on a white horse, or is that just symbolic of a glorified return? After all, we know that in history kings often rode into cities on horses, especially when they were intending war. So does coming down from heaven on a white horse simply symbolize a kingly entrance? Or is it something more direct about the importance of animals and their link to Jesus?

This example brings us back to the question of whether material in the Bible is symbolic or literal. Some denominations believe that some of the stories are allegorical and some are not. Many feel that the Old Testament is more of a spoken word passed down from generation to generation, and that the New Testament is more accurate and literal. Other denominations, however, take every word in the Bible as literal truth. I believe that the Bible consists primarily of truths, as we have been exploring, but that some stories appear as life lessons or examples of how to conduct ourselves. After all, Jesus often spoke in parables.

We will compare relevant stories about heaven in the Bible, discussing how they connect or compare as common links within common themes. We will look closely at what has been said related to the book of Revelation and to the topic of heaven in general.

The journey to uncover the biblical support for a conclusion that animals have a place in heaven is one in which we are building on a cumulative effect of scripture. Rather than relying on just one conclusive verse, we are considering an entire concept by examining all that the Bible says. This is the spirit in which we will pore over the stories related to heaven here.

For example, in the Old Testament, Christ's life is prophesied approximately three hundred times, as thought by most theologians. And when Christ roamed the earth, he spoke of the scriptures of the Old Testament, as we know them today. The prophet Daniel spoke of events that have a similarity to the events in the book of Revelation. Isaiah speaks in detail about Christ and what his life will look like. Isaiah also speaks about the new heaven and the new earth, as it will be after the second coming of Christ. These connections help validate and give clarity to God's message to us.

Throughout the centuries, philosophers and theologians have birthed the belief that the commoner could not understand the Bible without these enlightened teachers to guide our understanding. As a result, over the years, you get cultural differences that bury hidden spiritual meanings into theology, instead of the more obvious concepts. Perhaps this approach separates the Christian intellect from the laymen, a sort of elitist concept. Here's what author Randy Alcorn, a respected theologian on the subject of heaven and author of twenty-seven books, has to say about this in his book *Heaven*:

> This distinction still continues in some circles, with literal interpretations seen as suspect, and allegorical and symbolic

interpretations deemed more spiritual and intellectually appealing.

By the way, I highly recommend his book for more detailed dialogue in support of the delight of heaven for all.

So let's venture through the fog of heaven, doing our best to learn more about what is to come on the "other side," according to the Bible. We'll consider next what the apostle Luke states in a verse from the book of Acts:

> *Whom the heaven must receive until the times of restitution of all things, which God hath spoken by the mouth of all his holy prophets since the world began.*
> —**Acts 3:21 KJV**

The "whom" in this verse is Christ. He resides in heaven until it is time to restore all things. And the "restitution of all things" is well documented and prophesied in many areas of both the Old Testament as well as the New Testament. Just what form that restitution will take, however, is a topic of much discussion and debate.

Destination Beyond Death

Four different accepted theologies tie the end times and our being released from the bondage from this life to the heavenly inheritance we so hope to unite with as a glorious truth. But first, let's consider what the Bible says about the transition to heaven. According to the apostle Paul addressing the Corinthians:

> *We are confident, I say, and would prefer to be away from the body and at home with the Lord.*
> —**2 Corinthians 5:8 NIV**

This verse leads me to feel confident that in the instant that one passes away, his spirit/soul goes to be with the Lord immediately! That's consistent with what you often hear at a funeral about how the deceased person has "gone to be with the Lord," or "is in heaven with God," or "has gone to a better place." Where is that, exactly, according to the Bible? According to the Bible, at death, the human spirit/soul goes either to heaven or to hell. Again, some people believe there is a real heaven and hell, while others feel that hell is eternal misery or perhaps an eternal separation from God.

Let us examine one such story told by Jesus, where a rich man and Lazarus are conscious after death.

> *And it came to pass, that the beggar died, and was carried by the angels into Abraham's bosom: the rich man also died, and was buried; and in hell he lifted up his eyes, being in torments, and seeth Abraham afar off, and Lazarus in his bosom. And he cried and said, Father Abraham, have mercy on me, and send Lazarus, that he may dip the tip of his finger in water, and cool my tongue; for I am tormented in this flame. ... Then he said, I pray thee therefore, father, that thou wouldest send him to my Father's house: For I have five brethren; that he may testify unto them, lest they also come into this place of torment.*
> —Luke 16:22–24, 27–28 KJV

As the story continues, the rich man asks Abraham to warn his brothers of this place. Abraham's response is that he will not warn them, for they have had many warnings from Moses and the prophets. Abraham states that if he were to send Lazarus, as a man raised from the dead, to warn his brothers, it would not convince them, for they have ample evidence now to learn of this condition.

I understand that the idea of an actual place such as hell is difficult to think about. I also understand that Jesus is notorious for speaking in parables when telling stories. Is Jesus telling us that plenty of miracles throughout history have made it obvious that God is good and that he wants abundance for us all? He is letting us know that the rich man apparently missed this message. Is Jesus indicating that there is a real hell and a real heaven and that one is conscious after death? Or is he giving us a lesson so that we will not miss the important messages he is here to minister to us? After all, the prophets have been pointing to future events for millenniums.

As uncomfortable as the last set of verses may have been, we still saw an inkling of heaven in this last illustration. We can still request entry to this destination. Jesus verifies this for us in the next illustration.

When the criminal on the cross next to Jesus asked to be remembered when he comes into his kingdom, Christ answered:

> *Jesus answered him, "Truly I tell you, today you will be with me in paradise."*
> —**Luke 23:43 NIV**

The apostle Paul said in Philippians 1:23 NIV:

> *I am torn between the two: I desire to depart and be with Christ, which is better by far ...*

The apostle Luke speaks of Jesus in Acts 3:21 NIV:

> *He must remain in heaven until the time comes for God to restore everything, as he promised long ago through his holy prophets.*

And in Ecclesiastes 12:7 NIV in the Old Testament:

> *And the dust returns to the ground it came from, and the spirit returns to God who gave it.*

As we saw earlier, God has given the animals spirits (Job 12:10, Psalm 104:30, Ecclesiastes 3:21). I believe, then, that it is safe to say that these conditions in these verses will apply to our spirits/souls as well as the animals. More significant, these verses truly tie up the first difficult question as to where we go, according to the Bible, immediately after death. Our spirits/souls go to the current extraterrestrial intermediate heaven, where Christ resides at this time, along with God, the cherubim, the angels, etcetera. So there is evidence in the Bible that as soon as the body dies, the spirit/soul is released and gathered to be with God and Christ.

This evidence would appear to put an end to the idea of there being a period or state of resting in the grave while awaiting the second coming. That concept is more aligned with the current thinking in the Jewish religion because Jews are still waiting for their messiah. For Christians, however, this could explain why those who experience near-death experiences (NDE) see the tunnel of light and are drawn to God, as they describe it. If you believe in NDEs, then perhaps this is an example of the process of moving through to the "other side." By the way, did you know that in almost all NDEs, the person experiences the presence of animals as well? I find that little detail interesting!

So according to the Bible, one who dies, if that person is living under God's game plan, will be in this spiritual heaven. The reason some theologians call this an "intermediate heaven" is that the Bible goes into great detail about the final days of the planet, and how Christ will return, and how the planet will be restored to a likeness of the original Garden of Eden, with Christ at the helm. That means that when you pass away, you are not at your final destination. As we say in the airline industry, it is not a nonstop fight. You have to make a connection. That's the theory anyway.

Ah, we are now talking about a final destination. How is it going to materialize and where is it going to be physically? It's time to move on to the theories about Armageddon.

Post-Christ Era, Round Two

Allow me to introduce a new term I have named: "P-CERT." It is an acronym for "Post-Christ Era, Round Two." The first coming of Christ was when he walked the earth two millenniums ago. After the second coming of Christ is what I define as "round two." What lies in between these two eras is what is in question.

We are in an age of the Church at this time, which means that the people who follow Christ, referenced as "his Church," are in a time of expanding the word of God to the masses. Ah, but all things must come to an end, correct? Or is it a new beginning? Regardless of what your belief system about this subject may be, most of us feel the presence of a looming Armageddon. In fact, this is common for many societies throughout the ages. Whether it is fifty years from now or one thousand years from now, Armageddon is always looming over humankind. Hollywood often glamorizes the idea. Well, we have a book in the Bible more colorful than any Hollywood movie. It is the book of Revelation.

The book of Revelation is all about Armageddon. In lavish form, it describes how the planet, as we know it today, will come to an end. As you may know, or will be glad to discover, it is also about hope, happiness, and the victory over death and evil. Christ is foretold to be returning. Regardless of the set or sequence of events that surround his return, once he does return, the prophecies are fulfilled. Now we are talking about a post-Christ era. This era has its own set of prophecies, as we have read about in Hosea 2 and in Isaiah 11. The key point is that after all the drama of the book of Revelation has been played out, no matter what theology you accept in the making of the next era after Armageddon, it is a post-Christ era. It is round two for Christ. It is a final destination, for all creation, restored!

It's time to zero in on P-CERT prophesy ...

> *He will wipe away every tear from their eyes. There will be no more death or mourning or crying or pain, for the old order of*

> *things has passed away. He who was seated on the throne said, "I am making everything new!" Then he said, write this down, for these words are trustworthy and true.*
> —**Revelation 21:4–5 NIV**

And then we have this verse set from Hosea, which we have previously examined:

> *In that day I will make a covenant for them with the beasts of the field and the birds of the air and the creatures that move along the ground. Bow and sword and battle I will abolish from the land, so that all may lie down in safety. I will betroth you to me forever; I will betroth you in righteousness and justice, in love and compassion. I will betroth you in faithfulness, and you will acknowledge the LORD.*
> —**Hosea 2:18–20 NIV**

The evidence that this passage provides, consistent with the book of Revelation, is that all creation will be brought back (betrothed) to God, and all will acknowledge God. That "all creation" certainly means to me that the animals are included!

It is also interesting to note in this set of verses that the Hebrew translation for the word for "betroth" is number 781, *aras,* and means "to be engaged for matrimony." You see, in Revelation, God speaks through the apostle John and refers to the second coming of Christ as a matrimonial event.

> *Let us rejoice and be glad and give him glory! For the wedding of the Lamb has come ...*
> —**Revelation 19:7 NIV**

Throughout the Bible, and in the book of Revelation in particular, Christ is coming back to gather his flock to the heavens and eternity. This is what the second coming is all about. The analogy used in the book of Revelation, as well as many other references in the Bible, is also matrimonial. Christ will come for his bride. His "bride" is the "Church," and the "Church" is analogous to the followers in Christ. It is to be a grand union indeed, and according to Hosea 2:18–19, this grand union includes the animals. Sometimes I wonder, given this verse alone, how anyone could doubt that animals go to heaven.

But there is more. Later, in this same set of verses of Hosea, as well as in Isaiah, we will see that acknowledging God is also spoken of in the book of Revelation as "singing praises to God." The reference mentions that all beings, including animals, will praise God. That is not allegorical. It is prophesied and predicted.

The wild animals honor me ...
—Isaiah 43:20 NIV

So when the book of Revelation tells of this, it is "trustworthy and true." It is backed up by other prophecies and scriptures in the Bible, both Old and New Testaments. It is here where heaven lies, in P-CERT times of eternity.

Now we're going to venture into more detail regarding the end times theology. I believe that a better understanding of this fascinating book of Revelation will facilitate a greater comprehension about heaven and the post-Christ era. Remember, the apostle John wrote the book of Revelation in approximately 90 AD, while he was in prison in Patmos, Greece. According to many theologians, it is written in apocalyptic form. But that is only partially correct. It is written figuratively, literally, and poetically. Because of these variances, there are four accepted theories that theologians agree to disagree on as to how it all plays out. Personally, I do not concern myself so much with the particulars of these theories as much as I care about the "endgame" in and of itself. It is the final product that draws our interest—the "peace ever after" theology, the "no more tears," the "wolf will lie down with the lamb." These lines or quotes in the Bible set us up for a grand conclusion, don't they?

Before we break down the four theories, it will be helpful to define a few common terms. For easier comprehension, I am giving you generalities, not formal definitions.

Preterism is the belief that biblical prophecies about the end times are in reference to events in the first century. A few examples: the Antichrist is Emperor Caesar Nero, who burned Rome in the first century and put the blame on the Christians in the hopes of encouraging their persecution, which, by the way, he was responsible for starting. As explained in *Four Views of the End Times*, by Timothy Paul Jones, the highly valuable resource for those looking to learn more about end times theories, and which I am using to reference this information about the four beliefs, there was no written system for numbers at that time. They would spell out the number or write out the number in letters. And in this case of Preterism, the tribulation is about the Jewish persecution by the Romans, with the final destruction of their temple in 70 AD.

The **rapture** is an event where Christ returns and gathers up all Christians off the planet at once. The unbelievers will remain on the planet to face a period of mayhem.

The **tribulation** is a period of time when the population left behind goes through mayhem and chaos here on earth.

The **antichrist** is the opposition to defeating evil.

The **millennium,** or thousand-year reign, refers to an era where Christ reigns on earth for a thousand-year period after his second coming.

The **new earth** is when the planet is restored to the likeness of God's original design, the Garden of Eden. It is thought to occur after the tribulation and the period of mayhem. It is to be physically on the earth we occupy at this time, however restored.

The **new heaven** is, in some theologies, an extraterrestrial place we go after being on the new earth for the millennium of Christ's reign.

The four different theologies that we are about to outline include figurative and literal descriptions and variations as to how this all plays out ... and in what order. When I mention P-CERT, I am referring to that time after the grand finale, when good defeats evil and there is eternal peace. Wherever and whenever you decide that is, the animals will be there. Both God himself and the great prophet Isaiah and Hosea state this clearly in the Bible.

The Four Theologies of the End Times

The four most commonly accepted theologies of the end times are dispensational premillennialism, historical premillennialism, amillennialism, and postmillennialism. Please remember, as we go through the differences in these theologies, that they are all based on scripture. Let me reword that: they are all based on interpretation of scripture. Of course, these theories are the subject of hundreds if not thousands of books written by those more qualified than I am. However, I try to use these questions as my guiding light in my research: Is this in God's nature? And does this maintain a common theme throughout the Bible? Was it prophesied? Was this God's original intent? What does the Bible say that it means to God, not we mere mortals? And most of all, is this in line with what Jesus taught rather than what religion teaches? That, along with the research and direct interpretation from the original language, is how I have come to my conclusions.

Presenting the four theologies of the end times in brief, as referenced from Timothy Paul Jones's pamphlet, *Four Views of the End Times*:

Dispensational Premillennialism (DP): This theology, which became popular in approximately 1860, is a belief system that Christ will return physically after a seven-year tribulation. The rapture occurs first, prior to the tribulation. After the seven-year period, Christ returns and the millennial reign on earth begins. After a thousand-year period, the devil is thrown into the lake of fire and we all move on to the new heaven. Those not raptured prior to the tribulation will have a second chance to earn their way to heaven in the midst of this great mayhem period. Variations to this theology are mid-tribulation and pre-tribulation. This means that Christ will rapture all the Christians prior to or during the middle of the seven-year period.

The main idea here is that Christ will come twice during his second coming, once during the rapture and once during the end of the tribulation. Another important point of this theory is that the establishment of Israel as an independent state in 1948 fulfills an end times prophecy. This is due to the theology that all references to Israel in the book of Revelation refer to the nation of Israel. It also infers that some Jews, as well as others left behind, will return to Christ during the tribulation period.

Personally, I cannot say that I subscribe to this theology. It calls for those left behind being given a second chance, which those who died prior to the rapture did not get. That is not aligned with what Jesus taught and diminishes Christ dying on the cross for all. It's also important to note that "dispensational" means that God rules differently at different times. But as I have pointed out with scriptural backing, God doesn't change. Remember, too, that everyone in the entire Bible who asks for forgiveness receives it. God is always merciful and full of grace. Jesus came to speak of the new covenant and to remind us all that God is great and he is here for us.

Historical Premillennialism (HP): The difference between this group and the DP theology is that the Christians will be on the planet during the tribulation. The tribulation period will weed out false believers. The second coming of Christ will occur after the tribulation but before the millennial reign. HPs believe that the Church replaces the nation of Israel in scripture related to Revelation. They believe that the millennial reign of Christ is a literal event that will follow the tribulation and the time of reckoning, or judgment. It is to be an earthly event with a physical reign of Christ and includes the restoration of all creation to its original goodness here on earth. This theory states that the believers in Christ are the Church and therefore are the referenced current or true Israel. The Church is the new "chosen one." Therefore, the references to Israel in Revelation are symbolic to mean the Church.

Amillennialism: Those who subscribe to this theory believe that Christ will return soon and that there is no actual physical thousand-year reign by Jesus on earth. In the hearts of his followers, the millennium is symbolic of Christ's reign between his life on earth and his return in the second coming. The triumph over Satan is through Christ's death and resurrection. Through Christ, Satan's power is restricted. As mentioned in *Four Views of the End Times,* persecution of Christians throughout history, such as in the case of wars, disasters, and dictatorship, is considered the tribulation.

Again, the reference to Israel, in the book of Revelation, refers to God's people on earth. Since Revelation is considered to be written in apocalyptic language, this theology considers numbers as representative of concepts, not a literal numbering system. At the time of the writing of Revelation, the Hebrews, the Romans, and the Greeks all lacked a written numbering system. Author Del Washington notes in his book *The Original Code in the Bible*:

> For centuries mankind did not have any numbers or digits in their language structure. Instead, for thousands of years, early civilizations used the letters of their alphabets to express numbers.

A specific example is that of the Emperor Nero, an enemy of Christians at the time. The numbers representing N+E+R+O equal the number 666. Because of this idea, it was thought that Nero was the Antichrist.

In more general terms, concepts for amillennialists include the following: a six represents incompleteness, a twelve represents the perfection of God's people, and the number one thousand represents a long period. So there is no millennial reign. Christ will return at some point in the future, when evil will be defeated and the great judgment will come between those who follow or followed Christ and those who did not or don't.

It is thought that the father of this belief system was Saint Augustine of Hippo in the fifth century. Others who followed this theory include Martin Luther and John Calvin. Augustine of Hippo wrote the following in the *City of God* (and was quoted in *Four Views of the End Times* as well):

> During the thousand years when the devil is bound, the saints also reign for a thousand years. Without any doubt, these two time-periods are identical and point to the time between the first and second coming of Christ.

Postmillennialism: Jesus will return after the millennium. Therefore, the rapture and the second coming are going to occur at the same time. The tribulation is the conflict between good and evil since Jesus's death and resurrection. As part of this theory, Christians are to spread the word of Christ and to share the gospel. Tribulation is the gospel being opposed. The millennium is the period of peace when all have heard the gospel's message.

The One Verse Set that may Tell it All

As you can see, there are many differences among these four theologies of the end times. But does it change the idea of animals having a place in the afterlife? I do not believe that it does. In fact, I believe that no matter which end times theology you believe in, or if you find credence in any of them at all, one Bible verse emphatically points to animals being included in the picture of heaven and the afterlife under any scenario. It's also the verse set that I most frequently referenced when I first began researching this material and was asked by doubters to give them one Bible verse that says animals go to heaven.

For the second time but equally important, I would like to present Isaiah 11:6-9 NIV:

> *The wolf also shall live with the lamb, and the leopard shall lie down with the goat, and the calf and the lion and the yearling together; and the little child shall lead them. And the cow will feed with the bear; their young will lie down together; and the lion shall eat straw like the ox. The infant will play near the hole of the cobra, and the young child shall put its hand into the viper's nest. They will neither hurt nor destroy on all my holy mountain, for the earth will be full of the knowledge of the LORD as the waters cover the sea.*

Of course, this passage alone was not always enough to silence the protests of all the doubters! That is why I dedicated seven years of research into the evidence that supports my belief that God will not forget his animals in the afterlife.

Through my hours of study in the Bible, I was motivated by the desire to bring comfort to those who had lost a cherished animal. I thought about people who may be isolated in society or who are not confident with others but whose pets meant the world to them. I thought about many homeless people, whose pet serves as their only true friend and follower. I thought about those who are sad, angry, or down on their luck, where the only love they can experience is for and from their pet. I thought about elderly people whose families are too busy or who live too far away to visit regularly, whereas an animal in this case can be a great source of company, comfort and family.

For many people in these and other life situations, an animal may be all they have or the only source of love they are exposed to. A pet can bring out love in a person who appears incapable of loving others of the same species. A pet can display and give to its owner unconditional love, just as God's love is unconditional to us. As we've said many times, when a pet dies, it can be devastating.

So again, I contend that there is purpose in the animal kingdom that we cannot fathom. I refuse to sell God short and say that he cannot bring animals back to the glorious endgame. It is not all about us. You see, sometimes, no matter how we hope to live well in the eyes of God, we still think like humans. Even Jesus has pointed that out to his disciples, as evidenced in Mark 8:33 NIV:

You do not have in mind the things of God, but the things of men.

And to the Pharisees and to teachers of the law he said, as told in Mark 7:6–8 NIV:

Isaiah was right when he prophesied about you hypocrites; as it is written: "'These people honor me with their lips, but their hearts are far from me. They worship me in vain; their teaching are but rules taught by men.' You have let go of the commands of God and are holding on to the traditions of men."

Few churches teach anything about animals. Anytime they turn their attention to theories about heaven and the end times, they so easily leave animals out of the equation. In that, they are greatly mistaken. And that leads me back to Isaiah.

Clergy have actually told me that Isaiah 11:6–9 is not about heaven at all. They argue that it is about the thousand-year reign on earth. So let's look back at what we just learned about the dispensational and historical millennialists. They believe there is going to be a literal one thousand years on earth after the second coming of Christ and before we move to the extraterrestrial heaven. The animals will be there because Isaiah said so, which not even these doubting clergy will dispute. But they go on to tell me that the animals will *not* be there after the thousand-year reign.

"Why?" I ask. I have yet to get a real answer backed up in the Bible. For clarification, they believe that after the second coming, animals will be there on the new earth (as we have established from the prophecies of Isaiah), but when it is time to move to the final destination of the new heaven, God will suddenly eliminate the animals and take only us. In other words, God, in his love for all he created, is going to just leave the island, with a bunch of live beings on it, and move to heaven with only us? Really?

Coming Full Circle

I simply can't accept that such an act is in line with God's nature. You see, this is where I come full circle. As we have seen illustrated in this chapter, there is so much written in the Bible about heaven and how great it is going to be. No matter what theology one adopts, at some point, according to Christianity, the world as we know it will be over and some form of end times theology will play itself out. Those on God's game plan are going to be in heaven. According to the Bible, Christ returns and betroths all things unto himself and restores a place in the likeness of the Garden of Eden. We know from the Bible that when the earth was made, it was full of animals, and that God thought it was "good." When God flooded the planet, except for Noah and his family, the animals were 50 percent of that plan too. When Jesus was born, he was born in a manger ... with animals. He spent forty days and forty nights in the wilderness speaking with God—and with the devil, I might add—amongst the wild beasts, and the angels, out of harm's way. And in the P-CERT times, after all is said and done—bleep, no animals? Can that really be a viable scenario for theologians to champion?

We know that what Isaiah was professing was not in present time. No lion eats straw now. It is after the second coming of Christ, when all evil is defeated. Think about that for a moment. Those who argue that animals will not gain entry to heaven are saying that all of evil is defeated, except one more act of God—restricting the animals from the second leg of the journey to heaven. Again, this is simply not consistent with God's nature. And it is not scripturally backed up. There is simply too much assumption in their theory. That's why I still confidently point to that verse in Isaiah as the one that professes that animals will be right there with us at the endgame. Isaiah painted a picture of what paradise will once again look like, and I choose to take it literally.

Oh, and as I've said before, to those who doubt this conclusion, give me one verse that says the animals will not be in heaven. There is not one.

A Place of Paradise

What is great about Christianity is that heaven is going to be a place one can look forward to with great anticipation. The new kingdom of heaven as the new heaven and new earth will be a place of beauty, as was the Garden of Eden. It will be a restored location with all the splendor contained here on earth and in your life, except that all the sin and traumas of this world will be gone. As our friend Randy Alcorn writes in his book *Heaven,* while quoting theologian René Pache:

> In other words, the emphasis in the present heaven is on the absence of the earth's negatives, while in the future heaven it is the presence of earth's positives, magnified many times through the power and glory of resurrected bodies on a resurrected Earth, free at last from sin and shame and all that would hinder both joy and achievement.

Jesus makes this statement, furthering a visual for us of what heaven looks like:

> *In my Father's house are many rooms; if it were not so, I would have told you. I am going there to prepare a place for you. And if I go and prepare a place for you, I will come back and take you to be with me that you also may be where I am. You know the way to the place where I am going.*
> —John 14:2–4 NIV

Heaven will be a place of paradise enhanced with some of the great advancements of our era, such as the finest music ever heard. It will be filled with "joyful noise."

> *Then I heard every creature in heaven and on earth and under the earth and on the sea, and all that is in them, singing: "To him who sits on the throne and to the Lamb be praise and honor and glory and power, for ever and ever!" The four living creatures [cherubim] said, "Amen," and the elders fell down and worshiped.*
> —**Revelation 5:13–14 NIV**

We humans as well as the animals will be there, praising God. Our resurrected bodies will be ourselves in our prime and we will be in the presence of Christ and those who preceded us. As the great theologian Augustine of Hippo stated in his later years (as quoted in Randy Alcorn's book *Heaven*):

> We have not lost our dear ones who have departed from this life, but have merely sent them ahead of us, so we also shall depart and shall come to that life where they will be more than ever dear as they will be better known to us, and where we shall love them without fear of parting.

If you have lost a pet, imagine your animal in these terms just quoted by Saint Augustine. Or perhaps, better yet, let us be reminded about what the apostle Paul said to the Corinthians:

> *There are also heavenly bodies and there are earthly bodies; but the splendor of the heavenly bodies is one kind, and the splendor of the earthly bodies is another. The sun has one kind of splendor, the moon another and the stars another; and the star differs from the star in splendor. So will it be with the resurrection of the dead. The body that is sown perishable, it*

> *is raised imperishable; it is sown in dishonor, it is raised in glory; it is sown in weakness, it is raised in power; it is sown a natural body, it is raised a spiritual body.*
> —**1 Corinthians 15:40–44 NIV**

Isaiah speaks of the messianic era (P-CERT times), when the wolf will lie with the lamb, the lion will eat grass, and the child will not be hurt by the snake. God will gather the spirit of all flesh once they expire. God loves all that he created and "the glory of the Lord shall last forever and he will rejoice in all of his works." God will betroth the animal kingdom unto himself again, for all of creation belongs to God. In the end, we will be returned to our splendor, your pets will be returned to their splendor, and there will be a united presence of us all in the glory of a kingdom we can call heaven. This is the nature of God's heaven.

CELESTIAL BEINGS

Chapter 8

CELESTIAL BEINGS

> *After he drove the man out, he placed on the east of the Garden of Eden cherubim and a flaming sword flashing back and forth to guard the way to the tree of life.*
> —**Genesis 3:24 NIV**

It's time to refute another argument against animals having a place in heaven. This defense, which I have heard from clergy, goes something like this: *Animals don't go to heaven because they are not made in God's image.*

When I hear this argument, I will concede that we humans are made in God's image and that animals are different in that regard. Yet they were certainly made in a way pleasing to God, their Creator. Did not God say that it's "good" after each animal group was created? He certainly was not rejecting their images or likenesses at that time.

However, there's another way to respond to this assertion that animals will be barred from heaven because they are not made in God's image or likeness. That response begins with this question: where does it say that a being has to be made in God's image to get into heaven?

The Genesis verse that I quoted in the commencement of this chapter is about a being that is in heaven; however, it is not made in God's image. It is the "cherubim," plural for cherub. Cherubim are part of a group of celestial beings. To name a few, there are seraphim, cherubim, thrones, archangels and angels, and of course Satan—none of which are made in God's image.

Seraphim, according to Isaiah 6:2–7, have six wings with which they use two to cover their faces. They surround the Lord in heaven, and they sing praises to the Lord and call out to each other, saying, "Holy, holy, holy is the Lord of the hosts; the whole earth is full of his glory." The verse is also stating that these creatures give glory to the Lord.

The cherubim, according to Genesis 3:24 as well as Ezekiel 28:14, are attendants of God. They guard the Garden of Eden to keep Adam and Eve out after the fall. They are represented in gold, as commanded by God, in the temple of Solomon on the cover of the ark of the covenant. They are also placed on the curtains in the temple that tore at the same instant that Christ released his spirit to God on the cross. The cherubim are the ones with four heads: that of a human (some theologians believe it to be the head of an angel), an eagle, an ox, and a lion.

As I have learned in researching *The HarperCollins Encyclopedia of Catholicism*, "Thrones" (Colossians 1:16) are beings in heaven that are steadfast, and they facilitate God's justice upon us. "Archangels" and "angels," it should be noted, are not considered to be made in God's image. Archangels are messengers who bear divine decrees. The word "archangel" occurs twice in the New Testament: in Jude 9, where Michael is referred to as the archangel who "contends with the devil," and in Thessalonians 4:16, where there is a reference to the archangel's call that will come on the day the Lord returns from heaven. The prophet Enoch names the seven archangels as Uriel, Raguel, Michael, Seraqael. Gabriel, Haniel, and Raphael.

As for the angels, they perform many functions, such as protection and interceding with God on behalf of humans and animals. We will tell the story in the next chapter about a prophet named Balaam and the angel with the sword who interceded on behalf of his poor donkey. Angels are not made in God's image, yet they hold a higher place in the hierarchy than we do. Here is a verse describing Jesus. Remember,

Jesus was made a deity reincarnate as man. He is in the flesh of man so he is "lower" than the angels.

> *Thou madest him a little lower than the angel; thou crownedst him with glory and honor, and didst set him over the works of thy hand.*
> —Hebrews 2:7 KJV

Remember also that the angels see the face of God (Matthew 18:10), whereas, as we have mentioned, we are forbidden to see God's face while still mere mortals.

Satan, as we discussed earlier, was an angel. He, however, is now a fallen one. We now see that there are *many* creatures in heaven not made in God's image. There are beings with four heads, albeit with the heads of animals. There are beings with six wings. It is looking quite strange, isn't it?

These celestial beings are mentioned throughout the Bible up to and including the book of Revelation. Even though Revelation is often referred to as apocalyptical writing, these creatures are a part of God's story consistently throughout non-apocalyptical writings. So there is literal evidence in the book of Revelation, as well as the rest of the Bible, that point to the possibilities of animals being included in the paradise of heaven despite not being in God's image or likeness.

We will now dig deeply into the biblical evidence and use translations into the original language to find further clues. We will also see how the Bible speaks of animals that actually praise God, animals that edify God.

All Praise God

> *Beasts, and all cattle; creeping things, and flying fowl: Kings of the earth, and all people; princes, and all judges of the earth: both young men, and maidens; old men, and children:*

> *Let them praise the name of the Lord: for his name alone is excellent; his glory is above the earth and heaven.*
> —**Psalm 148:10–13 KJV**

> *My mouth shall speak the praise of the LORD: and let all flesh [Basar] bless his holy name for ever and ever.*
> —**Psalm 145:21 KJV**

> *Let everything that has breath praise the LORD. Praise the LORD.*
> —**Psalm 150:6 NIV**

In this last verse, notice the words "everything" and "breath." The number in the *Strong's Concordance* for "everything" is 3605: *kowl*. It means "the whole, all, any, everything." The word for "breath" in this particular case is number 5397: *n'shamah* or *neshamah*. As defined in *Strong's Concordance*, it means "a puff, i.e., wind, angry or vital breath, divine inspiration, intellect, or (concr.) an animal." It goes on to say, "Neshamah is literally a 'breathing being.'"

> *Each of the four living creatures had six wings and was covered with eyes all around, even under his wings. Day and night they never stop saying, "Holy, holy, holy is the Lord God Almighty, who was, and is, and is to come." Whenever the living creatures give glory, honor and thanks to him who sits on the throne and who lives for ever and ever.*
> —**Revelation 4:8–9 NIV**

According to Randy Acorn in his book *Heaven*:

> The word translation for "living creatures" here is *zoon.* Throughout most of the New Testament the word is translated as "animal" and is used to indicate animals sacrificed in the temple and wild, irrational

animals (Hebrews 13:11; 2 Peter 2:12; Jude 1:10). In the Old Testament, the Septuagint used *zoon* to translate the Hebrew words for animals, including the "living creatures" of the sea (Genesis 1:21; Ezekiel 47:9). In extrabiblical writings, *zoon* commonly referred to ordinary animals and was used for the Egyptians' divine animals and the mythological bird called the Phoenix (1 Clement 25:2–3). In virtually every case, this word means not a person, not an angel, but an *animal*.

So we are now looking at the word translation for "living creature." *Zoon*, we are discovering, means animals. The word is mentioned eight times in Revelation. From Psalm 150:6 NIV, "Let everything that has breath praise the Lord," we know for sure that animals have breath. And since these living creatures praise God from the present heaven, then animals must be there too.

If one was to argue that the book of Revelation is figurative, consider this: (1) we know Christ has a real body and is now present in the current heaven; (2) these particular living (animal-like) creatures mentioned in Revelation are thought by theologians to be cherubim because they are described much as they are in several other areas of the Bible. We will look at one example in Ezekiel 10:14–20 in a moment. Earlier in this chapter, we noted that cherubim are also mentioned as the guardians of the Garden of Eden and as God's bodyguards, and they were replicated and placed on the ark of the covenant and the curtains in the temples. They are close to God but are not angels.

The important point for us to emphasize again is that the cherubim are not made in God's image. They existed prior to the Garden of Eden. In Revelation 4:7, they are described just as they are in Ezekiel 10. Therefore, with the consistencies of the Bible prior to Revelation, they are not figurative. Why, then, is it hard to imagine things not made in God's likeness being present in heaven? The Bible clearly tells us that there are such beings. In the KJV, these living creatures are translated as "beasts." Still, they are animals who articulate and praise God. I believe that it is accurate to say that when a verse says that "all living things" (*zoon*) praise God from heaven, it includes animals and all the beings that God created as "good."

Now let's look at an exciting passage in Ezekiel:

> *And every one had four faces: the first face was the face of a cherub, and the second face was the face of a man, and the third the face of a lion, and the fourth the face of an eagle. And the cherubims were lifted up. This is the living creature I saw by the river of Chebar. And when the cherubims went, the wheels went by them: and when the cherubims lifted up their wings to mount up from the earth, the same wheels also turned not from beside them. When they stood, these stood; and they were lifted up, these lifted up themselves also: for the spirit of the living creature was in them. Then the glory of the Lord departed from off the threshold of the house, and stood over the cherubim. And the cherubims lifted up their wings, and mounted up from the earth in my sight: when they went out, the wheels also were beside them, and every one stood at the door of the east gate of the Lord's house; and the glory of the God of Israel was over them above. This is the living creature that I saw under the God of Israel by the river of Chebar; and I knew they were the cherubims.*
> —Ezekiel 10:14–20 KJV

Note that the word in Hebrew for "cherub" is number 3742: *kerub*. *Strong's Concordance* defines it as "of uncertain derivation, a cherub or imaginary figure. plural: cherubim." Now we have a better understanding of these strange creatures. God created these beings with faces representing many of his creatures: a man, a lion, an eagle. Again, God did not leave out representation of the animal kingdom! Why would he leave them out of the afterlife? Apparently, the animals are already there, serving God in this incredible, unimaginable fashion.

The Guards of Heaven

These "four creatures" definitely have a kingly role in the game of thrones, as we now see. Lifting God in a chariot into the celestial kingdom surely commands awareness of their existence. As we have seen, Ezekiel is verifying that they are indeed cherubim. They are basically God's security guards, sitting at the right and left side of Christ and of God on the throne. They are also a part of the apocalyptical tale in the book of Revelation.

> *And before the throne there was a sea of glass like unto crystal: and in the midst of the throne, and round about the throne, were four beasts full of eyes before and behind. And the first beast was like a lion, and the second beast like a calf, and the third beast had a face of a man, and the fourth beast was like a flying eagle.*
> —Revelation 4:6–7 KJV

Many theologians believe that the writer of Revelation, John, is describing the four beasts exactly as Ezekiel described them. Therefore, they would be considered cherubim even though he did not address them as such. Regardless, these beings are still guarding the throne of God. The difference is that they are now praising God as well.

Here's the main point: they are heavenly hosts, celestial beings; they have the heads of both man and animal. They represent all creatures. These animal-like creatures occupy and guard heaven. Interestingly, they are regarded highly enough that certain circles of theologians attach the characterization of each one of the faces of a cherub to the four writers of the gospel: Matthew, Mark, Luke, and John. Matthew represents the human/angel, Mark represents the lion, Luke represents the ox, and John represents the eagle.

As you may know, one of history's greatest displays of mosaic artwork lies in St. Peter's Basilica in the Vatican. It covers the entire dome interior of the ceiling above the tomb of St. Peter. The dome ceiling is divided into four parts representing these four apostles—and they are pictured with their respective representations of the cherub. Since the cherubim protect God, they are inlaid with the apostles because the apostles protected the word of God as proclaimed by Jesus.

That's one stunning visual reminder of the dramatic significance of animals and animal-like creatures in God's world. Though his animals may not be made in his image or likeness, it does not lessen their status. They praise God, they serve God, and they have a secure place in heaven along with all of God's creatures.

GOD'S ANIMAL KINGDOM

Chapter 9

GOD'S ANIMAL KINGDOM

A righteous man regardeth the life of his beast: but the tender mercies of the wicked are cruel.
—**Proverbs 12:10 KJV**

As we have pored through dozens and dozens of biblical verses and supporting research, I have invited you to contemplate these questions and issues related to animals going to heaven. I have challenged you to look upon things through a different lens or a new light, and I have held up the false assumptions and misunderstanding that many well-intentioned individuals have carried with them for years, for generations, or perhaps even for centuries.

Our journey of exploration is not yet complete. As we come closer to winding down our discussion, we're going to take a slightly different approach. Now that we have examined a body of evidence that strengthens our position, let us journey through some of the stories of the Bible for the pure enjoyment of it. Rather than engaging the intellect, let's take this opportunity to be entertained by more animal stories from the Bible. And besides, there may be a few more beads to enhance our new necklace of understanding.

Perhaps these stories will expand our awareness of a God of love and compassion, a God that loves all of us, a God who wants us to experience abundance in this lifetime, a God who has a much bigger plan for *all* that he created. We have already learned a great deal about how much

God talks about the animals in the Bible. God uses the animals for his purposes, and they matter to him. Remember, his eyes are on the sparrow. He is the ultimate Creator, the source of all intention, the one who gives a spirit and soul to *all* living things. Now we're going to focus a bit more about how *he* feels about his animal kingdom.

So relax. Put down your close-up lens that you've been calling upon to examine the evidence I have presented. As you walk with me through the field of God and his animal kingdom, open up room to simply absorb these stories and reflect on what they all mean in your heart ... and in the heart of God.

The Patron Saint of the Animals

I can't think of a better way to begin reflecting on the love of God for his animals than by looking at the example of Francis of Assisi, known as the patron saint of animals. Saint Francis of Assisi lived in the thirteenth century in Italy. He was known for his Christlike kindness to all: the poor, the lepers, and of course the animals. (Incidentally, this is the saint that the current pope emulated by taking his name. Pope Francis is the 266th and current pope of the Catholic Church.) I will offer a few stories about Saint Francis's ministry.

As Saint Francis and his companion friars ventured through the small towns of Italy, he gained a reputation for his moments of devotion to the animals. He truly believed that he could minister to these other creatures of God as well as to other people. When he and his friends reached a place called Pian d'Arca, they came upon a field filled with a multitude of birds. Drawn to their wonderment, he stopped and announced to his companions that he was going to preach to the flock.

Here's how Ivan Gobry describes the moment in the informative book *Saint Francis of Assisi*:

> He walked into the field and the multitude of winged creatures, instead of flying away, remained on the ground,

turned toward him, as though they were expecting him. Then, filled with joy, he spoke to them: "My brothers, you birds, you have good reason to thank God your Creator, and to praise him, always and everywhere; for he has given you the freedom to fly where you will; he has endowed you with a double and triple garment; he preserved your ancestors in Noah's ark, so that your species would not disappear from the face of the earth; furthermore you are indebted to him for the air in which you fly. Then too, you neither sow nor reap, and yet God feeds you ..."

During the entire time of this discourse, the birds nodded, opened their beaks without singing, fluttered their wings without flying, and tilted their heads gracefully. When the preacher finished and had made the sign of the cross over them, they all took flight, while making the air resound with their harmonious songs, which charmed and enraptured the listeners.

Did you notice his reference to God preserving the birds' ancestors in Noah's ark? Saint Francis certainly remembered that God would not let his animals "disappear from the face of the earth." And I wonder if Saint Francis remembered this verse as he ministered to the community of birds:

> *If ye continue in the faith grounded and settled, and be not moved away from the hope of the gospel, which ye have heard, and which was preached to every creature which is under heaven; whereof I Paul am made a minister ...*
> **—Colossians 1:23 KJV**

Perhaps a better-known story about Saint Francis, told throughout the ages, is that of the wolf of Gubbio. In this story, as Saint Francis is passing through the town of Gubbio, he hears of a beast that is terrorizing the town. This wolf is killing livestock as well as men of the city. No one is exiting the city walls due to the terror of this animal. Much to the astonishment of the townsmen, Saint Francis agrees to approach the wolf and put a stop to the violence. He confronts the wolf without conflict and even draws affection from this beastly character. He proceeds to communicate with the wolf. As Ivan Gobry describes in *Saint Francis of Assisi*:

> "A whole populace is grumbling about you; this entire city detests you. But I want to make peace between them and you, Brother wolf. You will no longer do them any harm, and they will forget your past misdeeds. Then neither men nor dogs will pursue you any more."

The wolf wags his tail and follows Saint Francis into the city walls. Saint Francis presents him to the spectators and explains to them that if they feed him for the rest of his life, he will be docile and full of gratitude. He then takes the paw of the wolf and it becomes so. The wolf never becomes aggressive again and lives out its life peacefully among the people of Gubbio. Eventually, the wolf dies of old age and is the fame of the town to this day.

Numerous times throughout his saintly and humble life, Saint Francis was witnessed ministering to animals. As mentioned in *Saint Francis of Assisi*, he was known to have asked others to "purchase the freedom of lambs that were being led to slaughter, in memory of the most meek Lamb who willed to be led to death in order to redeem sinners." He was legendary for his preaching to fish, birds, and all creatures of nature, commanding their full attention.

In Ivan Gobry's book that we have been referencing, he quotes Saint Bonaventure recalling Saint Francis's pious affection this way:

> By going back to the first principle of all things, he had conceived a lively friendship for them all, calling even the lowest creatures brothers and sisters, for he knew that he and they proceeded from the same principle.

Through his many acts of devotion to animals, Saint Francis no doubt was most renowned for his ability to enjoy the praises of the birds of the air. Of course, he delighted in all the creatures that came from his maker. He returned great servitude to all those he met throughout his pilgrimages. He never encountered a creature unworthy of his affection and his grace.

You can learn more about Saint Francis by reading *Saint Francis of Assisi* and many other books about him. His life is also the subject of the movie *Brother Sun, Sister Moon*. How privileged this planet would be to have more of the likes of Saint Francis of Assisi! And what a powerful contrasting image we can draw from the manner in which he connected with the animal kingdom to the way in which many people in our world today regard and relate to God's lower creatures.

The Portrayal of Hunters in the Bible

Do you remember Henry David Thoreau's reflections about nature? Let's look at some samples about hunting animals that he has mentioned in his classic book *Walden*:

> He goes thither at first as a hunter and fisher, until at last, if he has the seeds of a better life in him, he distinguishes his proper objects, as a poet or naturalist it may be, and leaves the gun and fish-pole behind. The mass of men are still and always young in this respect. In some countries a hunting parson [sic] is no uncommon sight. Such a one might make a good shepherd's dog, but is far from being a Good Shepherd.
>
> ... I have found repeatedly, of late years, that I cannot fish without falling a little in self-respect.
>
> ... True, he can and does live, in a great measure, by preying on other animals; but this is a miserable way— as any one who will go to snaring rabbits or slaughtering

lambs, may learn—and he will be regarded as a benefactor of his race who shall teach man to confine himself to a more innocent and wholesome diet. Whatever my own practice may be, I have no doubt that it is a part of the destiny of the human race, in its gradual improvement, to leave off eating animals, as surely as the savage tribes have left off eating each other when they came in contact with the more civilized.

Before we look at what the Bible may have to say about hunting, I would first like to tell my friends and others among this audience who happen to be hunters that I am sorry to have to address this subject on your behalf, for I do not judge. My love for all of you still stands. I understand that there are those of you who hunt to feed your family, which is far different from hunting to put a trophy on the wall or hunting for sport. I admit that there was nothing so tranquil as my own days with my father out in the deep blue sea, currents gently rocking the boat, fishing for the entire day and watching the dolphins frolic about in my presence.

Now that I have engaged in this journey of self-discovery about the nature of God's animal kingdom, however, I have come to see the issue of hunting differently. So while we're focusing on *feeling* in response to different stories and dimensions of God's connection to his animals, I want to engage in this brief inquiry.

So what does the Bible say on the subject of hunting? The first recorded hunter of the Bible was Nimrod, a descendant of Ham, one of Noah's sons. Nimrod was thought to be the greatest warrior on the earth (Genesis 10:8) at one point in history. He was a great hunter as well (Genesis 10:9). There was one problem with Nimrod's destiny.

> *The first centers of his kingdom were Babylon, Erech, Akkad and Calneh, in Shinar. From that land he went to Assyria, where he built Nineveh, Rehoboth Ir ...*
> —**Genesis 10:11 NIV**

To reiterate, Nimrod's kingdoms were Babylon, Assyria, and Nineveh, to name a few. The Babylonian Empire opposed God throughout the Bible. It is referenced in the book of Revelation as being destroyed for good. As for Assyria, many historians view this kingdom as the home of the first true terrorists of the world. In the book of Micah, a "source of peace" will come from the small town of Bethlehem and defeat God's enemies in Assyria and the gates of Nimrod (Micah 6:5–6).

A second hunter, Ishmael, is the first son of Abraham by his maidservant, Hagar. Abraham is of the lineage of Shem, another son of Noah. He was a skillful archer. He and his descendants lived in open hostility toward all their relatives (Genesis 25:18).

Then there was Esau, the son of Isaac, son of Abraham. Esau was a twin brother to Jacob. Esau became a great hunter, whereas Jacob preferred to stay home (Genesis 25:27). Esau became godless and immoral and is not looked upon favorably throughout scripture.

You may be familiar with the story of Jacob's sons, Simeon and Levi. They were rejected and denied their inheritance from Jacob due to their hunting for sport and having weapons of violence. They "crippled oxen for sport" (Genesis 49:5–6 NLT).

There is another, more ambiguous hunter mentioned in the Bible:

> *I looked and there before me was a white horse! Its rider held a bow, and he was given a crown, and he rode out as a conqueror bent on conquest.*
> —**Revelation 6:2 NIV**

It is important to note that this rider on the white horse should not be confused with the rider on the white horse mentioned in Revelation 19:

> *I saw heaven standing open and there before me was a white horse, whose rider is called Faithful and True. With justice he judges and makes war. His eyes are like blazing fire, and on his head are many crowns.*
> —**Revelation 19:11–12 NIV**

You see, the first rider holds a bow and is a hunter of souls. In this particular verse in the book of Revelation, he is sometimes mistakenly identified as Christ. But he holds a bow and is bent on conquest. In fact, he is the great deceiver, Satan himself. It is the second rider, of course, who is Christ. In the great Reverend Billy Graham's book *Approaching Hoofbeats*, he mentions that in the Greek language the crown worn by the rider in Revelation 6 is called *sephanos*, which means "the crown of victory worn by a conqueror." The crowns Christ wears in Revelation 19:12, on the other hand, are *diadema*, the "crowns of royalty."

I find it interesting that throughout the entire Bible, Satan is portrayed as a hunter of souls, a deceiver, and God's opponent. Christ, in contrast, is a shepherd of souls. Is it just a coincidence that when animal hunters are depicted in the Bible, they are portrayed as those who did not follow God's game plan? They were not men of God, and there was a darkness associated with them. As we have noted previously, when we look closely at scripture, we find that the Jewish religion concludes that hunting is inhumane and forbidden. And since Jesus was a Jew, I am sure he did not hunt, nor did he destroy. He was a healer, and he forgave all. In essence, is that not what the Christian religion is trying to emulate?

Perhaps hunting is just an accepted part of our culture. Whatever your own position may be, I simply invite you to consider those particular stories of the Bible.

God's Rules include His Animals

In Genesis chapter 24, we find the story about Rebecca and Isaac. Abraham's servant is sent out to find a wife for Isaac, Abraham's son. This is of great significance in the evolution of the Bible story because it is from this lineage that Jesus will be born. The servant is praying for success in his journey and decides that the woman who offers water to his camels will be worthy of being a good wife. Remember the proverb about how a righteous man cares for his animals? Well, it got Rebecca a husband

and a significant role in the Bible story ... for watering and caring for an animal. Reflect on how this act of kindness was of value to God.

The Bible also reminds us often of rules that God instills upon humans, in which he does not forget to include the other creatures.

> *If anyone takes the life of a human being, he must be put to death. Anyone who takes the life of someone's animal must make restitution—life for a life.*
> —Leviticus 24:17–18 NIV

Interestingly, this is where we got the idea of "an eye for an eye," because as verse 19 goes on to say, "If anyone injures his neighbor, whatever he has done must be done to him: fracture for fracture, eye for an eye, tooth for tooth." In our past discussion about covenants, we emphasized how the resurrection of Jesus brings a new covenant. In this particular case, Jesus clearly teaches that the new law is of one of love and forgiveness, and he famously coins the line "turn the other cheek." So it is out with "eye for an eye" and in with "turn the other cheek." Jesus has come to fulfill all the prophecies and to offer total forgiveness and future glory to all.

However, God of the Old Testament time period was still attempting to instill righteousness into the Israelites. Yet along the way, he remembers the animals.

> *Whatever the land yields during the Sabbath year (the year of rest) will be food for you—for yourself, your manservant and maidservant, and the hired worker and temporary resident who live among you, as well as for your livestock and the wild animals in your land.*
> —Leviticus 25:6–7 NIV

> *I set apart for myself every firstborn in Israel, whether man or animal. They are mine. I am the LORD.*
> —Numbers 3:13 NIV

Next we'll turn our attention to Moses and his struggle to organize the Israelites while they were under his control after the exodus from Egypt. You see, God provided food for the Israelites while stranded in the wilderness. It was called "manna," and it was like "coriander seed and it tasted like wafers made with honey," as it is worded in the *Life Application Bible: New International Version* commentary. It could be made into bread.

The people complain about this, telling Moses that at least the Egyptians fed them meat, and for that, they were better off in Egypt. Seeing how ungrateful the Israelites are for this food provided by God—without taking a life, I might add—God becomes angry. A frustrated Moses asks God where he can find meat for these people. This is God's response:

> *Now a wind went out from the LORD and drove quail in from the sea. It brought them down all around the camp to about three feet above the ground, as far as a day's walk in any direction. All that day and night and all the next day the people went out and gathered quail. No one gathered less than ten homers. Then they spread them out all around the camp. But while the meat was still between their teeth and before it could be consumed, the anger of the LORD burned against the people, and he struck them with a severe plague.*
> **—Numbers 11:31–33 NIV**

The poisoned quail is just the beginning of the rebellion of the people of Moses. At one point, God is frustrated at the lack of faith and compliance among the Israelites, as evidenced by this response:

> *The ox knows his master, the donkey his owner's manger, but Israel does not know, my people do not understand.*
> **—Isaiah 1:3 NIV**

You see, the donkey and the ox are under the inclination God intended of them; however, his people are not following a favorable inclination. God continues to administer guidance and to set rules for his people, yet mankind continues to struggle with those rules.

The Story of Balaam and his Donkey

Now let's bring in some stories of how the animals actually serve God. Are you familiar with the story about Balaam and his donkey? Balaam is a servant of God but chooses to take matters into his own hands and changes the course in which God had sent him. In other words, he makes the decision that his idea is worthy of a change in the game plan.

Meanwhile, his donkey sees an angel in the road and continues on the original path. In response, Balaam beats the donkey three times for not going where he directed. Watch what happens next:

> *The LORD opened the donkey's mouth, and she said to Balaam, "What have I done to you to make you beat me three times?" Balaam answered the donkey, "You have made a fool of me! If only I had a sword in my hand, I would kill you right now." The donkey said to Balaam, "Am I not your own donkey, which you have always ridden, to this day? Have I been in the habit of doing this to you?" "No," he said. Then The LORD opened Balaam's eyes, and he saw the angel of the Lord standing in the road with his sword drawn. So he bowed low and fell facedown. The angel of the LORD asked him, "Why have you beaten your donkey these three times? I have come here to oppose you because your path is a reckless one before me. The donkey saw me and turned away from me these three times. If she had not turned away, I would certainly have killed you by now, but I would have spared her."*
> —**Numbers 22:28–32 NIV**

We have an angel coming to the aid of a prophet gone astray. Or is it a case of the angel coming to the aid of an animal? Either way, the angel would have spared the donkey and not the prophet, even if the donkey had not seen the angel and had obeyed Balaam. It's also interesting to note that this is the only example in the written Bible of an angel arriving to intercede with a sword in hand. The only other mention of an angel with a sword is in 1 Chronicles 21:30, in which King David claims that he fears the "sword of an angel." The sword of an angel in this story in the book of Numbers is a sword in hand to aid an animal. That tells us a lot about how God values his animals. And if you look at the story as a whole, it's about a donkey who obeys God and saves Balaam's life. That sounds inspiring to me.

When I reflect on this story, I am reminded of my experience in training dogs to be of service. In the world of training seeing-eye service dogs, when a dog chooses to not walk straight with his master to avoid a low branch in harm's way, it is called "intelligent disobedience." I like to call it "deliberate disobedience," and to me it is an example of how valuable animals can be to us. Whether it is the donkey or a blind person's seeing-eye dog, an animal is a precious gift from God. We should view all animals as such, as well as one another, might I add.

In these illustrations, we are reminded of how God uses both humans and animals for his purpose. This attributing evidence is another reason that I believe we would be selling God short if we made a judgment assuming that the animals do not matter to God either now or in the future. After all, it was God who said, "I will show mercy to whom I will show mercy and I will show compassion to whom I will show compassion" (Exodus 33:19). It sure looks to me as if Balaam's donkey was the recipient of God's compassion and mercy.

Here's another story that happens to involve a donkey as well as a lion. In this story, a prophet who had direct orders from God chooses to listen to another prophet who deceives him, instead of listening to God. As a result, he crosses paths with a lion sent by God.

> *As he went on his way, a lion met him on the road and killed him, and his body was thrown down on the road, with both the donkey and the lion standing beside it.*
> —**1 Kings 13:24 NIV**

Hearing of this calamity, the man who had dinner with the prophet previously goes after him.

> *Then he went out and found the body thrown down on the road, with the donkey and the lion standing beside it. The lion had neither eaten the body nor mauled the donkey.*
> —1 Kings 13:28 NIV

In the *Life Application Study Bible, New International Version,* we find this interpretation:

> The fact that the lion and the donkey were standing by the prophet's body showed that this was a divine judgment. Normally the lion would have attacked the donkey and/or devoured the man.

The way I see this illustration, both the lion and Balaam's donkey are instruments of God's game plan. They are operating under an inclination from God. They have been put to use by God. Never underestimate the power of God to use any of his creation to fulfill his purpose.

The Story of Kind David and the Ewe

On a softer, more compassionate note, here is a story that compares a man's love for his pet to a man's love for a woman. A prophet is sent to King David, one of the Bible's greatest and most revered characters, to help him learn a lesson. You see, King David has fallen passionately in love with another man's wife, Bathsheba. As a result, he sends the husband into the front lines of war in the hope that he will be killed. King David's scheme is successful, and God is displeased. So he sends Nathan, a prophet, to speak with King David.

> *The LORD sent Nathan to David. When he came to him, he said, "There were two men in a certain town, one rich and the other poor. The rich man had a very large number of sheep and cattle, but the poor man had nothing except one little ewe lamb he had bought. He raised it, and it grew up with him and his children. It shared his food, drank from his cup and even slept in his arms. It was like a daughter to him. Now a traveler came to the rich man, but the rich man refrained from taking one of his own sheep or cattle to prepare a meal for the traveler who had come to him. Instead, he took the ewe lamb that belonged to the poor man and prepared it for the one who had come to him." David burned with anger against the man and said to Nathan, "As surely as the LORD lives, the man who did this deserves to die! He must pay for that lamb four times over because he did such a thing and had no pity." Then Nathan said to David, "You are the man! This is what the LORD, the God of Israel, says: 'I anointed you king over Israel, and I delivered you from the hand of Saul. I gave your master's house to you, and your master's wives into your arms. I gave you the house of Israel and Judah. And if all this had been too little, I would have given you even more. Why did you despise the word of the LORD by doing what is evil in his eyes? You struck down Uriah the Hittite with the sword and took his wife to be your own. You killed him with the sword of the Ammonites.'"*
> **—2 Samuel 12:1–9 NIV**

At first glance, this story may seem simple. It is being illustrated through a parable. God is mad at King David for doing something so evil out of his selfish, lustful desire for someone else's wife. Just for fun, let's detour and consider how many commandments were broken here: (1) King David committed murder; (2) he coveted another man's belonging; and (3) he committed adultery. As a result, King David will deal with a tremendous calamity in his future. However, he does not desert his devotion to God, and he continues to ask for forgiveness. God hears his prayers and forgives him. His son Solomon, as we saw earlier, becomes a great leader and one of the better-known characters of the Bible.

Ah, but could there be a secondary theme buried in this story? Nathan is setting up King David with a parable to point out his shortcomings in this matter, as we know. Why, then, did he use the illustration of the pet ewe? It was common in that day for people to have pet lambs and to treat them with this degree of kindness. Nathan used the tenderness of a man's love for his pet because he is sure that King David will understand this depth of compassion. Because King David does see this example as an outrage, he clearly states that the "rich man" should be put to death for the taking of this precious pet from this poor man. That's quite a judgment in favor and in defense of a poor little ewe lamb. King David is declaring that taking this pet away from its owner and using it for dinner is punishable by death.

I recognize that the primary point of this story is that it is wrong to take something so valuable and loved from someone else, and so unjustly at that. But have you met or do you know of people who love an animal so much that they let it drink from their cup and let it sleep in their arms? How about those who have a difficult time connecting to other humans but who can display their love to an animal? If animals have the power to teach us how to love, imagine the trauma that ensues in the mind of one when there looms the possibility of losing this pet. Like King David in this story, they are feeling the depth of the awareness that a person's pet may be his greatest asset.

Since we're looking at King David, it's a good time to include a story about his son, King Solomon. As we noted, Solomon became a great king, ruler, and poet of the Bible. He prayed for wisdom. God thought that was brilliant, so he rewarded him handsomely. Solomon is given great wisdom. The Bible tells of Solomon having more wisdom than any other.

> *He taught about animals and birds, reptiles, and fish. Men of all nations came to listen to Solomon's wisdom, sent by all the kings of the world, who had heard his wisdom.*
> —1 Kings 4:33–34 NIV

Apparently, according to God, it was considered great wisdom to have knowledge of the animals' world. That's worth reflecting on.

The Story of the Ravens

When the prophet Elijah told an evil king of an impending drought from God, he had to escape to the east side of the Jordan River. God provided ravens to feed him.

> *You will drink from the brook, and I have ordered the ravens to feed you there.*
> —1 Kings 17:4 NIV

Later, Elijah's fate is taken into God's hands.

> *As they were walking along and talking together, suddenly a chariot of fire and horses of fire appeared and separated the two of them, and Elijah went up to heaven in a whirlwind.*
> —2 Kings 2:11 NIV

Elijah did not die in his lifetime. He is one of two characters of the Bible who never had to experience death. Enoch was the other. Well, I wouldn't mind a ride to heaven like that, horses and all. I am sure that I am not worthy, but it doesn't hurt to ask … or hope … or pray for something so grand. Oh, and did you take note of the horses from heaven in this illustration?

The Story of Job

This is a wonderful account where God uses the animal kingdom to provide an important lesson for Job. You see, Job is a wealthy and righteous man who begins to experience overwhelming calamity. His friends try to console him. They believe that he needs to repent for his sins. Job does believe he is being punished, but he does not believe that he has committed any great sins. He becomes frustrated. As explained in the *Life Application Bible: New International Version*, "When God finally speaks to Job, we learn that the lesson from the book of Job is that 'knowing' God is better than 'knowing' answers. God is not arbitrary or uncaring and pain is not always punishment."

In other words, Job's problems are not punishment from God. However, Job is impatient for answers and resolve. What is so unique about the book of Job is that it has many descriptions from God, by God, about how spectacular he made the animal kingdom. God describes various animals in all their glory. God does this on Job's behalf, as described in the same *Life Application Bible:*

> God asked Job several questions about the animal kingdom in order to demonstrate how limited Job's knowledge really was. God was not seeking answers from Job. Instead, he was getting Job to recognize and submit to God's power and sovereignty. Only then could he hear what God was really saying to him.

God has reminded us in scripture that he has all knowledge. He wants to guide Job to understanding more about his ways. He wants to bestow more wisdom upon Job.

> *His ways are greater than your ways, his thoughts are greater than your thoughts.*
> —Isaiah 55:9 NIV

> *He will not grow tired or weary, and his understanding no one can fathom.*
> —Isaiah 40:28 NIV

As the story continues, Job's friends are telling him that he is suffering because he must have sinned or that God needs to "purify" him. Job goes on quite a journey as a result. However, Job does attempt to listen to God and to learn from him. As God teaches Job these life lessons, he narrates about the animal kingdom like a proud father. His speeches are poetic!

Here is God's narration about the horse:

> *Did you give the horse his strength or clothe his neck with a flowing mane? Do you make him leap like a locust, striking terror with his proud snorting? He paws fiercely, rejoicing in his strength, and charges into the fray. He laughs at fear, afraid of nothing; he does not shy away from the sword. The quiver rattles against his side, along with the flashing spear and lance. In frenzied excitement he eats up the ground; he cannot stand still when the trumpet sounds.*
> —Job 39:19–25 NIV

By challenging Job about the animal kingdom, God is showing Job that he has a lot of nerve (to put it politely) questioning God when God is the creator of such miracles in nature. These are miracles involving creatures that could outrun, outfox, outfly, and simply out-survive any human. God is reminding Job of the glory that he created in the animals, and that the world is what it is because of God, and that only God fully understands all things within. After all, remember the opening line of the Bible?

> *In the beginning God created the heavens and the earth.*
> —Genesis 1:1 NIV

Luckily, Job becomes a good student and gains more knowledge about God's nature. As a result, Job humbles himself. His family and his possessions are restored. Ultimately, he receives even greater blessings.

I certainly feel humbled by this lesson. I am deeply appreciative that I can turn to the Bible for incredible poetic references to the animal kingdom and learn life lessons as well. They seem to go together somehow.

Let us discover more about God's poetic license in the book of Job. We have seen how proud God is of his horse. He also is proud of the eagle, the donkey, and the behemoth. In Job 40:19 NIV, God is actually quoted as saying that the behemoth (thought by some experts to be an elephant) "ranks first among all the works of God!" Doesn't that sound like a proud father?

> *Do you hunt the prey for the lioness and satisfy the hunger of the lions when they crouch in their dens or lie in wait in the thicket? Who provides food for the raven when its young cry out to God and wander about for lack of food? Do you know when the mountain goats give birth? Do you watch when the doe bears her fawn? Do you count the months till they bear? Do you know the time they give birth? They crouch down and bring forth their young; their labor pains are ended. Their young thrive and grow strong in the wilds; they leave and do not return. Who let the wild donkey go free: Who untied his ropes? I gave him the wasteland as his home, the salt flats as his habitat. He laughs at the commotion in the town; he does not hear a driver's shout. He ranges the hill for his pasture and searches for any green thing. Will the wild ox consent to serve you? Will he stay by your manger at night? Can you hold him to the furrow with a harness? Will he till the valleys behind you? Will you rely on him for his great strength? Will you leave your heavy work to him? Can you trust him to bring your grain and gather it to your threshing floor? The wings of the ostrich flap joyfully, but they cannot compare with the pinions and feathers of the stork. She lays her eggs on the ground and lets them warm in the sand, unmindful that a foot may crush them, that some wild animals may trample them. She treats her young harshly, as if they were not hers; she cares not that her labor was in vain, for God did not endow her with wisdom*

> *or give her a share of good sense. Yet when she spreads her feathers to run, she laughs at the horse and rider. ... Does the hawk take flight by your wisdom and spread his wings toward the south? Does the eagle soar at your command and build his nest on high?*
>
> Job 38:39–Job 39:27 NIV

If you're moved by these verses, I recommend that you spend more time looking through the book of Job. It is an excellent book of the Bible for obtaining a glimpse of how God feels about the animal world that he created. From the slight remark concerning pets to poetic description of more exotic species, God has plenty to say about some of the attributes that animals have—and the attributes that we do not have!

> *But ask the beasts, and they shall teach thee; and the fowls of the air, and they will tell thee: Or speak to the earth, and it shall teach thee: and the fishes of the sea shall declare unto thee. Who knoweth not in all these that the hand of the LORD hath wrought this? In whose hand is the soul of every living thing, and the breath of all mankind.*
>
> —Job 12:7–10 KJV

The Story of Jonah

Jonah and the whale is one story that even most nonreligious people have heard about. If you take the time to look at the story closely, you will discover that it is not a story about a fish or whale but rather a story about a fallen city and all the inhabitants of the city. Of course, there are those little connections to the animal kingdom as well.

Jonah is a prophet of God and is asked to go to the city of Nineveh. As you may recall, Nineveh has become wicked in its ways, according to God. Jonah despises this city and runs "away from the Lord" (Jonah 1:3). He boards a boat to escape, but God excites the seas and Jonah ends up a man overboard. God then provides "a great fish to swallow Jonah, and Jonah was inside the fish for three days and three nights" (Jonah 1:17 NIV). Jonah desperately prays to God for forgiveness.

> *And the LORD commanded the fish, and it vomited Jonah onto dry land.*
> —Jonah 2:10 NIV

God then commands Jonah to go to Nineveh and tell the people there that their city will be destroyed within forty days if they do not change their ways. The Ninevites, as well as their king, believe God. All of them fast and put on sackcloth, a rough, coarse garment worn as a symbol of mourning or penitence.

> *Do not let any man or beast, herd or flock, taste anything; do not let them eat or drink. But let man and beast be covered with sackcloth. Let everyone call urgently on God. Let them give up their evil ways and their violence. Who knows? God may yet relent and with compassion turn from his fierce anger so that we may not perish.*
> —Jonah 3:7–9 NIV

God is aware that the occupants of Nineveh have repented, so he does not "bring upon them the destruction" that he had threatened. Jonah seems displeased, for he still does not like this city. Jonah proceeds to go east of Nineveh to reflect in anger that God saved this place. God then provides a vine to shade Jonah's head and give comfort. However, the next morning God provides a worm (Jonah 4:7) to chew the vine so that it withers. The sun blazes on Jonah, and as he grows faint, he is also angry. God says to Jonah, "Do you have the right to be angry about the vine?"

> *But the LORD said, "You have been concerned about this vine, though you did not tend it or make it grow. It sprang*

> *up overnight and died overnight. But Nineveh has more than a hundred and twenty thousand people who cannot tell their right hand from their left, and many cattle as well. Should I not be concerned about that great city?"*
> —Jonah 4:10–11 NIV

God does have a way with words, doesn't he? Moreover, it's interesting to see how that familiar line "right hand from the left" originated in the Bible. This is an illustration of how God grants mercy to a violent and wicked city because the people asked for it. Because the king of Nineveh was aware of God's ways, he tells his people and all of their animals to fast and cover in sackcloth. A worm is called into command by God to take away the shady vine God had provided for Jonah. He is showing Jonah that compassion should be granted to all those who ask. He even reminds Jonah that he should not desire that a great city, and all those therein, including their cattle, should perish. God included his concern for the numerous cattle as well. We know that the animals are victims of people's fallen actions in this condition on earth, so the cattle certainly would have perished if the people of Nineveh had not repented. God emphasizes this to Jonah.

If this does not convince you that God is concerned for the animals in a community as well, let's take a look at an earlier situation in Bible history concerning Babylon. To the contrary, the Babylonians were not repenting, and this is what God has to say about them as he is dictating to Habakkuk:

> *The violence you have done to Lebanon will overwhelm you, and your destruction of animals will terrify you. For you have shed man's blood; you have destroyed lands and cities and everyone in them.*
> —Habakkuk 2:17 NIV

Once again, God is fully aware of the suffering of animals, and he acts on their behalf. When we allow ourselves to take inventory of just how many times in the Bible we see that this is true, and to ponder God's love for his animals, our hearts can't help but be filled with gratitude.

The Story of Daniel

In this story, Nebuchadnezzar, king of Babylon, rides into Jerusalem and besieges it. He chooses some Israelites for his service, and among them is Daniel. God gave Daniel "knowledge and understanding of all kinds of literature and learning. And Daniel could understand visions and dreams of all kinds" (Daniel 1:17 NIV). So Daniel is considered valuable to the king and has the privilege to dine at his table. It so happens that Daniel is from a sect of Israelites who were vegetarian, and he requests not to defile himself with the "royal food" (Daniel 1:8 NIV). Daniel goes further. He convinces the official in charge to test this diet on ten other servants to see if they will look healthier in the end of a trial period. This turns out to be a success for Daniel.

> *At the end of the ten days they looked healthier and better nourished than any of the young men who ate the royal food. So the guard took away their choice food and wine they were to drink and gave them vegetables instead.*
> —Daniel 1:15–16 NIV

Ah, take heed of the power of vegetarianism! Even if you're not inclined to see this story in that vein, there are ample lessons to be learned from the book of Daniel. You see, Daniel is not without trials and tribulations. As the story continues, Daniel finds himself under the rule of King Darius. This king issues a decree to worship an idol. Daniel does not comply, so he is cast into a den of lions for worshiping his God.

> *Daniel answered, "O king, live forever! My God sent his angel, and he shut the mouths of the lions. They have not hurt me,*

> *because I was found innocent in his sight. Nor have I ever done any wrong before you, O king."*
> —**Daniel 6:21–22 NIV**

Because of this miracle, Daniel finds himself in the good graces of the king. However, this is an act of God, and Daniel is allowed to continue to interpret dreams and predict the future. What is more intriguing about the book of Daniel is that it has direct parallels to the book of Revelation. In fact, many theologians believe the book of Daniel lends itself to further support and validation of the apocalyptic nature of the book of Revelation. Of course, what I find most interesting is how animals are duly represented in both, just as they are represented in so many important moments and moving stories of the Bible. They communicate with God, and God gives them purpose and value.

I'll mention one more reference to Daniel. A medical doctor and active Christian of the early twentieth century, Dr. E. D. Buckner, wrote a book about animals being in heaven: *The Immortality of Animals: And the Relation of Man as Guardian, from a Biblical and Philosophical Hypothesis*. It was published in 1903, but you can still buy it today. In 1903, this is what Dr. Buckner had to say about Daniel's experience in the lion's den:

> Nothing but an immaterial principle within could hear and obey the direct command of an immaterial nature like God or His angels. If the material organism of animal comes from matter, then it must be obvious that the mental and vital organism which pervades every living being must come from the immaterial attributes of the Creator, and is eternal. It is claimed by the Church that man is immortal because he can communicate with God. We take the same Bible and prove that God communicated with lower animals, which would indicate a divine nature in them for the same reason.

God does not Forget

In this chapter, we've covered a lot of ground in our survey of stories that illustrate God's love for his animals and how he holds his animal kingdom in the highest regard. I hope you've had an opportunity to reflect upon the ones that you find the most impactful.

As for me, I found myself especially stirred upon reading and rereading the book of Job. It made me ponder again the pain that many animal lovers experience when they want to believe that their loved ones with hooves or paws or beaks are going to heaven but then someone of authority tells them it won't be happening. I can't help wondering why those naysayers are not humble like Job. Why are they so afraid of sharing heaven with an animal? Isaiah says, "In that day the lion will eat straw." So why are they afraid to share heaven with a lion?

I will admit that when it comes to creatures going to heaven, I can't answer every related question: "Will all the insects be in heaven?" "What about worms?" "What about the animals that kill each other for food?" But I have learned from the book of Job that I do not have to have all the answers. I just have to "know" God and trust in him. By "knowing" God, I am learning about his nature. Again, God cares for all of his creation, and there is plenty of evidence that the animals will be along for God's ride into the future state of Eden. I believe God wants all of us to know him. He certainly wanted Job to know him, yet he wanted Job to have abundance as well.

My prayer is that the collective consciousness of our current condition on earth will someday come to the aid of the animal kingdom, just as it has for such needs as human rights and the end of slavery. Is it too much to ask for—a peaceful kingdom here on earth as it is in heaven? Are we not capable of that? Can we drop our pride and arrogance just for a moment to "listen" to what God might say in defense of a part of something that he created? You see, we do not have all the answers. What God "betroths unto himself" may be different from what humans think he will betroth.

It has been a long road through this journey of discovery that we've traveled in seeking to answer the age-old question of whether animals go to heaven. We have looked at many of the covenants and plagues, and many of the blessings, that have all included the animals. We have seen repeatedly that animals play a prominent role in the story of mankind, and that God has them in his purpose. We have seen poetry in their grandness. For God said it is good. God does not forget.

EPILOGUE

Epilogue

A quote from Jesus:

Come to me, all you who are weary and burdened, and I will give you rest. Take my yoke upon you and learn from me, for I am gentle and humble in heart, and you will find rest for your souls. For my yoke is easy and my burden is light.
—Matthew 11:28–30 NIV

We conclude this journey after much analysis into a subject matter that has potential to calm matters of the heart. For many of us, our animals are a part of our families. Our desires, concerns, and hopes that they will be in a better place when they die are real emotions that tug at our heartstrings. In search of comfort, we've spent the last several chapters carefully studying the biblical evidence pointing to the conclusion that God will not forget his animals and he reserves a place for them in heaven. We revealed the true meaning of dominion and how we as humans are meant to be stewards of the animals rather than ignoring their sentience on behalf of our own selfish needs or regarding them as mere furniture in the room. We've gone back to the Garden of Eden and the story of Noah to understand the importance God has always placed on his animal kingdom and how he has valued and protected them. We've considered the story of Jesus, not only in noting how animals were present and visible in so many of his important stories but also in recognizing his link to the animal world as the last sacrificial lamb. We've addressed questions about whether animals have souls and whether they have to be saved to gain entrance into heaven or if it matters that they are not of God's image or likeness. Oprah has a line she loves to use: "Things that I know for sure." Well, here are some things that I know for sure: Animals will not be forgotten by God. Animals have souls. I see it in their eyes!

I completed the writing of the first draft of this book late one night. After seven long years of intense research, you can imagine how elated I felt as I awoke the next morning knowing that I was finished! I had stayed up so late that I did not answer a particular phone call the next morning due to my fatigue. When I finally did return the call, I found myself shaking my head and thinking once again of the urgent need for the information and understanding that we have been exploring together.

Here is the true account of what happened. On the face of my iPhone, I saw that the missed call was from a friend I had not heard from in a while. She and I have common interests in the world of dog training, and she has been a vegetarian for years. She is also a strong and active Christian. I returned the call. After a few quick exchanges to get caught up, she proceeded to tell me about the sermon in her church the night before. The subject of the sermon was the end times and what that might look like. At the closing of the sermon, the pastor threw a final punch that definitely got the attention of many. He had been saying things such as "Jesus's second coming will be in a blink of an eye, and like a thief in the night, so be ready." Then he concluded his sermon with this final line: "And kiss your pets good night before you go to bed, because they will not be coming with you."

My friend was startled and then shaken, to say the least. Her first thought after hearing his advice was this: *As my dogs are asleep in their crates and I am raptured, my dogs will be left in their crates to starve to death ... while the mayhem on the planet begins? What kind of God is that?* She unsuccessfully fought to withhold tears.

As she walked to her car in the church parking lot, she saw that others who had listened to the sermon were also in tears.

One woman said, "There will be no tears in heaven, so we won't remember them, perhaps?" Well, that did not make the idea of our pets being left behind any easier to swallow for my friend. Her tears ran all night.

Still perplexed the next morning, she remembered that I had been studying the question of whether or not animals go to heaven and decided to reach out to me. As you can imagine, I had several conversations with her over a two-day period. I attempted to help her as much as I could. I believe I had some success. What scared and disturbed me most about what I had heard is the fact that my friend walked away from this experience saying to herself, "What kind of God is that?" It hurt me to think about those who are loyal to Christ being given a reason to question their religion and their God. And the source of that questioning and doubt came from the pulpit! I also knew there was a pretty good chance that the pastor would not become aware of how others were impacted by what he had said. When something like this is said in church, animal lovers are usually too embarrassed to reveal that they care this much for an animal to be bothered by such remarks.

I did not speak to the pastor (but I hope he reads this book!). If I had approached him directly, I bet you can guess the questions I would be prepared to *respectfully* ask of him on behalf of my doubting friend: How do you back up your assertion in scripture that our pets will not be in heaven? What is your biblical reference for that statement? I might tell the pastor, as well as any naysayer, that what I brought forth from years of research about this subject comes from a place in the Bible that spoke to me. After all, aren't we told as Christians that the Word of God (the Bible) is a *living and active* document (Hebrews 4:12) and that we should *stay in the Word* (continue to read it) and let it *speak* to us? If someone representing a church body has not studied this subject as you and I are today, perhaps a safer, more appropriate answer would be to say that they simply do not know whether animals go to heaven. Otherwise, we may be forced to reflect on this question: Are you causing one of your flock to be lost?

> *In the same way your father in heaven is not willing that any of these little ones should be lost.*
> —Matthew 18:14 NIV

The truth is that I have encountered many other clergy who have communicated similar messages and who stubbornly profess to know the "truth" about animals and heaven without looking at or understanding what the Bible says on this subject. In some cases, the opposition to what I have concluded has been so strong, and so uncomfortable for me, that it has led me to become a bit separated from organized religion, at least for a while. However, I remain devoted to Jesus. He will always be my knight in shining armor ... and my Messiah!

I have been told that I should not be making such a trivial subject as animals going to heaven of substantial concern because it could "crowd out" the real message of the Bible. Well, dear reader, I will leave it up to you to decide whether this subject is one that deserves your full attention and consideration. After all, this is not a salvation issue. I ask, by reading this book, does it make you love more or sin more?

It is about time for our journey to end. I am grateful for your willingness to ride along with me. I hope that the evidence that I have presented has allowed your heart to feel comfort in the biblical perspective that animals will be included in the afterlife. There is no reason that they should *not* be included—no evidence that can be drawn to conclude that they do not go to heaven.

As my journey of writing this book comes to a close, who have I become? I have certainly found my own comfort in my heart knowing that animals will be a part of the redemptive plan destined by God. I am happy that I have found the strength to continue this project through completion so that I can share it with others who, like myself, long for answers and healing. Many of us live with a void, wondering whether God truly cares for the meek and the "single sparrow." Now we can have confidence to say, "Not one sparrow that falls to the ground will be forgotten by God" (Luke 12:6).

As I have dug further and further into my research about the nature of animals and their place in God's kingdom, I have also discovered that I've had a harder time eating meat. As I found myself looking into factory farming, excessive breeding, slaughter practices, dolphin and whaling issues, and hunting, my conscience began to unravel. I have to admit that I had not previously given much thought to these issues. But because of my own "hunt" for knowledge, I slowly became a vegetarian and am currently moving toward becoming vegan. Yes, I simply have developed a difficult time eating flesh. After all, there is ample evidence in the medical community that this diet is better for your health, and I have already seen improvements in mine. And why not try to live a life as God originally intended for us?

In summary, as Reverend Andrew Linzey put it, as quoted in the excellent resource book *They Shall Not Hurt or Destroy*, by Vasu Murti:

> Can it really be so difficult to grasp that the God who performs the demanding and costly task of redeeming sinful man will not also be able to restore the involuntary animal creation, which groans under the weight of another's burden?

The Bible should be a source of comfort. It should not be something to fear. The Bible is the best seller of all time. It is a great piece of literature. It contains every genre imaginable: history, poetry, epic war stories, romance, self-help, enlightenment, superheroes, science fiction, horror, Armageddon. All these genres contain some aspect of our animal kingdom. Referencing the Bible as our guide, we see that God would surely be disappointed at one who displays a lack of compassion for anything he created with sentience. Jesus said we should love one another. We should not cause suffering to any being.

As we have seen, the Bible remembers the animal world. Fear not, for God has his eye on the sparrow. Heaven is for the animals too.

We have read many verses for the animals.
This one is for you, dear reader:

The LORD your God is with you, he is might to save. He will take great delight in you, he will quiet you with his love, he will rejoice over you with singing.
—**Zephaniah 3:17 NIV**

May God shed his grace on thee.

ANIMALS NOT FORGOTTEN

Animals Not Forgotten
A Poem by Melinda Cerisano

To all the birds of the air,
To all the fishes of the sea,
And to all the animals of the land,
Throughout my life, on your behalf,
I hope to do all that I can.

I hope to encourage all of mankind
To live a life according to God's original plan,
For the animal kingdom is ruled by man's fall,
But that does not mean we can make all the calls.
We forget that creation, and all that is within,
God made for himself, but gave us the option to sin.

What a gift it was when God made the dove,
The first domesticated animal,
So God could show us Christ's love.

And how he loved the horse,
An animal who would stand by man
And transport him through life's entire course.
Through battle and fury, wars and distant escapes,
The horse was there, to aid in man's fate.

But as history will show, man's fate went astray,
For pillage and violence became part of the fray.
But are not we better, now aware
Of how this trend is getting us nowhere?

Love and kindness should be the goal
So that all of the beings can live as a whole
In this beautiful playground God lent to us all.
So let's thrive to make peace;
That should be our first call.

So when any man or animal cries for our grace,
Try not to forget: there's a tear on his face.
If we ignore the call to mercy and act as if there is no cry,
God too will shed a tear if he sees that we don't even try.

It is God who gave us such pleasures in life
So that we as humans will never be left alone in our strife.
Like a little dog who will give us unconditional affection
And don't forget the devotion of a German shepherd's protection.

So when you think about an animal shelter
Or a whale or dolphin in a large tank of water,
For those within are enslaved due to no fault of their own,
Try to think about their future, and give them a better home.

The world is getting older now;
It's time we evolve to a peaceful kingdom somehow.
As Jesus said, "Let's be kind to all that God made"
And not let our ability to create peace be one trait that we let fade.

God wants your soul;
He is really the one in control.
He does not forget a single sparrow
So the road we can walk is going to be narrow.

But I swear that God loves us all,
So be of a higher spirit and answer his call
To love him, and yourself, and all of the animals too
So that peace on the planet can begin to ensue.

So the next time you look into the eyes of frustration,
See God's face and believe in a final destination
Of a suffering little being, or that of a lonely or abandoned pet.
A glorious final place—to God they are all heaven sent!

Appendix A
OTHER OPINIONS

For as long as men massacre animals, they will kill each other. Indeed, he who sows the seed of murder and pain cannot reap joy and love.
—Pythagoras, mathematician

The time will come when men such as I will look upon the murder of animals as they now look on the murder of men.
—Leonardo da Vinci, artist and scientist

If a group of beings from another planet were to land on Earth—beings who consider themselves as superior to you as you feel yourselves to be to other animals—would you concede them the rights over you that you assume over other animals?
—George Bernard Shaw, playwright, Noble Prize winner of 1925

In their behavior toward creatures, all men are Nazis. Human beings see oppression vividly when they're the victims. Otherwise they victimize blindly and without a thought.
—Isaac Bashevis Singer, author, Noble Prize winner of 1978

Our task must be to free ourselves ... by widening our circle of compassion to embrace all living creatures and the whole of nature and its beauty.
—Albert Einstein, physicist, Noble Prize winner of 1921

Nothing will benefit human health and increase chances of survival for life on Earth as much as the evolution to a vegetarian diet.
—Albert Einstein, physicist, Noble Prize winner of 1921

I am in favor of animals' rights as well as human rights. That is the way of a whole human being.
—Abraham Lincoln, sixteenth U.S. President

The greatness of a nation and its moral progress can be judged by the way its animals are treated.
—Mahatma Gandhi, statesman and philosopher

To my mind, the life of a lamb is no less precious than that of a human being.
—Mahatma Gandhi, statesman and philosopher

Non-violence leads to the highest ethics, which is the goal of all evolution. Until we stop harming all other living beings, we are still savages.
—Thomas Edison, inventor

Appendix B
BIBLICAL VERSES BY CATEGORY

Special note: I have provided this appendix for your convenience to use as a quick reference for identifying verses according to their category. I hope to facilitate settings for future study by providing this means of reference versus the need to search through the entire body of work. Please note that it is my intent to quote Bible verses as accurately as possible. However, with the advent of such volumes as the New King James Version, the New Darby Translation, and the New Living Translation versus the New Living Translation Second Edition (se), for example, there may be variances in text. In some cases, the text is identical; however, when processing of poetic alignment, digital mobile device formatting, or updating the development of annual revisions, examples such as capitalization or punctuation may have been altered within similar versions of the same translation.

In conclusion, some translations include unique characteristics within the content of style. For example, the presence of italicized words in the KJV indicates words inserted by the English translators, which were not present in referenced original documents, for the facilitation of understanding. Lastly, many Bibles do not follow the rules of modern punctuation and grammar. You may note grammatical differences or perceived errors within translations. However, in the spirit of maintaining the accuracy of each translation, I have displayed the Bible verses exactly as they are in my references, to the best of my ability.

The Original Verses of Discovery that Birthed this Book

Genesis 1:30 KJV: And to every beast of the earth, and to every fowl of the air, and to every *thing* that creepeth upon the earth, wherein *there is* life, I *have given* every green herb for meat: and it was so.

[After I discovered verses that favored animals going to heaven, I checked the KJV to see if it was consistent. I found that this verse had a footnote after "there is life" that noted that the original translation is "soul."]

Hosea 2:18–19 NIV: In that day I will make a covenant for them with the beasts of the field and the birds of the air and the creatures that move along the ground. Bow and sword and battle I will abolish from the land, so that all may lie down in safely. [19]I will betroth you to me forever; I will betroth you in righteousness and in justice, in love and compassion.

[This is the verse in which God promises to all beasts, birds, and things that creepeth that he will provide safety and righteousness in the day of the Messiah.]

Proverbs 12:10 KJV: A righteous *man* regardeth the life of his beast: but the tender mercies of the wicked *are* cruel.

Ecclesiastes 3:21 KJV: Who knoweth the spirit of man that goeth upward, and the spirit of the beast that goeth downward to the earth?

Joel 1:18 KJV: How do the beasts groan! The herds of cattle are perplexed, because they have no pasture; yea, the flocks of sheep are made desolate.

[I was amazed by the fact that God was addressing the animals as sentient beings.]

Joel 1:20 KJV: The beast of the field cry also unto thee: [I was amazed that God hears the animal cry out to him.]

Joel 2:22 KJV: Be not afraid, ye beasts of the field: for the pastures of the wilderness do spring, for the tree beareth her fruit, the fig tree and the vine do yield their strength.

Romans 8:20–21 KJV: For the creature was made subject to the vanity, not willingly, but by reason of him who hath subjected *the same*, in hope, ²¹because the creature itself also shall be delivered from the bondage of corruption into the glorious liberty of the children of God. [This is the verse about the animals being victims of Adam's indiscretion. They were not willing participants of the vanity. They too are children of God.]

About Jesus

Zechariah 9:9 NIV: See, your king comes to you, righteous and having salvation, gentle and riding on a donkey, on a colt, the foal of a donkey.

John 3:16 DNT: For God so loved the world, that he gave his only-begotten Son, that whosoever believes on him may not perish, but have life eternal.

John 3:17 DNT: For God has not sent his Son into the world that he may judge the world, but that the world may be saved through him.

About Scripture

Matthew 22:29 KJV: Jesus answered and said unto them, Ye do err, not knowing the scriptures, nor the power of God.

John 8:31–32 KJV: If ye continue in my word, *then* are ye my disciples indeed. ³²And ye shall know the truth, and the truth shall make you free.

John 17:17 KJV: Sanctify them through thy truth: thy word is truth.

Romans 15:4–6 KJV: For whatsoever things were written aforetime were written for our learning, that we through patience and comfort of the scriptures might have hope. ⁵Now the God of patience and consolation grant you to be likeminded one toward another according to Christ Jesus: ⁶That ye may with one mind and one mouth glorify God, even the Father of our Lord Jesus Christ.

1 Corinthians 2:12–13 NIV: We have not received the spirit of the world but the Spirit who is from God, that we may understand what God has freely given us. [13]This is what we speak, not in words taught us by human wisdom but in words taught by Spirit, expressing spiritual truths in spiritual words.

Colossians 1:23 KJV: If ye continue in the faith grounded and settled, and *be* not moved away from the hope of the gospel, which ye have heard, and which was preached to every creature which is under heaven; whereof I Paul am made a minister;

2 Timothy 3:16–17 KJV: All scripture is given by inspiration of God, and *is* profitable for doctrine, for reproof, for correction, for instruction in righteousness: [17]That the man of God may be perfect, thoroughly furnished unto all good works.

All that God Creates Belongs to Him

Numbers 3:13 NIV: ... I set apart for myself every firstborn in Israel, whether man or animal. They are to be mine. I am the LORD.

Deuteronomy 10:14 KJV: Behold, the heaven and the heaven of heavens is the LORD'S thy God, the earth *also*, with all that therein is.

Job 1:21 KJV: ... The LORD gave and the LORD taketh away.

Job 41:11 NIV: ... Everything under heaven belongs to me.

Job 12:10 KJV: In whose hand *is* the soul of every living thing, and the breath of all mankind.

Psalm 50:10–12 KJV: For every beast of the forest is mine, *and* the cattle upon a thousand hills. [11]I know all the fowls of the mountains: and the wild beasts of the field *are* mine. [12]If I were hungry, I would not tell thee: for the world is mine, and the fullness thereof.

Ezekiel 18:4 KJV: Behold, all souls are mine;

Animal Cruelty

Genesis 49:5–7 NLT: Simeon and Levi are two of a kind—⁶O my soul, stay away from them. May I never be a party to their wicked plans. For in their anger they murdered men, and they crippled oxen just for sport. ⁷Curse on their anger, for it is fierce; a curse be their wrath, for it is cruel.

Numbers 22:25–33 NLT: When the donkey saw the angel of the LORD standing there, it tried to squeeze by and crushed Balaam's foot against the wall. So Balaam beat the donkey again. ²⁶Then the angel of the LORD moved farther down the road and stood in a place so narrow for the donkey to get by at all. ²⁷This time when the donkey saw the angel, it lay down under Balaam. In a fit of rage Balaam beat it again with his staff. ²⁸Then the LORD caused the donkey to speak. "What have I done to you that deserves your beating me three times?" it asked Balaam. ²⁹"Because you have made me look like a fool!" Balaam shouted. "If I had a sword with me, I would have killed you!" ³⁰"But I am the same donkey you always ride on," the donkey answered. "Have I ever done anything like this before?" "No," he admitted. ³¹Then the LORD opened Balaam's eyes, and he saw the angel of the LORD standing in the roadway with a drawn sword in his hand. Balaam fell face down on the ground before him. ³²"Why did you beat your donkey those three times?" the angel of the LORD demanded. "I have come to block your way because you are stubbornly resisting me. ³³Three times the donkey saw me and shied away; otherwise, I would certainly have killed you by now and spared the donkey."

Habakkuk 2:17 NIV: The violence you have done to Lebanon will overwhelm you, and your destruction of animals will terrify you. For you have shed man's blood; you have destroyed lands and cities and everyone in them.

Animals as Companions

Genesis 2:18–19 NIV: The Lord God said, "It is not good for the man to be alone. I will make a helper suitable for him." [19]Now the LORD God had formed out of the ground all the beasts of the field and the birds of the air. He brought them to the man to see what he would name them; and whatever the man called each living creature, that was its name.

Mark 1:13 NIV: and he was in the desert forty days, being tempted by Satan. He was with the wild animals, and angels attended him.

Animals are Sentient

Psalm 104:29 LITV: You hide your face *and* they are troubled;

Joel 1:18 KJV: How do the beasts groan! the herds of cattle are perplexed, because they have no pasture; yea, the flocks of sheep are made desolate.

Joel 1:20 KJV: The beasts of the field cry also unto thee:

Luke 16:20–21 NIV: At his gate was laid a beggar named Lazarus, covered with sores [21]and longing to eat what fell from the rich man's table. Even the dogs came and licked his sores.

Animals have Souls

Genesis 1:20–21 DAR: And God said, Let the waters swarm with swarms of living souls, and let fowl fly above the earth in the expanse of the heavens. [21]And God created the great sea monsters, and every living soul that moves with which the waters swarm, after their kind, and every winged fowl after its kind. And God saw that it was good.

Genesis 1:24 LITV: And God said, Let the earth bring forth the soul of life according to its kind: cattle, and creepers, and its beasts of the earth, according to its kind. And it was so.

Genesis 2:7 LITV: And Jehovah God formed the man *out of* dust from the ground, and blew into his nostril the breath of life; and man became a living soul.

[The word "soul" in this verse is the same word in Hebrew used in the previous set of verses, Genesis 1:20–21 and 24, in which God made the animals.]

Genesis 2:19 LITV: And he brought them to the man, to see what he would call it. And all which the man might call it, each living soul, that was its name.

Genesis 35:18 KJV: And it came to pass, as her soul was departing (for she died) that she called his name ...

[The word for "soul" here in Hebrew is the same as it is when used for animals. Therefore, this verse points to the evidence that both animals and mankind have both bodies and souls and are dualistic beings.]

Job 12:7–10 KJV: But ask now the beasts, and they shall teach thee; and the fowls of the air, and they shall tell thee: [8]Or speak to the earth, and it shall teach thee: and the fishes of the sea shall declare unto thee. [9]Who knoweth not in all these that the hand of the LORD hath wrought this? [10]In whose hand *is* the soul of every living thing, and the breath of all mankind.

Animals Praise God

Nehemiah 9:6 KJV: Thou, *even* thou, *art* LORD alone; thou hast made heaven, the heaven of heavens, with all their host, the earth, and all *things* that *are* therein, the seas, and all that *is* therein, and thou preservest them all; and the host of heaven worthshippeth thee.

Isaiah 43:20–22 NIV: The wild animals honor me, the jackals and the owls, because I provide water in the desert and streams in the wasteland, to give drink to my people, my chosen, [21]the people I formed for myself that they may proclaim my praise. [22]"Yet you have not called upon me, O Jacob, you have not wearied yourselves for me, O Israel."

Psalm 148:10–13 KJV: Beasts, and all cattle; creeping things, and flying fowl: [11]Kings of the earth, and all people; princes, and all judges of the earth: [12]Both young men, and maidens; old men, and children: [13]Let them praise the name of the LORD: for his name alone is excellent; his glory *is* above the earth and heaven.

Psalm 145:21 KJV: My mouth shall speak the praise of the LORD: and let all flesh bless his holy name for ever and ever.

Psalm 150:6 NIV: Let everything that has breath praise the LORD. Praise the Lord.

Joel 1:20 KJV: The beasts of the field cry also unto thee: for the rivers of waters are dried up, and the fire hath devoured the pastures of the wilderness.

Revelation 5:13–14 NIV: Then I heard every creature in heaven and on earth and under the earth and on the sea, and all that is in them, singing: "To him who sits on the throne and to the Lamb be praise and honor and glory and power, for ever and ever!" [14]The four living creatures said, "Amen," and the elders fell down and worshiped.

The Dead Sea Scrolls: The Splendour of the Spirits, Manuscript B Fragment 2:

> (1) ... them, and they shall bless Your Holy Name with blessing[s ... (2) and they shall bless] You, all creatures of flesh in unison, whom [You] have creat[ed ... (3) be]asts and birds and reptiles and the fish of the seas, and all ... (4) [Y]ou have created them all anew ...

[This is a fragment found in Qumran, Israel. It is a part of the famed Dead Sea Scrolls as indicated by Robert H. Eisenman and Michael Wise in their book, *The Dead Sea Scrolls Uncovered*, 2004, p. 230.]

Animal Sacrifice

Leviticus 6:27 NIV: Whatever touches any of the flesh will become holy, and if any of the blood is spattered on a garment, you must wash it in a holy place.

Isaiah 1:10–17 NIV: Hear the word of the LORD, you rulers of Sodom; listen to the law of our God, you people of Gomorrah! [11]"The multitudes of your sacrifices—what are they to me?" says the LORD. "I have more than enough of burnt offerings, of rams and the fat of fattened animals; I have no pleasure in the blood of bulls and lambs and goats. [12]When you come to appear before me, who has asked this of you, this trampling of my courts? [13]Stop bringing meaningless offerings! Your incense is detestable to me. New Moons, Sabbaths and convocations—I cannot bear your evil assemblies. [14]Your New Moon festivals and your appointed feasts my soul hates. They have become a burden to me; I am weary of bearing them. [15]When you spread out your hands in prayer, I will hide my eyes from you; even if you offer many prayers, I will not listen. Your hands are full of blood; [16]wash and make yourselves clean. Take your evil deeds out of my sight! Stop doing wrong, [17]learn to do right! Seek justice, encourage the oppressed."

Isaiah 43:23–24 NIV: You have not brought me sheep for burnt offerings, nor honored me with your sacrifices. I have not burdened you with grain offering nor wearied you with demands for incense. [24]You have not bought any fragment calamus for me, or lavished on me the fat of your sacrifices. But you have burdened me with your sins and wearied me with your offenses.

Isaiah 66:3 NIV: But whoever sacrifices a bull is like one who kills a man, and whoever offers a lamb, like one who breaks a dog's neck; whoever makes a grain offering is like one who presents a pig's blood, and whoever burns memorial incense, like one who worships an idol. They have chosen their ways, and their souls delight in their abominations.
[In these last three verses of Isaiah, Isaiah is condemning the sacrifice of animals because these people have lost the meaning of sacrifice itself. They are freely sinning and offering sacrifices without repenting and remembering that God hates sin. God, according to Isaiah, is stating that he hates sin and the spilling of blood as well, in the case of human and animal sacrifice. God even goes as far as stating that to break a dog's neck is the same as murder. Remember, it is Isaiah who describes a time in the new world, post the second coming of Christ, as a place where the wolf will lie down with the lamb and the lion will eat grass as does the ox.] See Dietary Laws.
Hebrews 9:22 NIV: In fact, the law requires that nearly everything be cleansed with blood, and without the shedding of blood there is no forgiveness.

Animals' Spirits/Spirit of God

Genesis 1:2 KLV: And the earth was without form, and void; and darkness *was* upon the face of the deep. And the Spirit of God moved upon the face of the waters.
Numbers 27:15–16 KJV: And Moses spake unto the LORD, saying, [16]Let the Lord, the God of the spirits of all flesh, set a man over the congregation.
Job 33:4 KJV: The Spirit of God hath made me, and the breath of the Almighty hath given me life.
Psalm 104:30 LITV: You send out Your Spirit, *and* they are created; and You renew the face of the earth.

[This verse is specifically speaking of animals.]

Ecclesiastes 3:21 KJV: Who knoweth the spirit of man that goeth upward, and the spirit of the beast that goeth downward to the earth?

Ecclesiastes 12:7 NIV: and the dust returns to the ground it came from, and the spirit returns to God who gave it.

John 19:30 LITV: Then when Jesus took the vinegar, He said, It has been finished. And bowing *His* head, *He* delivered up the spirit.

1 Thessalonians 5:23 KJV: And the very God of peace sanctify you wholly; and *I pray God* your whole spirit and soul and body be preserved blameless unto the coming of our Lord Jesus Christ.

Animals will not be Forgotten by God

Psalm 36:6 KJV: Thy righteousness is like the great mountains; thy judgments *are* a great deep: O LORD, thou preservest man and beast.

Psalm 145:13 NIV: Your kingdom is an everlasting kingdom, and your dominion endures throughout all generations. The LORD is faithful to all his promises and loving toward all he has made.

Matthew 10:29 NIV: Are not two sparrows sold for a penny? Yet not one of them will fall to the ground apart from the will of your Father.

Luke 12:6–7 NIV: Are not five sparrows sold for two pennies? Yet not one of them is not forgotten by God. [7]Indeed, the very hairs on your head are all numbered. Don't be afraid; you are worth more than many sparrows.

Romans 8:19–22 LITV: For the earnest expectation of the creation is eagerly expecting the revelation of the sons of God. [20]For the creation was not willingly subjected to vanity, but through Him subjecting it, on hope; [21]that also the creation will be freed from the slavery of corruption to the freedom of the glory of the children of God. [22]For we know that all the creation groans together and travails together until now.

Caring for Animals

Exodus 20:10 KJV: But the seventh day *is* the sabbath of the LORD thy God: *in it* thou shalt not do any work, thou, nor thy son, nor thy daughter, thy manservant, not thy maidservant, nor thy cattle, nor thy stranger that is within thy gates:

Deuteronomy 22:10 KJV: Thou shall not plow with an ox and an ass together.

Deuteronomy 25:4 KJV: Thou shalt not muzzle the ox that treadeth out *the corn*.

Proverbs 12:10 KJV: A righteous *man* regardeth the life of his beast: but the tender mercies of the wicked *are* cruel.

1 Timothy 5:18 KJV: For the scriptures saith, Thou shalt not muzzle the ox that treadeth out *the corn*. And, the labourer is worthy of his reward.

Celestial Beings

Genesis 3:24 KJV: So he drove out the man; and he placed at the east of the garden of Eden Cherubims, and a flaming sword which turned every way, to keep the way of the tree of life.

Ezekiel 10:14–20 KJV: And every one had four faces: the first face was the face of a cherub, and the second face *was* the face of a man, and the third the face of a lion, and the fourth the face of an eagle. [15]And the cherubims were lifted up. This *is* the living creature I saw by the river of Chebar. [16]And when the cherubim went, the wheels went by them: and when the cherubims lifted up their wings to mount up from the earth, the same wheels also turned not from beside them. [17]When they stood, *these* stood; and they were lifted up, *these* lifted up themselves *also*: for the spirit of the living creature *was* in them. [18]Then the glory of the LORD departed from off the threshold of the house, and stood over the cherubims. [19]And the cherubims lifted up their wings, and mounted up from the earth in my sight: when they went out, the wheels also *were* beside them, and *every one* stood at the door of the east gate of the LORD'S house; and the glory of the God of Israel *was* over them above. This *is* the living creature that I saw under the God of Israel by the river of Chebar; and I knew they *were* the cherubims.

Hebrews 2:7 KJV: Thou madest him a little lower than the angels; thou crownedst him with glory and honor, and didst set him over the works of thy hands:

Revelation 4:6–9 KJV: And before the throne *there was* a sea of glass like unto crystal: and in the midst of the throne, and round about the throne, *were* four beasts full of eyes before and behind. [7]And the first beast *was* like a lion, and the second beast like a calf, and the third beast had a face of a man, and the fourth beast *was* like a flying eagle. [8]And the four beasts had each of them six wings about *him;* and *they* were full of eyes within: and they rest not day and night, saying, Holy, holy, holy, Lord God Almighty, which was, and is, and is to come. [9]And when those beasts give honor and thanks to him that sat on the throne, who liveth for ever and ever …

Revelation 5:13–14 NIV: Then I heard every creature in heaven and on earth and under the sea, and all that is in them, singing: "To him who sits on the throne and to the Lamb be praise and honor and glory and power, for ever and ever!" [14]The four living creatures said, "Amen," and the elders fell down and worshiped.

Covenants with Animals

Genesis 9:3–5 NIV: Everything that lives and moves will be food for you. Just as I gave you the green plants, I now give you everything. [4]"But you must not eat meat that has its lifeblood still in it. [5]And for your lifeblood I will surely demand an accounting. I will demand an accounting from every animal.

And from each man, too, I will demand an accounting for the life of his fellow man."

Genesis 9:8–17 DAR 1890: And God spoke to Noah, and to his sons with him, saying, ⁹And I, behold, I establish my covenant with you, and with your seed after you; ¹⁰and with every living soul which is with you, fowl as well as cattle, and all the animals of the earth with you, of all that has gone out of the ark—every animal of the earth. ¹¹And I establish my covenant with you, neither shall all flesh be cut off any more by the waters of a flood, and henceforth there shall be no flood to destroy the earth. ¹²And God said, This is the sign of the covenant that I set between me and you and every living soul that is with you, for everlasting generations: ¹³I set my bow in the clouds, and it shall be for a sign of the covenant between me and the earth. ¹⁴And it shall come to pass when I bring clouds over the earth, that the bow shall be seen in the cloud, ¹⁵and I will remember my covenant which is between me and you and every living soul of all flesh; and the waters shall not henceforth become a flood to destroy all flesh. ¹⁶And the bow shall be in the cloud; and I will look upon it, that I may remember the everlasting covenant between God and every living soul of all flesh that is upon the earth. ¹⁷And God said to Noah, This is the sign of the covenant which I have established between me and all flesh that is upon the earth.

Leviticus 24:17–18 NIV: "If anyone takes the life of a human being, he must be put to death. ¹⁸Anyone who takes the life of someone's animal must make restitution—life for a life."

Leviticus 25:6–7 NIV: Whatever the land yields during the sabbath year will be food for you—for yourself, your manservant and maidservant, and the hired worker and temporary resident who live among you, ⁷as well as for your livestock and the wild animals in your land.

Dietary Laws

Deuteronomy 14:21 NIV: ... Do not cook a young goat in its mother's milk.

Leviticus 11:46–47 NIV: "These are the regulations concerning animals, birds, every living thing that moves in the water and every creature that moves about the ground. [47]You must distinguish between the unclean and the clean, between the living creatures that may be eaten and those that may not be eaten."

[Please note: The dietary laws are in greater detail than can be portrayed in this appendix. Hebrew dietary laws and rituals eventually evolved to replace the sacrificial system as a means for atoning sin. For Christians, Christ's blood is the atonement.]

Leviticus 22:28 NIV: Do not slaughter a cow or sheep and its young on the same day.

Acts 15:19–20 NIV: "It is my judgment, therefore, that we should not make it difficult for the Gentiles who are turning to God. [20]Instead we should write to them, telling them to abstain from food polluted by idols, from sexual immorality, from the meat of strangled animals and from blood."

[This is Peter explaining the Noahide Law to the Jewish council.]

Dominion/Rule

Genesis 1:26 DNT: And God said, Let us make man in our image, after our likeness; and let them have dominion over the fish of the sea, and over the fowl of the heavens, and over the cattle, and over the whole earth, and over every creeping thing that creepeth on the earth.

Genesis 1:28 DNT: And God blessed them; and God said to them, Be fruitful and multiply, and fill the earth, and subdue it; and have dominion over the fish of the sea, and over the fowl of the heavens, and over every animal that moveth on the earth.

1 Kings 4:24–25 KJV: For he had dominion over all *the region* on this side the river, from Tiphsah even to Azzah, over all the kings on this side the river: and he had peace on all sides round about him. [25]And Judah and Israel dwelt safely, every man under his vine and under his fig tree, from Dan even to Beersheba, all the days of Solomon.

Psalm 72:6–8 KJV: He shall come down like rain upon the mown grass: as showers *that* water the earth. [7]In his days shall the righteous flourish; and abundance of peace so long as the moon endureth. [8]He shall have dominion also from sea to sea, and from the river unto the ends of the earth.

Psalm 72:12–14 KJV: For he shall deliver the needy when he crieth; the poor also, and *him* that hath no helper. [13]He shall spare the poor and needy, and shall save the souls of the needy. [14]He shall redeem their soul from deceit and violence: and precious shall their blood be in his sight.

Psalm 145:13 NIV: Your kingdom is an everlasting kingdom, and your dominion endures throughout all generations. The LORD is faithful to all his promises and loving toward all he has made.

Dualism (Man and Animal have both a Body and Soul/Spirit)

Genesis 35:18 KJV: And it came to pass, as her soul was departing (for she died) that she called his name ...

Ezekiel 37:1–14 NIV: The hand of the LORD was upon me, and he brought me out by the Spirit of the LORD and set me in the middle of a valley; it was full of bones. [2]He led me back and forth among them, and I saw a great many bones on the floor of the valley, bones that were very dry. [3]He asked me, "Son of man, can these bones come alive?" I said, "O sovereign LORD, you alone know." [4]Then he said to me, "Prophesy to these bones and say to them, 'Dry bones, hear the word of the

LORD! ⁵This is what the Sovereign Lord say to these bones: I will make breath enter you, and you will come to life. ⁶I will attach tendons to you and make flesh come to life. Then you will know that I am the LORD.'" ⁷So I prophesied as I was commanded. And as I was prophesying, there was a noise, a rattling sound, and the bones came together, bone to bone. ⁸I looked, and tendons and flesh appeared on them and skin covered them, but there was no breath in them. ⁹Then he said to me, "Prophesy to the breath; prophesy, son of man, and say to it, 'This is what the Sovereign LORD says: Come from the four winds, O breath, and breathe into these slain, that they may live.'" ¹⁰So I prophesied as he commanded me, and breath entered them; they came to life and stood up on their feet—a vast army. ¹¹Then he said to me: "Son of man, these bones are the whole house of Israel. They say, 'Our bones are dried up and our hope is gone; we are cut off.' ¹²Therefore prophesy and say to them: 'This is what the Sovereign LORD says: O my people, I am going to open your graves and bring you up from them; I will bring you back to the land of Israel. ¹³Then you, my people, will know that I am the LORD, when I open your graves and bring you up from them. ¹⁴I will put my Spirit in you and you will live, and I will settle you in your own land. Then you will know that I the LORD have spoken, and I have done it, declares the LORD.'"

God Bethroths/Reconciles the Animals to Himself

Hosea 2:18–19 NIV: In that day I will make a covenant for them with the beasts of the field and the birds of the air and the creatures that move along the ground. Bow and sword and battle I will abolish from the land, so that all may lie down in safety. ¹⁹I will betroth you to me forever; I will betroth you in righteousness and justice, in love and compassion.

John 3:17 KJV: For God sent not his Son into the world to condemn the world; but that the world through him might be saved.

Acts 3:21 NIV: He must remain in heaven until the time comes for God to restore everything, as he promised long ago through his holy prophets.

2 Corinthians 5:15 KJV: And *that* he died for all, that they which live should not henceforth live unto themselves, but unto him which died for them, and rose again.

2 Corinthians 5:18–19 NIV: All this is from God, who reconciled us to himself through Christ and gave us the ministry of reconciliation: [19]that God was reconciling the world to himself in Christ, not counting men's sins against them. And he has committed to us the message of reconciliation.

Ephesians 1:10 KJV: That in the dispensation of the fullness of times he might gather together in one all things in Christ, both which are in heaven and which are on earth; *even* in him.

Colossians 1:19–20 NIV: For God was pleased to have all his fullness dwell in him, [20]and through him to reconcile to himself all things, whether things on earth or things in heaven, by making peace through his blood, shed on the cross.

Hebrews 1:1–4 NIV: In the past God spoke to our forefathers though the prophet at many times and various ways, [2]but in these last days he has spoken to us by his Son, whom he appointed heir of all things, and through whom he made the universe. [3]The Son is the radiance of God's glory and the exact representation of his being, sustaining all things by his powerful word. After he had provided purification for sins, he sat down at the right hand of the Majesty in heaven. [4]So he became as much superior to the angels as the name he has inherited is superior to theirs.

1 John 2:2 KJV: And he is the propitiation for our sins, and not for ours only, but also for *the sins of* the whole world.

Revelation 19:7 NIV: Let us rejoice and be glad and give him glory! For the wedding of the Lamb has come, and his bride has made herself ready.

God's Face

Exodus 33:20 NIV: "But," he said, "you cannot see my face, for no one may see me and live."

Psalm 17:15 NIV: And I—in righteousness I will see your face; when I awake, I will be satisfied with seeing your likeness.

Psalm 104:29 LITV: You hide Your face *and* they are troubled.
 [This verse is about the animals only.]

Matt 18:10 NIV: "See that you do not look down on one of these little ones. For I tell you that their angels in heaven always see the face of my Father in heaven."

God Mentions Animals

Numbers 3:13 NIV: for all the firstborn are mine. When I struck down the firstborn of Egypt, I set apart for myself every firstborn in Israel, whether man or animal. They are mine. I am the LORD.

Job 12:7–10 KJV: But ask the beasts, and they shall teach thee; and the fowls of the air, and they will tell thee: [8]Or speak to the earth, and it shall teach thee: and the fishes of the sea shall declare unto thee. [9]Who knoweth not in all these that the hand of the LORD hath wrought this? [10]In whose hand is the soul of every living thing, and the breath of all mankind.

Job 38:39–41–Job 39:1–18 NIV: "Do you hunt the prey for the lioness and satisfy the hunger of the lions [40]when they crouch in their dens or lie in wait in the thicket? [41]Who provides food for the raven when its young cry out to God and wander about for lack of food?" [1]"Do you know when the mountain goats give birth? Do you watch when the doe bears her fawn? [2]Do you count the months till they bear? Do you know the time they give birth? [3]They crouch down and bring forth their young; their labor pains are ended. [4]Their young thrive and grow strong in the wilds; they leave and do not return. [5]Who let the wild donkey go free? Who untied his ropes? ⁶I gave him the wasteland as his home, the salt flats as his habitat. ⁷He laughs at the commotion in the town; he does not hear a driver's shout. ⁸He ranges the hills for his pasture and searches for any green thing. ⁹Will the wild ox consent to serve you? Will he stay by your manger at night? ¹⁰Can you hold him to the furrow with a harness? Will he till the valleys behind you? ¹¹Will you rely on him for his great strength? Will you leave your heavy work to him? ¹²Can you trust him to bring your grain and gather it to your threshing floor? ¹³The wings of the ostrich flap joyfully, but they cannot compare with the pinions and feathers of the stork. ¹⁴She lays her eggs on the ground and lets them warm in the sand, ¹⁵unmindful that a foot may crush them, that some wild animals may trample them. ¹⁶She treats her young harshly, as if they were not hers; she cares not that her labor was in vain, ¹⁷for God did not endow her with wisdom or give her a share of good sense. ¹⁸Yet when she spreads her feathers to run, she laughs at the horse and rider.

Job 39:19–24 NIV: "Did you give the horse his strength or clothe his neck with flowing mane? ²⁰Do you make him leap like a locust, striking terror with his proud snorting? ²¹He paws fiercely, rejoicing in his strength, and charges into the fray. ²²He laughs at fear, afraid of nothing; he does not shy away from the sword. ²³The quiver rattles against his side, along with the flashing spear and lance. ²⁴In frenzied excitement he eats up the ground; he cannot stand still when the trumpet sounds."

Isaiah 1:3 NIV: The ox knows his master, the donkey his owner's manger, but Israel does not know, my people do not understand.

God's Mercy

Exodus 33:19 NIV: ... I will have mercy on whom I will have mercy, and I will have compassion on whom I will have compassion.

1 Samuel 16:7 NIV: ... The LORD does not look at the things man looks at. Man looks at outward appearance, but the LORD looks at the heart.

Psalm 145:9 KJV: "The LORD is good to all: and his tender mercies *are* over all his works."

Jonah 1:2 DNT: Arise, and go to Nineveh the great city, and cry against it; for their wickedness is come up before me.

Jonah 3:7–8 KJV: And he caused *it* to be proclaimed and published through Nineveh by the decree of the king and his nobles, saying, Let neither man nor beast, herd nor flock, taste anything: let them not feed, nor drink water: [8]But let man and beast be covered with sackcloth, and cry mightily unto God: yea, let them turn everyone from his evil way, and from the violence that *is* in their hands.

[And the conclusion as a result of the people obeying this order ...]

Jonah 3:9–10 DNT: Who knoweth but that God will turn and repent, and will turn away from his fierce anger, that we perish not? [10]And God saw their works, that they turned from their evil way; and God repented of the evil that he had said he would do unto them, and he did [it] not.

Jonah 4:10–11 NIV: But the Lord said, "You have been concerned about this vine, though you did not tend it or make it grow. It sprang up overnight and died overnight. [11]But Nineveh has more than a hundred and twenty thousand people who cannot tell their right hand from their left, and many cattle as well. Should I not be concerned about that great city?"

God's Nature

Genesis 6:5–6 DNT: And Jehovah [God] saw that the wickedness of Man was great on the earth, and every imagination of the thoughts of his heart only evil continually. ⁶And Jehovah repented that he had made Man on the earth, and it grieved him in his heart.

Numbers 11:32–33 NIV: All that day and night and all the next day the people went out and gathered quail. No one gathered less than ten homers. Then they spread them out all around the camp. ³³But while the meat was still between their teeth and before it could be consumed, the anger of the LORD burned against the people, and he struck them with a severe plague.

[This is a story about God's people living in the desert after the exodus from Egypt. They were given manna to eat and they were not satisfied. They complained that at least they got meat from the Egyptians while in slavery. This angered God so he poisoned the meat of the quail.]

Exodus 33:19 NIV: … I will have mercy on whom I will have mercy, and I will have compassion on whom I will have compassion.

Psalm 36:6–7 KJV: Thy righteousness is like the great mountains; thy judgments are a great deep: O LORD, thou preservest man and beast. ⁷How excellent is thy loving kindness …

Proverbs 25:2 KJV: It is in the glory of God to conceal a thing: but the honour of kings is to search out a matter.

Isaiah 40:28 NIV: … He will not grow tired or weary, and his understanding no one can fathom.

Isaiah 55:8–9 KJV: For my thoughts *are* not your thoughts, neither *are* your ways my ways, saith the LORD. ⁹For *as* the heavens are higher than the earth, so are my ways higher than your ways, and my thoughts than your thoughts.

Isaiah 55:11 KJV: So shall my word be that goeth forth out of my mouth: it shall not return unto me void, but it shall accomplish that which I please, and it shall prosper *in the thing* whereto I sent it.

Jeremiah 32:27 KJV: Behold, I *am* the LORD, the God of all flesh: is there anything too hard for me?

Matthew 22:29 KJV: Jesus answered and said unto them, Ye do err, not knowing the scriptures, nor the power of God.

Mark 8:33 NIV: ... "You do not have in mind the things of God, but the things of men."

Hebrews 1:1–3 NIV: In the past God spoke to our forefathers through the prophets at many times and various ways, ²but in these last days he has spoken to us by his Son, whom he appointed heir of all things, and through whom he made the universe. ³The Son is the radiance of God's glory and the exact representation of his being, sustaining all things by his powerful word.

God Regrets Animal Sacrifice

Isaiah 1:10–11 NIV: Hear the word of the LORD, your rulers of Sodom; listen to the law of our God, you people of Gomorrah! ¹¹"The multitudes of your sacrifices—what are they to me?" says the LORD. "I have more than enough of burnt offerings, of rams and the fat of fattened animals; I have no pleasure in the blood of bulls and lambs and goats."

Isaiah 66:3 NIV: But whoever sacrifices a bull is like one who kills a man, and whoever offers a lamb, like one who breaks a dog's neck; whoever makes a grain offering is like one who presents a pig's blood, and whoever burns memorial incense, like one who worships an idol. They have chosen their ways, and their souls delight in their abominations; ...

Hebrews 13:11–16 NIV: The high priest carries the blood of animals into the Most Holy Place as a sin offering, but the bodies are burned outside the camp. ¹²And so Jesus also suffered outside the city gate to make the people holy through his own blood. ¹³Let us, then, go to him outside the camp, bearing the disgrace he bore. ¹⁴For here we do not have an enduring city, but we are looking for the city that is to come. ¹⁵Through Jesus, therefore, let us continually offer to God a sacrifice of praise—the fruit of lips that confess his name. ¹⁶And do not forget to do good and to share with others, for with such sacrifices God is pleased.

Heaven

2 Kings 2:11 NIV: As they were walking along and talking together, suddenly a chariot of fire, and horses of fire, appeared and separated the two of them, and Elijah went up to heaven in a whirlwind.

Isaiah 40:5 KJV: And the glory of the Lord shall be revealed, and all flesh shall see it together: for the mouth of the Lord hath spoken it.

John 14:1–4 NIV: "Do not let your hearts be troubled. Trust in God; trust also in me. ²In my Father's house are many rooms; if it were not so, I would have told you. I am going there to prepare a place for you. ³And if I go and prepare a place for you, I will come back and take you to be with me that you also may be where I am. ⁴You know the way to the place where I am going."

Luke 16:22–31 KJV: And it came to pass, that the beggar died, and was carried by the angels into Abraham's bosom: the rich man also died, and was buried; ²³and in hell he lifted up his eyes, being in torments, and seeth Abraham afar off, and Lazarus in his bosom. ²⁴And he cried and said, Father Abraham, have mercy on me, and send Lazarus, that he may dip the tip of his finger in water, and cool my tongue; for I am tormented in this flame. ²⁵But Abraham said, Son, remember that thou in thy lifetime receivedth thy good things, and likewise Lazarus evil things: but now he is comforted, and thou art tormented. ²⁶And besides all this, between us and you there is a great gulf fixed: so that they which would pass from hence to you cannot: neither can they pass to us, that *would come* from thence. ²⁷Then he said, I pray thee therefore, father, that thou wouldest send him to my father's house: ²⁸For I have five brethren; that he may testify unto them, lest they also come into this place of torment. ²⁹Abraham saith unto him, They have Moses and the prophets; let them hear them. ³⁰And he said, Nay, father Abraham: but if one went unto them from the dead, they will repent. ³¹And he said unto him, If they hear not Moses and the prophets, neither will they be persuaded, though one rose from the dead.

Acts 3:21 NIV: He must remain in heaven until the time comes for God to restore everything, as he promised long ago through his holy prophets.

Luke 10:18 NIV: He [Jesus] replied, "I saw Satan fall like lightning from heaven."

Luke 23:43 NIV: Jesus answered him, "I tell you the truth, today you will be with me in paradise."

1 Corinthians 13:12 NIV: ... Now I know in part; then I shall know fully, even as I am fully known."

1 Corinthians 15:35–44 NIV: But someone may ask, "How are the dead raised? With what kind of body will they come?" ³⁶How foolish! What you sow does not come to life unless it dies. ³⁷When you sow, you do not plant the body that will be, but a seed, perhaps of wheat or of something else. ³⁸But God gives it a body as he has determined, and to each kind of seed he gives its own body. ³⁹All flesh is not the same: Men have one kind of flesh, animals have another, birds another and fish another. ⁴⁰There are also heavenly bodies and there are earthly bodies; but the splendor of the heavenly bodies is one kind, and the splendor of the earthly bodies is another. ⁴¹The sun is one kind of splendor, the moon another and the stars another; and star differs from star in splendor ⁴²So will it be with the resurrection of the dead. The body that is sown is perishable, it is raised imperishable; ⁴³it is sown in dishonor, it is raised in glory; it is sown in weakness, it is raised in power; ⁴⁴it is sown a natural body, it is raised a spiritual body.

2 Corinthians 5:8 KJV: We are confident, I *say*, and willing rather to be absent from the body, and to be present with the Lord.

Philippians 1:23 NIV: I am torn between the two: I desire to depart and be with Christ, which is better by far; ...

Revelation 5:13–14 NIV: Then I heard every creature in heaven and on earth and under the earth and on the sea, and all that is in them, singing: "To him who sits on the throne and to the Lamb be praise and honor and glory and power for ever and ever!" [14]The four living creatures [cherubim] said, "Amen," and the elders fell down and worshiped.

Hunters

Nimrod:

Genesis 10:8–12 NIV: Cush was the father of Nimrod, who grew to be a mighty warrior on the earth. [9]He was a mighty hunter before the LORD; that is why it is said, "Like Nimrod, a mighty hunter before the LORD." [10]The first centers of his kingdom were Babylon, Erech, Akkad and Calneh, in Shinar. [11]From that land he went to Assyria, where he built Ninevah, Rehobeth Ir, Calah [12]and Resen, which is between Nineveh and Calah; that is a great city.

Micah 5:6 NIV: They will rule the land of Assyria with the sword, the land of Nimrod with drawn sword. He will deliver us from the Assyrian when he invades our land and marches into our borders.

[Those living in these cities under Nimrod are God's enemies. Remember, the Babylonian Empire is destroyed in the book of Revelation.]

Ishmael:

Genesis 25:18 NIV: His descendants settled in the area from Havilah to Shur, near the border of Egypt, as you go toward Asshur. And they lived in hostility toward all their brothers.

Esau:

Genesis 25:27 NIV: The boys grew up and Esau became a skillful hunter, a man of the open country, while Jacob was a quiet man, staying among the tents.

Hebrews 12:16 NIV: See that no one is sexually immoral, or is godless like Esau, who for a single meal sold his inheritance rights as the oldest son.

Simeon and Levi:

Genesis 49:5–7 NIV: "Simeon and Levi are brothers—their swords are weapons of violence. ⁶Let me not enter their council, let me not join their assembly, for they have killed men in their anger and hamstrung oxen as they pleased. ⁷Cursed be their anger, so fierce, and their fury, so cruel!"

Satan:

Revelation 6:2 NIV: I looked, and there before me was a white horse! Its rider held a bow, and he was given a crown, and he rode as a conqueror bent on conquest.

[This is the hunter of souls. He is not to be confused with the verse in Revelation 19:11, which is about the other rider on a white horse: Christ Jesus.]

Jesus with Animals

Luke 2:7 KJV: And she brought forth her firstborn son, and wrapped him in swaddling clothes, and laid him in a manger; because there was no room in the inn.

Mark 1:12–13 NIV: At once the Spirit sent him out into the desert, [13]and he was in the desert forty days, being tempted by Satan. He was with the wild animals, and angels attended him.

Revelation 19:11 NIV: I saw heaven standing open and there before me was a white horse, whose rider is called Faithful and True.

Jesus's Verse on Animal Sacrifice

Hebrews 9:13–15 NIV: The blood of goats and bulls and the ashes of a heifer sprinkled on those who are ceremonially unclean sanctify them so that they are outwardly clean. [14]How much more, then, will the blood of Christ, who through the eternal Spirit offered himself unblemished to God, cleanse our consciences from act that lead to death, so that we may serve the living God! [15]For this reason Christ is the mediator of a new covenant, that those who are called may receive the promised eternal inheritance—now that he has died as a ransom to set them free from the sins committed under the first covenant.

Kindness to Animals

Genesis 24:14 NLT: This is my request. I will ask one of them for a drink. 'Yes, certainly, and I will water your camels too!'—let her be the one you have appointed as Isaac's wife. By this I will know that you have shown kindness to my master.

Genesis 33:17 NIV: Jacob, however, went to Succoth, where he built a place for himself and made shelters for his livestock. That is why the place is called Succoth.

More Animal Stories

Numbers 22:25–33 NLT: When the donkey saw the angel of the LORD standing there, it tried to squeeze by and crushed Balaam's foot against the wall. So Balaam beat the donkey again. [26]Then the angel of the LORD moved farther down the road and stood in a place so narrow for the donkey to get by at all. [27]This time when the donkey saw the angel, it lay down under Balaam. In a fit of rage Balaam beat it again with his staff. [28]Then the LORD caused the donkey to speak. "What have I done to you that deserves your beating me three times?" it asked Balaam. [29]"Because you have made me look like a fool!" Balaam shouted. "If I had a sword with me, I would have killed you!" [30]"But I am the same donkey you always ride on," the donkey answered. "Have I ever done anything like this before?" "No," he admitted. [31]Then the LORD opened Balaam's eyes, and he saw the angel of the LORD standing in the roadway with a drawn sword in his hand. Balaam fell face down on the ground before him. [32]"Why did you beat your donkey those three times?" the angel of the LORD demanded. "I have come to block your way because you are stubbornly resisting me. [33]Three times the donkey saw me and shied away; otherwise, I would certainly have killed you by now and spared the donkey."

1 Kings 4:33–34 NIV: ... He also taught about animals and birds, reptiles, and fish. [34]Men of all nations came to listen to Solomon's wisdom, sent by all the kings of the world, who had heard his wisdom.

1 Kings 13:24 NIV: As he went on his way, a lion met him on the road and killed him, and his body was thrown down on the road, with both the donkey and the lion standing beside it.

1 Kings 13:28 NIV: Then he went out and found the body thrown down on the road, with the donkey and the lion standing beside it. The lion had neither eaten the body nor mauled the donkey.

1 Kings 17:4 NIV: You will drink from the brook, and I have ordered the ravens to feed you there.

2 Samuel 12:1–9 NIV: The LORD sent Nathan to David. When he came to him, he said, "There were two men in a certain town, one rich and the other poor. ²The rich man had a very large number of sheep and cattle, ³but the poor man had nothing except one little ewe lamb he had bought. He raised it and it grew up with him and his children. It shared his food, drank from his cup and even slept in his arms. It was like a daughter to him. ⁴Now a traveler came to the rich man, but the rich man refrained from taking one of his own sheep or cattle to prepare a meal for the traveler who had come to him. Instead, he took the ewe lamb that belonged to the poor man and prepared it for the one who had come to him." ⁵David burned with anger against the man and said to Nathan, "As surely as the LORD lives, the man who did this deserves to die! ⁶He must pay for that lamb four times over because he did such a thing and had no pity." ⁷Then Nathan said to David, "You are the man! This is what the LORD, the God of Israel, says: 'I anointed you king over Israel, and I delivered you from the hand of Saul. ⁸I gave your master's house to you and your master's wives into your arms. I gave you the house of Israel and Judah. And if all this had been too little, I would have given you even more. ⁹Why did you despise the word of the LORD by doing what is evil in his eyes? You struck down Uriah the Hittite with the sword and took his wife to be your own. You killed him with the sword of the Ammonites.'"

Daniel 6:21–22 NIV: Daniel answered, "O king, live forever! ²²My God sent his angel, and he shut the mouths of the lions. They have not hurt me, because I was found innocent in his sight. Nor have I ever done any wrong before you, O king."

Jonah 2:10 NIV: And the LORD commanded the fish, and it vomited Jonah onto dry land.

Luke 16:20–21 NIV: At the gate was laid a beggar named Lazarus, covered with sores [21]and longing to eat what fell from the rich man's table. Even the dogs came and licked his sores.

Our Talents

1 Peter 4:10 NIV: Each one should use whatever gift he has received to serve others, faithfully administering God's grace in its various forms.

Plants for Food

Genesis 1:30 KJV: And to every beast of the earth, and to every fowl of the air, and to every thing that creepeth upon the earth, wherein *there is* life, *I have given* every green herb for meat: and it was so.

Daniel 1:11–16 NIV: Daniel then said to the guard whom the chief official had appointed over Daniel, Hananiah, Mishael, and Azariah, [12]"Please test your servants for ten days: Give us nothing but vegetables to eat and water to drink. [13]Then compare our appearance with that of the young men who eat the royal food, and treat your servants in accordance with what you see." [14]So he agreed to this and tested them for ten days. [15]At the end of the ten days they looked healthier and better nourished than any of the young men who ate the royal food. [16]So the guard took away their choice food and wine they were to drink and gave them vegetables instead.

Quotes from Jesus: General

Matthew 5:8 NIV: Blessed are the pure in heart, for they will see God.

Matthew 5:9–10 NIV: Blessed are the peacemakers, for they will be called sons of God. ¹⁰Blessed are those who are persecuted because of righteousness, for theirs is the kingdom of heaven.

Matthew 5:17 NIV: Do not think that I have come to abolish the Law or the Prophets; I have not come to abolish them but to fulfill them.

Matthew 10:28 KJV: And fear not them which kill the body, but are not able to kill the soul: but rather fear him which is able to destroy both the soul and the body in hell.

Matthew 12:11–12 NIV: He said to them, "If any of you has a sheep and it falls into a pit on the Sabbath, will you not take hold of it and lift it out? ¹²How much more valuable is a man than a sheep! Therefore it is lawful to do good on the Sabbath."

Matthew 22:29 KJV: Jesus answered and said unto them, Ye do err, not knowing the scriptures, nor the power of God.

Matthew 26:52 NIV: "Put your sword back in its place," Jesus said to him, "for all who draw the sword will die by the sword."

Matthew 11:28–30 NIV: "Come to me, all you who are weary and burdened, and I will give you rest. ²⁹Take my yoke upon you and learn from me, for I am gentle and humble in heart, and you will find rest for your souls. ³⁰For my yoke is easy and my burden is light."

Mark 7:6–8 NIV: He replied, 'Isaiah was right when he prophesied about you hypocrites; as it is written: "These people honor me with their lips, but their hearts are far from me. They worship me in vain; their teachings are but rules taught by men." You have let go of the commands of God and are holding on to the traditions of men.'

Mark 8:33 NIV: … "You do not have in mind the things of God, but the things of men."

Luke 6:37–38 NIV: "Do not judge, and you will not be judged. Do not condemn, and you will not be condemned. Forgive, and you will be forgiven. ³⁸Give, and it will be given to you. A good measure, pressed down, shaken together and running over, will be poured into your lap. For with the measure you use, it will be measured to you."

Luke 10:18 NIV: He [Jesus] replied, "I saw Satan fall like lightning from heaven."

Luke 15:10 NIV: In the same way, I tell you, there is rejoicing in the presence of the angels of God over one sinner who repents.

Luke 24:44 NIV: He said to them, "This is what I told you while I was still with you: Everything must be fulfilled that is written about me in the Law of Moses, the Prophets, and in the Psalms."

John 3:17 NIV: For God did not send his Son into the world to condemn the world but to save the world through him.

John 8:31–32 KJV If ye continue, *then* are ye my disciples indeed; ³²And ye shall know the truth, and the truth shall make you free.

Quotes from Jesus about Peace

Matthew 5:9 NIV: Blessed are the peacemakers, for they will be called sons of God.

Matthew 12:19–20 NIV: He will not quarrel or cry out; no one will hear his voice in the streets. ²⁰A bruised reed he will not break, and a smoldering wick he will not snuff out, till he leads justice to victory.

Matthew 22:34–40 DNT: But the Pharisees, having heard that he had put the Sadduccees to silence, were gathered together. ³⁵And one of them, a lawyer, demanded, tempting him, and saying, ³⁶'Teacher, which is the greatest commandment in the law? ³⁷And he said to him, Thou shalt love [the] Lord thy God with all thy heart, and with all thy soul, and with all thy understanding. ³⁸This is [the] great and first commandment. ³⁹And [the] second is like it, Thou shalt love thy neighbor as thyself. ⁴⁰On these two commandments the whole law and prophets hang.

Mark 9:50 KJV: Salt *is* good: but if the salt have lost his saltness, wherewith will ye season it? Have salt in yourselves, and have peace one with another.

Quotes from the Prophets Regarding Animals

Isaiah 11:6–9 NIV: The wolf will live with the lamb, the leopard will lie down with the goat, the calf and the lion and the yearling together; and a little child will lead them. [7]And the cow will feed with the bear; their young will lie down together; and the lion shall eat straw like the ox. [8]The infant will play near the hole of the cobra, and the young child shall put its hand into the viper's nest. [9]They will neither hurt nor destroy on all my holy mountain, for the earth will be full of the knowledge of the LORD as the waters cover the sea.

Isaiah 65:25 NIV: The wolf and the lamb will feed together, and the lion will eat straw like the ox, but dust will be the serpent's food. They will neither harm nor destroy on all my holy mountain.

Acts 3:21 NIV: He must remain in heaven until the time comes for God to restore everything, as he promised long ago through his holy prophets.

Revelation 21:4–5 NIV: "He will wipe away every tear from their eyes. There will be no more death or mourning or crying or pain, for the old order of things has passed away." [5]He who was seated on the throne said, "I am making everything new!" Then he said, "Write this down, for these words are trustworthy and true."

The Soul is in the Blood

Genesis 9:4–5 NIV: "But you must not eat meat that has its lifeblood still in it. [5]And for your lifeblood I will surely demand an accounting. I will demand an accounting from every animal. And from man, too, I will demand an accounting for the life of his fellow man."

Leviticus 17:10–11 DNT: And every one of the house of Israel, or of the strangers who sojourn among them, that eateth any manner of blood,—I will set my face against the soul that hath eaten blood, and will cut him off from among his people; ¹¹for the soul of the flesh is in the blood; and I have given it to you upon the altar to make atonement for your souls, for it is the blood that maketh atonement for the soul.

Hebrews 13:11–16 NIV: The high priest carries the blood of animals into the Most Holy Place as a sin offering, but the bodies are burned outside the camp. ¹²And so Jesus also suffered outside the city gate to make the people holy through his own blood. ¹³Let us, then, go to him outside the camp, bearing the disgrace he bore. ¹⁴For here we do not have an enduring city, but we are looking for the city that is to come. ¹⁵Through Jesus, therefore, let us continually offer to God a sacrifice of praise—the fruit of lips that confess his name. ¹⁶And do not forget to do good and to share with others, for with such sacrifices God is pleased.

The Ten Commandments

Exodus 19:12–13 NIV: "Put limits for the people around the mountain and tell them, 'Be careful that you do not go up the mountain or touch the foot of it. Whoever touches the mountain shall surely be put to death. ¹³He shall surely be stoned or shot with arrows; not a hand is to be laid on him. Whether man or animal, he shall not be permitted to live.' Only when the ram's horn sounds a long blast may they go up to the mountain."

Exodus 20:10 KJV: but the seventh day *is* the sabbath of the LORD thy God: *in it* thou shalt not do any work, thou, nor thy son, nor thy daughter, thy manservant, not thy maidservant, nor thy cattle, nor thy stranger that is within thy gates:

Tsa'ar ba'alei chayim (No Suffering to Animals)

Deuteronomy 22:10 KJV: Thou shall not plow with an ox and an ass together.
Deuteronomy 25:4 KJV: Thou shalt not muzzle the ox that treadeth out *the corn.*
1 Timothy 5:18 KJV: For the scripture saith, Thou shalt not muzzle the ox that treadeth out the corn. And, the labourer *is* worthy of his reward.

Visible And Invisible

Colossians 1:16–20 NIV: For by him all things were created: things in heaven and on earth, visible and invisible, whether thrones or powers or rulers or authorities; all things were created by him and for him. [17]He is before all things, and in him all things hold together. [18]And he is the head of the body, the church; he is the beginning and the firstborn from among the dead, so that in everything he might have supremacy. [19]For God was pleased to have all his fullness dwell in him, [20]and through him to reconcile to himself all things, whether things on earth or things in heaven, by making peace through his blood, shed on the cross.

The Tomato List (Verses used to Claim that Animals do not go to Heaven)

Mark 7:27–29 NIV: "First let the children eat all they want," he told her, "for it is not right to take the children's bread and toss it to their dogs." [28]"Yes, Lord," she replied, "but even the dogs under the table eat the children's crumbs." Then he told her, "For such a reply, you may go; the demon has left your daughter."

[Remember that Jesus's original language was Aramaic. This language is a metaphorical language. The dog is being analogous to the Gentiles. The woman in this verse is like the Gentiles, catching the crumbs of faith to Jesus.]

Acts 10:13 NIV: Then a voice told him, "Get up, Peter. Kill and eat."

[I would like to reiterate: This is the story of Cornelius the Roman centurion. Peter gets a vision of animals coming to and from heaven under a sheet. The animals are representing both clean and unclean as defined by dietary law at the current time. An angel then visits Peter and tells him to go see Cornelius. Peter is to bestow the Holy Spirit on Cornelius. But Cornelius is a Roman Gentile, and Peter is not allowed to eat with him or be in his presence in his home according to Jewish law. Cornelius has been chosen because he is a righteous man and is living by Noahide Law. Peter realizes the vision means that nothing is impure anymore and that all people, including Gentiles, are allowed to become Christians. Peter explains this to a Jewish council later in the book of Acts. He states that the animals represented both clean and unclean, meaning that both Jews and Gentiles may come to Christ. Cornelius was the first Gentile to be brought into the Christian brotherhood. Many see this verse as permission to abandon kosher law and that we Gentiles can eat any animal for food. This is a misunderstanding. This verse does not release us from our obligation to treat animals kindly. We are still under the biblical obligation to treat all living things with the respect and kindness that God has required.]

2 Peter 2:12 NIV: But these men blaspheme in matters they do not understand. They are like brute beasts, creatures of instinct, born only to be caught and destroyed, and like beasts they too will perish.

[This verse is representing these vile men who are saying things that are not thought out, nor are they correct. They are being compared to animals that are in the wild and who operate under instinct. According to Norm Phelps in his compassionate book *The Dominion of Love*:

> "This instinct is a part of the world that allows bigger and stronger animals to have victory over their prey and hence some animals die and perish under the harsh laws of the animals world."

Thanks to Adam, our animal world is now subjected to the eating of flesh to survive. Furthering Norm Phelp's idea, it does not mean that they will perish eternally. Yet, these men that the verse is referring to are acting inappropriately and therefore they are subjecting themselves to the ravages of others who could cause them to also perish. Sin begets sin.]

Jude 1:10 NIV: Yet these men speak abusively against whatever they do not understand; and what things they do understand by instinct, like unreasoning animals—these are the very things that destroy them.

[This is the same explanation as the above verse for 2 Peter 2:12.]

Appendix C
RECOMMENDED READING

Bibles

The Book. Wheaton, IL: Tyndale House Publishers Inc., 1988.
The Catholic Bible. New York: Oxford University Press, 1995.
The Hendrickson Parallel Bible. Peabody, MA: Thomas Nelson, Inc., Tyndale House Publishers, and the Zondervan Corporation, Hendrickson Publishers, 2005.
The Holy Bible: John Nelson Darby's New Translation. PocketBible. Cedar Rapids, IA: Laridian Electronic Publishing, 2003.
The Holy Bible King James Version. PocketBible. Cedar Rapids, IA: Laridian Electronic Publishing, 2003.
Holy Bible: The New Living Translation. PocketBible. Wheaton, IL: Laridian Electronic Publishing, 2004.
The Interlinear Bible, Hebrew-Greek-English. Greene, Jay P. Sr. Peabody, MA: Hendrickson Publishers, 2006.
Life Application Bible: New International Version. Wheaton, IL, and Grand Rapids, MI: Tyndale House Publishers, Zondervan Publishing House, 1991.
New American Standard Bible. Hebrew-Greek Key Word Study Bible. Chattanooga, TN: AMG Publishers, 2008.
Pocket Bible. Prod. Craig Rairdin. Cedar Rapids, IA: Laridian, Inc., 1988.
PocketBible App. Laridian, Inc. Prod. Craig Rairdin. Cedar Rapids, IA: Laridian Inc., 1988.

Books

Alcorn, Randy. *Heaven.* Wheaton, IL: Tyndale House Publishers Inc., 2004.

⎯⎯⎯. *Heaven: Biblical Answers to Common Questions.* Carol Stream, IL: Tyndale House Publishers, 2004.

Buckner, E. D. *The Immortality of Animals.* Philadelphia: George W. Jacobs & Co. Publishers, 1903.

Buddemeyer-Porter, Mary. *Animals, Immortal Beings.* Manchester, MO: Eden Publications LLC, 2005.

Eadie, Betty. *Embraced by the Light.* Placerville, CA: Gold Leaf Press, 1992.

Gobry, Ivan. *Saint Francis of Assisi.* Translated by Michael J. Miller. San Francisco: Ignatius Press, 2003.

Halley, Henry H. *Halley's Bible Handbook with the New Internatinal Version.* Grand Rapids, MI: Zondervan, 2000.

Jones, Deborah M. *Concern for Animals.* London: CTS Publishers, 2010.

⎯⎯⎯. *The School of Compassion: A Roman Catholic Theology of Animals.* Herefordshire: Gracewing, 2009.

Linzey, Andrew. *Animal Theology.* Champaign, IL: University of Illinois Press, 1994.

⎯⎯⎯. "The Bible and Killing for Food." *Between the Species*, Winter 1993.

⎯⎯⎯. *Christianity and the Rights of Animals.* New York: Crossroad Publishing Co., 1987.

Murti, Vasu. *They Shall Not Hurt or Destroy.* Cleveland, OH: Vegetarian Advocates Press, 2003.

Parcelle, Wayne. *The Bond.* New York: Harper Books, 2011.

Phelps, Norm. *The Dominion of Love.* New York: Lantern Books, 2002.

Priebe, Matthew. *Animals, Ethics, & Chistianity.* Matthew Priebe, 2005.

Ratzinger, Joseph. *Jesus of Nazareth.* New York: Doubleday, 2007.

Scott, Steven K. *The Greatest Words Ever Spoken.* Colorado Springs, CO: WaterBrook Press, 2008.

Scully, Matthew. *Dominion.* New York: St. Martin's Griffin, 2002.

Shanahan, Niki Behrikis. *There Is Eternal Life for Animals.* Tyngsborough, MA: Pete Publishing, 2002.

———. *Who Says Animals Go to Heaven?* Tyngsborough, MA: Pete Publishing, 2008.

Stanton, Arch. *Animals in Heaven: Fantasy of Reality.* Victoria, BC: Trafford Publishing, 2004.

Strobel, Lee. *The Case for Christ.* Grand Rapids, MI: Zondervan, 1998.

———. *The Case for Faith.* Grand Rapids, MI: Zondervan, 2000.

Animals in Heaven? DVD. Directed by Jack Van Impe. 2004; Troy, MI: Jack Van Impe Ministries, 2004.

Volpe, Tina, and Judy Carman. *The Missing Peace: The Hidden Power of Our Kinship with Animals.* Flourtown, PA: Dreamriver Press LLC, 2009.

Wilson, Terry. *All Creatures of Our God and King.* Manchester, MO: Eden Publications LLC, 2006.

Bibliography

Abegg Jr., Martin, Peter Flint, and Eugene Ulrich. *The Dead Sea Scrolls Bible.* San Francisco: HarperSanFrancisco, 1999.

Alcorn, Randy. *Heaven.* Carol Stream, IL: Tyndale House Publishers, 2004.

———. *Heaven: Biblical Answers to Common Questions.* Wheaton, IL: Tyndale House Publishers Inc., 2003.

Animals in Heaven? DVD. Directed by Jack Van Impe. Produced by Jack Van Impe Ministries International. Performed by Dr. Jack and Rexella Van Impe, 2004.

Bartlette, John. *Bartlette's Familiar Quotations.* Edited by Justin Kaplan. Boston: Little, Brown and Company, 2002.

Baxter, John. *The Academic Gameplan Workbook.* Clovis, CA: Self-published, 1999.

Bercot, David W., ed. *A Dictionary of Early Christian Beliefs.* Peabody, MA: Hendrickson Publishers, 1998.

Bindman, Yirmeyahu. *The Seven Colors of the Rainbow.* San Jose, CA: Resource Publications, 1995.

Bodo, Murray. *Francis: The Journey and the Dream.* Cincinnati, OH: St. Anthony Messenger Press, 1988.

Bristol Works, Inc. *Bible and Christian History Time Lines.* Torrence, CA: Rose Publishing, 2006.

Bruce, F. F. *New Testament History.* New York: Doubleday, 1969.

Buckner, E. D. *The Immortality of Animals.* Philadelphia: George W. Jacobs & Co. Publishers, 1903.

Buddemeyer-Porter, Mary. *Animals, Immortal Beings.* Manchester, MO: Eden Publications LLC, 2005.

———. *Will I See Fido in Heaven?* Vol. 4. Manchester, MO: Eden Publications LLC, 2006.

Cairns, Earle E. *Christianity through the Centuries.* Grand Rapids, MI: Zondervan, 1996.

Colson, Charles. *The Body: Being Light in Darkness.* Dallas, TX: Word Publishing, 1992.

Davies, Philip R., George J. Brooke, and Phillip R. Callaway. *The Complete World of the Dead Sea Scrolls.* London: Thames & Hudson Ltd., 2002.

Eadie, Betty. *Embraced by the Light.* Placerville, CA: Gold Leaf Press, 1992.

Edward, John. *After Life.* New York: Princess Books, 2003.

Eisenman, Robert H., and Michael Wise. *The Dead Sea Scrolls Uncovered.* New York: Barnes and Noble Books, 2004.

Englebert, Omer. *St. Francis of Assisi: A Biography.* Cinncinati, OH: Servant Books, 1979.

Eusebius. *The History of the Church.* Translated by Arthur Cushman McGiffert. Acheron Press, 2012. Kindle edition.

Gobry, Ivan. *Saint Francis of Assisi.* Translated by Michael J. Miller. San Francisco: Ignatius Press, 2003.

Graham, Billy. *Angels.* Dallas, TX: Thomas Nelson, 1995.

———. *Approaching Hoofbeats.* New York: Avon Books, 1983.

———. *Death and the Life After.* Dallas, TX: Word Publishing, 2001.

Greene, Jay P. Sr. *The Interlinear Bible, Hebrew-Greek-English.* Peabody, MA: Hendrickson Publishers, 2006.

Gronowitz, Antoni. *God's Broker.* New York: Richardson & Snyder, 1984.

Guralnik, David B. *Webster's New World Dictionary.* Cleveland, OH: William Collins Publishers, Inc., 1977.

Gurevich, Eliyahu. *Tosefta Berachot.* Las Vegas, NV: Self-published, 2010.

Habermas, Gary R., and J. P. Moreland. *Beyond Death.* Eugene, OR: Wipf & Stock Pubishers, 1998.

Halley, Henry H. *Halley's Bible Handbook with the New Internatinal Version.* Grand Rapids, MI: Zondervan, 2000.

Henry, Matthew. *Matthew Henry's Commentary on the Whole Bible.* Peabody, MA: Hendrickson Publishers, Inc., 2007.

Holmes, M. Jean. *Do Dogs Go to Heaven?* Tulsa, OK: JoiPax Publishing, 1999.

John Paul II. *Crossing the Threshold of Hope.* Edited by Vittorio Messori. New York: Alfred A. Knopf, 2008.

———. *God, Father and Creator: A Catechesis on the Creed.* Vol. 1. Boston: Pauline Books and Media, 1996.

———. *In My Own Words.* Edited by Anthony F. Chiffolo. New York: Gramercy Books, 1998.

———. *The Splendor of Truth.* Vatican City: Libreia Editice Vaticana, 1993.

Jones, Deborah M. *Concern for Animals.* London: CTS Publishers, 2010.

———. *The School of Compassion: A Roman Catholic Theology of Animals.* Herefordshire: Gracewing, 2009.

Jones, Timothy Paul. *Four Views of the End Times.* Torrance, CA: Rose Publishing, 2006.

Jones, Timothy Paul, Timothy Larson, and John McRay. *Bible and Christian History Time Line.* Torrance, CA: Rose Publishing, 2006.

Josephus, Flavius. *The Complete Works of Flavius Josephus.* Translated by William Whiston. Nashville: Thomas Nelson, 2003. Kindle edition.

Kaiser Jr., Walter C. *The Messiah in the Old Testament.* Grand Rapids, MI: Zondervan Publishing House, 1995.

Kirby, David. *Animal Factory.* New York: St. Martin's Press, 2010.

Konig, George, and Ray Konig. *100 Prophecies.* Lexington, KY: CreateSpace Independent Publishing Platform, 2008.

Kowalski, Gary. *The Bible According to Noah.* New York: Lantern Books, 2001.

Kurz, Gary. *Cold Noses at the Pearly Gates.* Topeka, KS: Gary Kurz, 1997.

LaHaye, Tim, and Jerry B. Jenkins. *Are We Living in End Times?* Wheaton, IL: Tyndale House Publishers Inc., 1999.

Libreria Editrice Vaticana. *Catechism of the Catholic Church.* New York: Doubleday, 1994.

Linzey, Andrew. *Animal Theology.* Champaign, IL: University of Illinois Press, 1994.

———. "The Bible and Killing for Food." *Between the Species*, Winter 1993.

———. *Christianity and the Rights of Animals*. New York: Crossroad Publishing Co., 1987.

Lockyer, Herbert. *All the Messianic Prophecies of the Bible*. Grand Rapids, MI: Zondervan, 1973.

Martin, Ralph. *The Catholic Church at the End of an Age*. San Francisco: Ignatius Press, 1994.

McBrien, Richard P. *Catholicism*. San Francisco: HarperSanFrancisco, 1994.

McBrien, Richard P., ed. *Encyclopedia of Catholicism*. New York: HarperCollins Publishers, 1989.

Murti, Vasu. *They Shall Not Hurt or Destroy*. Cleveland, OH: Vegetarian Advocates Press, 2003.

Newton, Richard. *Bible Animals*. Birmingham, AL: Solid Ground Christian Books, 2007.

Novak, David. *The Image of the Non-Jew in Judaism*. Portland, OR: The Littman Library of Jewish Civilization, 2011.

———. *Jewish-Christian Dialogue*. New York: Oxford University Press, 1989.

Parcelle, Wayne. *The Bond*. New York: Harper Books, 2011.

Phelps, Norm. *The Dominion of Love*. New York: Lantern Books, 2002.

Price, Steven D., ed. *The Quotable Horse Lover*. Guilford, CT: The Lyons Press, 2001.

Priebe, Matthew. *Animals, Ethics, & Chistianity*. San Bernardino, CA: Self-published, 2005.

Ratzinger, Joseph. *Jesus of Nazareth*. New York: Doubleday, 2007.

Rivers, Francine. *As Sure as the Dawn*. Carol Stream, IL: Tyndale House Publishers, 2002.

Rogers Jr., Cleon, and Cleon L. Rogers III. *The New Liguistic and Exegetical Key to the Greek New Testament*. Grand Rapids, MI: Zondervan, 1998.

Rosten, Leo. *Religions of America*. New York: Simon and Schuster Paperbacks, 1975.

Saint Augustine of Hippo. *The City of God*. Translated by Marcus Dods. Peabody, MA: Hendrickson Publishers, 2009.

---. *The Confessions of Saint Augustine.* Translated by John K. Ryan. New York: Doubleday, 1988.

San Diego Natural History Museum. *Dead Sea Scrolls.* San Diego, CA: San Diego University Press, 2007.

"Science of the Dead Sea Scrolls." San Diego Natural History Museum. Prod. the Dead Sea Scrolls Mudbrick Medis and Israel Antiquities Authority, 2007.

Scott, Steven K. *The Greatest Words Ever Spoken.* Colorado Springs, CO: WaterBrook Press, 2008.

Scully, Matthew. *Dominion.* New York: St. Martin's Griffin, 2002.

Shanahan, Niki Behrikis. *There Is Eternal Life for Animals.* Tyngsborough, MA: Pete's Publishing, 2002.

---. *Who Says Animals Go to Heaven?* Tyngsborough, MA: Pete's Publishing, 2008.

Shelley, Bruce L. *Church History in Plain Language.* Nashville: Thomas Nelson Publishers, 1995.

Smiley, Kathryn, and Robin H. Smiley. *Firsts: The Book Collector's Magazine,* January 2012, vol. 22, no. 1.

Smith, Chuck. *New Testament Study Guide.* Costa Mesa, CA: The Word For Today, 2005.

---. *What Is the World Coming To?* Costa Mesa, CA: The Word for Today, 1993.

Stanton, Arch. *Animals in Heaven: Fantasy of Reality.* Victoria, BC: Trafford Publishing, 2004.

Strobel, Lee. *The Case for Christ.* Grand Rapids, MI: Zondervan, 1998.

---. *The Case for Faith.* Grand Rapids, MI: Zondervan, 2000.

Strong, James. *The New Strong's Expanded Concordance of the Bible: Red-Letter Edition.* Nashville, TN: Thomas Nelson Publishers, 2001.

Thoreau, Henry David. *Walden.* Vook, Inc. Kindle edition. 2011.

Towle, Mike. *Quotable John Paul II.* Nashville, TN: TowleHouse Publishing, 2003.

Trigilio, John, and Kenneth Brighenti. *Catholicism for Dummies.* Hoboken, NJ: Wiley Publishing, Inc., 2003.

"Vegetarian Quotes," Vegetarian Choices. September 23, 2000. http://choices.cs.uiuc.edu/~f-kon/vegetarian.html (accessed February 2013).

Volpe, Tina, and Judy Carman. *The Missing Peace: The Hidden Power of Our Kinship with Animals*. Flourtown, PA: Dreamriver Press LLC, 2009.

Washington, Del. *The Original Code in the Bible*. Lanham, MD: Madison Books, 1998.

———. *Theomatics II*. Lanham, MD: Scarborough House, 1994.

Wilson, Terry. *All Creatures of Our God and King*. Manchester, MO: Eden Publications LLC, 2006.

Wray, T. J., and Gregory Mobley. *The Birth of Satan*. New York: Palgrave Macmillan, 2005.

REFLECTION

NOTES

NOTES

NOTES

NOTES

NOTES

Index

bold denotes photos

A

Abraham, 65, 66, 120, 155, 156
acaph (gathering of souls), 103
Adam
    animals as fearful of, 18, 19
    consequences of as extended to animals, 18
    as directed to name and rule over animals, 50
    God as asking Adam to give animals names, 23
    God placing animals in Garden of Eden as companions for, 14
    God's constraint on, 15
    God's first mention of, 75
    as key link to animals, 75–77, 83
    relationship of to animals, 15
    as using skins to cover nakedness, 18–19
afterlife
    animals as having place in, 130
    Hebrew belief in, 80–81
Alcorn, Randy, 118, 134, 135, 142
"all," Greek word for (*pas*), 98, 104, 106

"all flesh"
    Greek word for (*sarx*), 95, 98
    Hebrew word for (*basar*), 71, 95
    use of term, 95–100
"all that had life," use of in translations, 81
amillennialism, 129
anakephalaiomao (to gather as one), 104
angels, 110–112, 140–141
Angels (Graham), 110
Animal Behavior College, xx
animal cruelty
    biblical verses about, 193
    legislation, 36
animal sacrifice
    as atonement, 48
    biblical verses about, 197–198, 211
    description of practice of, 56–58
    for food only, 32
    God as regretting (biblical verses about), 211
    Jesus as last sacrifice, 56, 60
    Jesus's biblical verse about, 216

practice of as representing and
pointing to coming of
Messiah, 59
ritual of as compared to what
happened to Jesus, 56
sales of sacrificed animals in
temple market, 53, 55
animal souls
biblical verses about, 57, 194–195
evidence of, 78
life (soul) of animals is in blood,
34, 57
as mentioned twice in Genesis
1:20–21, 4
references to, 73–75
what original translation
reveals, 63–86
animal spirits, 4–5, 63–64, 198–199
animal stories
biblical verses about, 217–219
hunters, portrayal of in Bible,
153–156
ravens, 164
Saint Francis, patron saint of
animals, 150–153
story of Balaam and his donkey,
159–160
story of Daniel, 171–172
story of Job, 164–168
story of Jonah, 168–170
story of King David and ewe,
161–164
animals
all as having place on the ark,
30, 37
as being accountable for taking
of a life, 34
caring for (biblical verses
about), 200

as coexisting peacefully on
ark, 31
as companions (biblical verses
about), 194
as conscious of God's plan and
appreciative of God's
grace and mercy, 30
covenant as addressed to five
times, 84
covenants with (biblical verses
about), 201–202
doves considered first
domesticated animal, 49
few churches as teaching
anything about, 132
God as mentioning of (biblical
verses about), 207–208
God as not restricting his face
from, 102
God's rule as including, 156–159
as having free ticket to ride to
heaven, 112
Jesus with (biblical verses about),
215–216
kindness to (biblical verses
about), 216
as knowing God in way that
humans do not, 103
link between angels and, 110–112
as not being forgotten by God
(biblical verses about), 199
as not under same rules humans
are, 92
as not willing partners in offense
Adam and Eve created, 91
as praising God, 195–197
quotes from prophets regarding
(biblical verses about), 222
as resting on the Sabbath (Fourth
Commandment), 38

role of in Bible, 34
    as sentient (biblical verses about), 194
    slaughtering of according to kosher law, 39
    as source of food, 32
    as subject to earthly consequences, 30
"Animals Not Forgotten" (Cerisano), 185–186
antichrist, 126, 129
The Antiquities of the Jews, Book III (Josephus), 71
apokalupsis (revelation), 90
apokatastasis (restitution; to set in order; reconciliation), 99, 105
Approaching Hoofbeats (Graham), 156
Aramaic, one of original two languages of Old Testament, 65, 66
aras (betroth), 124
archangels, 140
Armageddon, 123
Augustine of Hippo, 135

B

Balaam, story of, 159–160
basar (all flesh), 71, 95
Bathsheeba, 161
benevolent rulers, humans as, over animals, 13, 26
Bible
    evolution of, 64–67
    main versions referenced, xxv
The Bible According to Noah (Kowalski), 49
biblical verses (by category), 189–226
blood
    of animals and of Jesus, 55–60
    draining of in kosher laws, 39
    eating of animal's blood known as "strangulation," 35
    of lamb as atonement, 48
    of lamb as saving God's believers, 48
    life (soul) of animals is in blood, 34
    as not to be eaten, 34, 35, 39
    souls as in (biblical verses about), 222–223
bow (come), 98
"breath of life"
    Hebrew word for (*neshamah*), 76–77
    and term "soul," 78
    use of in translations, 81
Brother Sun, Sister Moon (movie), 153
Buckner, E. D., 172
Bush, George, Sr., 36

C

Calvin, John, 93, 130
capital punishment, law of, 34
caretakers, humans as, of animals, 14
The Case for Faith (Strobel), 7
cattle industry, 36
celestial beings, 139–141, 145, 200–201
Cerisano, Melinda, 185
chayyah (living being), 75
cherub, Hebrew word for (*kerub*), 144
cherubim, 139, 140
Christian Classics Ethereal Library, 93
Christianity and the Rights of Animals (Linzey), 22
City of God (Augustine of Hippo), 130
clergy
    on Isaiah 11:6–9, 132

mistake made by, regarding
"breath of life" and
"soul," 78–81
who profess to know "truth"
about animals and
heaven, 180
"come," Greek word for (*bow*), 98
Cornelius, 40–44
Council of Carthage, 66
council of Laodicea and Carthage, 66
covenants with animals, biblical
verses about, 201–202
creature (or creation), Greek word for
(*ktisis*), 91

D

Daniel (prophet), 118
Daniel, story of, 171–172
DAR (Darby 1890 Version), xxv, 73
Darby 1890 Version (DAR), xxv, 73
Darby New Translation (DNT),
xxv, 74
Darius (king), 171
David (king), 21, 98, 101, 108, 160, 161–164
Dead Sea Scrolls (DSS), xxv, 73, 77, 196–197
death
destination beyond, 119–122
spirit as giving life after, 85–86
devil, 107–109
diadema (crowns of royalty), 156
dietary rules/laws, 35, 203
dispensational premillennialism
(DP), 127–128
*A Dissertation on the Duty of Mercy
and the Sin of Cruelty to Brute
Animals* (Primatt), 6

DNT (Darby New Translation),
xxv, 74
dominion
biblical verses about, 203–204
God as viewing of with
compassion and mercy, 23
God's idea of, 8
Hebrew translation as "rule," 20
true meaning of, 13–26
The Dominion of Love (Phelps), 58, 111
donkey
Balaam and, 159–160
Jesus's ride on, 52–53
dualism, 79, 204–205

E

Edison, Thomas, 188
Einstein, Albert, 187–188
Elijah, 164
Encyclopedia Britannica, 34
Encyclopedia Judaica, 35
end times, four theologies of, 127–130
English, translation of Bible, 66
Enoch, 140
Esau, 155, 215
Eve, 15, 18–19
ewe, story about, 161–164

F

food, plants for, biblical verses
about, 219
Four Views of End Times (Jones), 126, 127, 129, 130
Foxy (German shepherd), **xiii**

G

Gabriel (archangel), 140
Gandhi, Mahatma, 188

Garden of Eden
   animals as included in, 14
   animals as part of that plan, 133
   fall in resulting in severe departure from God's original plan, 18, 19
   importance of in understanding why animals are included in all of God's plans, 20
   and true meaning of dominion, 16
   as vegetarian state, 14, 23, 32
"gather"
   Greek word for (*anakephalaiomao*), 104
   Hebrew word for (*acaph*), 103
   Hebrew word for (*lagat*), 103
Genre magazine, 86
Gentiles, 38, 39, 42
Gobry, Ivan, 150, 152
God
   all as praising God, 141–144
   all that God creates belongs to Him (biblical verses about), 192
   betroths/reconciles the animals to himself (biblical verses about), 205–206
   face of (biblical verses about), 207
   as gathering up a spirit, 103–107
   as making covenant to animals, 18
   as making strict rules on animals' behalf, 32
   as mentioning animals (biblical verses about), 207–208
   mercy of (biblical verses about), 208–209
   nature of, 209–211
   as not forgetting, 173–174
   as preserving all, 100–103
   questioning the nature of, 7–9
   as regretting animal sacrifice (biblical verses about), 211
   remembering nature of, 16–19
   spirit of (biblical verses about), 198–199. *See also* God's spirit
God's game plan, 25–26
God's spirit
   all flesh as having, 95–100
   as never leaving, 70–73
   good stewards, humans as, of animals, 36
Graham, Billy, 110, 156
Greek, as original language of New Testament, 65, 67, 68
Green, Jay P., 73, 75, 101
Gubbio (wolf), 151–152

H

Halley, Henry Hampton, 68
Halley's Bible Handbook (Halley), 68
Haniel (archangel), 140
The HarperCollins Encyclopedia of Catholicism, 140
heaven
   animals as going to, the unwilling, 89–94
   in the Bible, 116–119
   biblical verses about, 212–214
   guards of, 145–146
   nature of, 115–136
   new heaven, 126
   as place of paradise, 134–136
   verses used to claim animals do not go to, 224–226
Heaven (Alcorn), 118, 134, 135, 142

Hebrew, one of original two
	languages of Old Testament,
	65, 66, 67, 68
Hebrew Bible, 65
Hebrews (people), 55
hell, 91, 120, 121
historical premillennialism (HP), 128
Holy Spirit, as in all flesh, 71
hunters
	biblical verses about, 214–215
	portrayal of in Bible, 153–156
hunting, as inhumane and forbidden
	in Jewish religion, 156
Hurwitz, Rabbi, 110

I

*The Immortality of Animals: And the
	Relation of Man as Guardian,
	from a Biblical and Philosophical
	Hypothesis* (Buckner), 172
"instinct," Greek word for
	(*physica*), 111
intelligent design, 69
Interlinear Bible, Hebrew-Greek-
	English (LITV), xxv, 73, 75, 101
intermediate heaven, 122
Isaac, 156
Ishmael, 155, 214
Israelites, 38, 48, 103, 157, 158

J

James (apostle), 66
James (king), 66
Jerome, 66
Jesus
	on animal sacrifice (biblical verse
		about), 216
	with animals (biblical verses
		about), 215–216
	animals and, 49–53
	biblical verses about, 191
	as coming to bring peace, 51–52
	as expressing will of God, 17
	general quotes from (biblical
		verses about), 219–221
	as good ruler, 26
	as having brought a new
		covenant, 26
	kindness and compassion of
		toward animal world, 54
	as last animal sacrifice, 56, 60
	meditation in the wilderness
		among wild animals, 49
	as Messiah, 49, 53
	prophecies as saying he will
		be born among the
		animals, 53
	as proposing idea of being good
		shepherd, 54
	quotes about peace (biblical
		verses about), 221
	ride of on donkey colt, 52–53
Jewish-Christian Dialogue (Novak), 35
Job, story of, 164–168
John (apostle), 66, 98, 124, 125, 145
John Paul II (pope), support from
	regarding animal souls, 86–87
John the Baptist, 49
Jonah, story of, 168–170
Jones, Timothy Paul, 126, 127
Josephus, Flavius, 71
Judaism
	and animals' blood, 35, 39
	on Genesis 3:21 and "skins"
		reference, 19
	Jewish law under Moses as
		residing law of, 39
	Oral Law of Judaism, 35
Jude, 66

K

kerub (cherub), 144
Ketubim (Writings), 65
Key Word Study Bible: Key Insights to God's Word, 81
kindness, to animals (biblical verses about), 216
King James Version (KJV), xxv, 66, 72, 74, 84
kosher laws, as evidence of animal protection, 39
kosmos (world), 105
Kowalski, Gary, 49
kowl (everything), 142
ktisis (creature or creation), 91

L

lagat (gather as in food), 103
last sacrificial lamb, genesis of term, 56
Last Supper, 58
Latin, translation of Bible, 66
Lazarus, 120
Leonardo da Vinci, 187
Levi, 155, 215
Life Application Bible: New International Version, 80, 158, 161, 165
Lincoln, Abraham, 188
Linzey, Andrew, 22, 181
lion, story about, 161
LITV (Interlinear Bible, Hebrew-Greek-English), xxv, 73, 75, 101
"living being," use of in translations, 81
living beings with souls, 75
"living creature," use of in translations, 81, 82, 142
"living soul," Hebrew phrase for (*nephesh chayyah*), 77, 110–111
lost sheep, 53–55
Luke (apostle), 66, 99, 100, 119, 121, 145
Luther, Martin, 130

M

Mark (apostle), 66, 145
mataiotes (vanity), 91
Matthew (apostle), 51, 66, 145
mercy, of God (biblical verses about), 208–209
Michael (archangel), 140
Millan, Cesar, xxi
millennium, 126
mistake, made by clergy, regarding "breath of life" and "soul," 78–81
Mosaic laws, 38, 39
Moses, 37–38, 81, 83, 91, 120, 158
Murti, Vasu, 181

N

naphash ("to breathe; respire; to be refreshes"), 78
NASB (New American Standard Bible), xxv, 74, 81, 84
Nathan, 161, 163
near-death experiences (NDE), 122
Nebiim (Prophets), 65
Nebuchadnezzar, 171
Nehemiah 9:6, 195
nephesh (soul), 73, 79, 81–83
nephesh chayyah (living soul), 77, 110–111
Nero (emperor), 129
neshamah (breath of life), 76–77

New American Standard Bible
(NASB), xxv, 74, 81, 84
new earth, 126
new heaven, 126
New International Version (NIV),
xxv, 74, 76, 84
New Living Translation (NLT),
xxv, 66
*New Strong's Exhausted Expanded
Concordance of the Bible:
Red-Letter Edition (Strong's
Concordance)*, 68
New Testament, described, 66
Nimrod, 154–155, 214
Nineveh, 155, 168, 169, 170
"no suffering to animals" (*tsa'ar
ba'alei chayim*), 35, 224
Noah and the ark
    animals as 50 percent of that
        plan, 133
    animals coexisting peacefully, 31
    background of, 29–30
    God telling Noah he may use
        animals for food, 32, 36
    souls of, 83–85
Noahide laws, 34–37, 38, 39, 40, 43,
44, 84
Noel (German shepherd), 3–4, 9
"not one sparrow is forgotten," 18,
54, 60, 150, 180, 181, 186
Novak, David, 35
n'shamah (or *neshamah*) (breath), 142

O

Old Testament, described, 65
Oral Law of Judaism, 35
The Original Code in the Bible
(Washington), 129

P

Pache, René, 134
pain (of animals), 5–6
Palm Sunday, 52
Parelli, Pat, xx
pas (all; all things), 98, 104, 106
Passover, 48, 56, 58
Paul (apostle), 50, 55–56, 66, 90, 91,
92, 96, 98, 119, 121, 135
P-CERT (Post-Christ Era, Round
Two), 123–127, 133, 136
peace, Jesus's quotes about (biblical
versus about), 221
Pentateuch, 65
Peter, 40–44, 66
Pharisees, 53, 54, 132
Phelps, Norm, 58, 111
physica (instinct), 111
plants for food, biblical verses
about, 219
pneuma (spirit), 70, 86
Post-Christ Era, Round Two
(P-CERT), 123–127, 133, 136
postmillennialism, 130
preterism, 126
Primatt, Humphrey, 6
Public Law 102-14, 102nd Congress, 1st
session, H.J. Res. 104, 36
Pythagoras, 187

R

Raguel (archangel), 140
Raphael (archangel), 140
rapture, 126, 127–128
ravens, story about, 164
Rebecca, 156
recommended reading, 227–229
"reconciliation," Greek word for
(*apokatallasso*), 105

"restitution," Greek word for (*apokatastasis*), 99
"revelation," Greek word for (*apokalupsis*), 90
Roxanne (Rottweiler mix), 115
ruwach (spirit), 70, 73, 85

S

sacrificial lamb, last, 47–60
Sadducees, 53
Saint Augustine of Hippo, 130
Saint Bonaventure, 152
Saint Francis of Assisi, 150–153
Saint Francis of Assisi (Gobry), 150, 152, 153
sarx (all flesh), 95, 98
Satan, 26, 107–110, 140, 141, 156, 215
scripture, biblical verses about, 191–192
sephanos (crown of victory worn by a conqueror), 156
Septuagint, 65
seraphim, 139
Seraqael (archangel), 140
Sermon 60 (John Wesley), 5, 94
Shanahan, Niki Behrikis, 97
Shaw, George Bernard, 187
Simeon, 155, 215
Singer, Isaac Bashevis, 187
Solomon (king), 20, 21, 72, 163
soul
  as in the blood (biblical verses about), 222–223
  as completely omitted in some translations, 57, 81
  of creation theory, 69–70
  Hebrew word for (*nephesh*), 73, 79, 81–83

word as left out of Noah scripture in some translations, 74–75, 84
sparrow, as not forgotten, 17, 18, 54, 60, 150, 180, 181, 186
spirit. *See also* animal spirits; God's spirits
  as completely omitted in some translations, 81
  of creation theory, 69–70
  Greek word for (*pneuma*), 70, 86
  Hebrew word for (*ruwach*), 70, 73, 86
St. Peter's Basilica, 145–146
stewards, being good stewards (humans for animals), 20–25
strangulation, 35, 36
Strobel, Lee, 7
Strong's Concordance, 68, 73, 78, 82, 90, 101, 103, 111, 142
Strong's Expanded Exhaustive Concordance, 41, 42

T

talents, ours, biblical verse about, 219
Tanakh, 65
Ten Commandments, 37–38, 84, 223
There Is Eternal Life for Animals (Shanahan), 97
"there is life," use of in translations, 81
"they," Greek word for (*zao*), 106
They Shall Not Hurt or Destroy (Murti), 181
Thoreau, Henry David, 153
three-tier theory, 107–110
thrones, 140
tomato list, biblical verses about, 224–226

Torah (Law), 35, 39, 65
Tosefta, 35
translations
    changes and omissions as a result of, 64
    and common assumptions regarding God's perspective of animal kingdom, 44
    dealing with issue of dualism, 79
    earliest, 66
    example of common error in, 72
    phrase-for-phrase, 67
    thought-for-thought, 67
    word-for-word, 67–69
tribulation, 126
tsa'ar ba'alei chayim (no suffering to animals), 35, 224

U

United States Dressage Federation, xx
Uriel (archangel), 140

V

vanity, Greek word for (*mataiotes*), 91
vegetarianism, 14, 23, 32, 35, 171, 181, 188
visible and invisible, biblical verses about, 224

W

Walden (Thoreau), 153
Washington, Del, 129
Wesley, John, 5, 93, 94
whale, Jonah and, 168–170
Winfrey, Oprah, 178
"world," Greek word for (*kosmos*), 105
Wycliffe, John, 66

Y

yasha (preserveth; salvation), 101

Z

zao (they), 106
Zechariah (person), 52
zoon (animals), 142, 143, 144

Verse Index

A

Acts, 40–44
Acts 3:20–21, 99
Acts 3:21, 106, 119, 121, 206, 213, 222
Acts 10:13, 225
Acts 10:15, 41
Acts 10:22, 41
Acts 10:28, 41
Acts 15:7–9, 42
Acts 15:19–20, 42, 203
Acts 15:20, 42

C

Colossians 1:16, 140
Colossians 1:16–20, 22, 224
Colossians 1:19–20, 105, 206
Colossians 1:23, 151, 192

D

Daniel 1:8, 171
Daniel 1:11–16, 219
Daniel 1:15–16, 171
Daniel 1:17, 171
Daniel 6:21–22, 171–172, 218
Deuteronomy, 39
Deuteronomy 4:31, 3
Deuteronomy 10:14, 192
Deuteronomy 14:21, 203
Deuteronomy 22:10, 24, 200, 224
Deuteronomy 25:4, 35, 200, 224

E

Ecclesiastes, 72
Ecclesiastes 3:18–21, 72
Ecclesiastes 3:21, 73, 122, 190, 199
Ecclesiastes 12:7, 72, 73, 121, 199
Ephesians 1:10, 104, 206
Exodus 19:12–13, 38, 223
Exodus 20:10, 24, 200, 223
Exodus 33:19, 160, 208, 210
Exodus 33:20, 207
Ezekiel, book of, 79
Ezekiel 10, 142
Ezekiel 10:14–20, 142, 144, 200
Ezekiel 18:4, 112, 192
Ezekiel 28:14, 140
Ezekiel 37:1–14, 80–81, 204–205

G

Genesis 1, 73
Genesis 1:1, 166
Genesis 1:2, 70, 198
Genesis 1:20, xix, 75
Genesis 1:20–21, 4, 74, 194
Genesis 1:21, 75
Genesis 1:24, 75, 195
Genesis 1:26, 13, 203

Genesis 1:28, 20, 22, 203
Genesis 1:29–30, 14–15, 76
Genesis 1:30, 190, 219
Genesis 2:7, 75–76, 77, 82, 83, 195
Genesis 2:17, 15
Genesis 2:18–19, 194
Genesis 2:19, 15, 75, 195
Genesis 3, 18
Genesis 3:14–21, 89
Genesis 3:21, 18, 19
Genesis 3:24, 139, 140, 200
Genesis 6:5–6, 30, 209–210
Genesis 6–9, 29
Genesis 6:19, 29
Genesis 7:15, 30
Genesis 9, 34
Genesis 9:1–7, 31
Genesis 9:3–5, 31–32, 201–202
Genesis 9:4, 35
Genesis 9:4–5, 222
Genesis 9:8–17, 33, 83–84, 202
Genesis 10:8, 154
Genesis 10:8–12, 214
Genesis 10:9, 154
Genesis 10:11, 154
Genesis 24:14, 216
Genesis 25:18, 155, 214
Genesis 25:27, 215
Genesis 33:17, 216
Genesis 35:18, 79, 195, 204
Genesis 49:5–6, 155
Genesis 49:5–7, 193, 215

H

Habakkuk 2:17, 170, 193
Hebrews 1:1–3, 106, 211
Hebrews 1:1–4, 206
Hebrews 2:7, 141, 201
Hebrews 4:12, 179

Hebrews 9:13–15, 216
Hebrews 9:22, 198
Hebrews 12:16, 215
Hebrews 13:11–12, 47
Hebrews 13:11–16, 55, 211, 223
Hosea 2, 123
Hosea 2:18–19, 18, 100, 125, 190, 205
Hosea 2:18–20, 124

I

Isaiah, 57, 99, 100
Isaiah 1:3, 57, 103, 158, 208
Isaiah 1:10–11, 57–58, 211
Isaiah 1:10–17, 197
Isaiah 6:2–7, 140
Isaiah 11, 123
Isaiah 11:6–9, 99, 131, 222
Isaiah 40:5, 95, 97, 212
Isaiah 40:28, 165, 210
Isaiah 43:20, 102–103, 125
Isaiah 43:20–22, 196
Isaiah 43:23–24, 197
Isaiah 46:9–11, 16–17
Isaiah 55:8–9, 7, 210
Isaiah 55:9, 165
Isaiah 55:11, 210
Isaiah 65:25, 222
Isaiah 66:3, 58, 198, 211

J

Jeremiah 32:27, 99, 210
Job 1:21, 34, 192
Job 12:7–10, 168, 195, 207
Job 12:10, 122, 192
Job 33:4, 71, 198
Job 38:39, 167–168
Job 38:39–41, 207–208
Job 39:19–24, 208
Job 39:19–25, 166

Job 39:27, 168
Job 40:19, 167
Job 41:11, 192
Joel 1:18, 190, 194
Joel 1:20, 190, 194, 196
Joel 2:22, 190
John 3:16, 59, 191
John 3:17, 52, 105, 191, 206, 221
John 6:63, 86
John 8:31–32, 191, 221
John 12:12–16, 117
John 14:1–4, 212
John 14:2, 134
John 17:2, 98
John 17:17, 191
John 19:30, 86, 199
Jonah 1:2, 209
Jonah 1:3, 168
Jonah 1:17, 169
Jonah 2:10, 169, 218
Jonah 3:7–8, 209
Jonah 3:7–9, 169
Jonah 3:9–10, 209
Jonah 4:7, 169
Jonah 4:10–11, 169–170, 209
Jude 1:10, 111, 226
Jude 9, 140

L

Leviticus, 39
Leviticus 6:27, 197
Leviticus 8:15, 56
Leviticus 11:46–47, 203
Leviticus 17:10–11, 32, 57, 222–223
Leviticus 22:28, 203
Leviticus 24:17–18, 157, 202
Leviticus 25:6–7, 157, 202
Luke 2:7, 215
Luke 3:6, 97

Luke 6:37, 52
Luke 6:37–38, 220
Luke 10:16, 108
Luke 10:18, 108, 213, 221
Luke 12:6, 60, 180
Luke 12:6–7, 17, 54, 199
Luke 15:10, 221
Luke 16:20–21, 194, 219
Luke 16:22–24, 120
Luke 16:22–31, 212–213
Luke 16:27–28, 120
Luke 23:43, 121, 213
Luke 24:44, 221

M

Mark 1:10, 49
Mark 1:12–13, 216
Mark 1:13, 50, 194
Mark 7:6–8, 132, 220
Mark 7:27–29, 224–225
Mark 8:33, 132, 211, 220
Mark 9:50, 25, 221
Matthew 5:8, 219–221
Matthew 5:9, 50, 221
Matthew 5:9–10, 220
Matthew 5:17, 53, 220
Matthew 5:39, 51
Matthew 6:26, 54
Matthew 10:28, 220
Matthew 10:29, 17, 199
Matthew 11:28–30, 51, 177, 220
Matthew 12:11–12, 54, 220
Matthew 12:15–21, 25
Matthew 12:19–20, 51, 221
Matthew 13:52, 115
Matthew 17:27, 54
Matthew 18:10, 108, 141, 207
Matthew 18:14, 180
Matthew 19:26, 16

Matthew 19:28, 55
Matthew 22:29, 191, 210, 220
Matthew 22:34–40, 51, 221
Matthew 26:52, 51, 220
Micah 5:6, 214

N

Numbers 3:13, 157, 192, 207
Numbers 11:31–33, 158
Numbers 11:32–33, 210
Numbers 22:25–33, 193, 217
Numbers 22:28–32, 159
Numbers 27:15–16, 70, 198
Numbers 27:16–17, 95

O

1 Chronicles 21:30, 160
1 Corinthians 2:12–13, 63, 192
1 Corinthians 13:12, 213
1 Corinthians 15:21–22, 92
1 Corinthians 15:35–44, 96, 213
1 Corinthians 15:40, 135–136
1 John 2:2, 106, 206
1 Kings 4:24–25, 20, 204
1 Kings 4:33–34, 163, 217
1 Kings 13:24, 160, 217
1 Kings 13:28, 161, 217
1 Kings 17:4, 164, 218
1 Peter 4:10, xii, 219
1 Samuel 16:7, 209
1 Thessalonians 5:23, 199
1 Thessalonians 5:23, 71
1 Timothy 5:18, 24, 200, 224

P

Philippians 1:23, 121, 213
Proverbs 12:10, 24, 149, 190, 200
Proverbs 25:2, ix, 210
Psalm 17:15, 108, 207

Psalm 36:6, 101, 199
Psalm 36:6–7, 210
Psalm 50:10–12, 21, 192
Psalm 65:2, 97, 98
Psalm 72:1–8, 20–21
Psalm 72:6–8, 204
Psalm 72:12–14, 20–21, 204
Psalm 104:24–30, 101–102
Psalm 104:29, 86, 104, 194, 207
Psalm 104:30, 122, 198–199
Psalm 145:9, 83, 89, 209
Psalm 145:13, 23, 199, 204
Psalm 145:21, 142, 196
Psalm 147:4, 16
Psalm 148:10, 141–142
Psalm 148:10–13, 196
Psalm 150:6, 142, 196

R

Revelation, 118, 123, 124, 125, 129, 142
Revelation 4:6–7, 145
Revelation 4:6–9, 201
Revelation 4:7, 142
Revelation 4:8–9, 142
Revelation 5:13–14, 135, 196, 201, 214
Revelation 6:2, 155, 215
Revelation 19:7, 124, 206
Revelation 19:11, 216
Revelation 19:11–12, 117, 155
Revelation 19:12, 156
Revelation 21:4–5, 123–124, 222
Romans 8, 93
Romans 8:19–22, 90, 199
Romans 8:20, 91, 93
Romans 8:20–21, 50, 191
Romans 8:21, 92, 93–94, 97
Romans 15:4–6, 191–192

T

2 Corinthians 5:8, 107, 119, 213
2 Corinthians 5:15, 106, 206
2 Corinthians 5:18–19, 206
2 Corinthians 5:19, 105
2 Kings 2:11, 164, 212
2 Peter 2:12, 225–226
2 Peter 2:23, 111
2 Samuel 12:1–9, 162, 218
2 Timothy 3:16–17, 192

Z

Zechariah 9:9, 191
Zechariah 9:9–10, 52–53
Zephaniah 3:17, 182

Please feel free to visit:

www.doanimalsgotoheaven.com

- Contact the author
- Discuss the book's content with others
- Learn about services and events for those interested in the continued examination of the animal afterlife or animal welfare issues.

Edwards Brothers Malloy
Oxnard, CA USA
September 21, 2015